SOLAR YOGA

In the hyper-technological
and fragmented world of the
21st century, it is essential for our
harmony and survival to go back
to the unifying source of all knowledge, the Light Divine.
This book presents a universal
method of reaching that source.
It owes its originality to a
longstanding East-West collaboration
of two devoted practitioners
of Solar Yoga.

SOLAR YOGA

An Illustrated Guide to Yoga Practice

YOGACHARYA JANAKIRAMAN
CAROLINE ROSSO CICOGNA

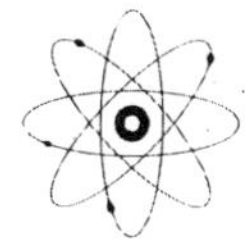

New Age Books

ISBN: 81-7822-247-7

Second Revised Edition: Delhi, 2005

(First Spanish Edition, 1992)
(First Indian Edition, 1990)
(First Italian Edition, 1990)

(The Illustrations and the Cover Painting are by Carmelo Vranich.)

Published by
NEW AGE BOOKS
A-44 Naraina Phase-I
New Delhi-110 028 (INDIA)
Email: nab@vsnl.in
Website: www.newagebooksindia.com

Printed in India
at Shri Jainendra Press
A-45 Naraina Phase-I, New Delhi-110 028

This book is offered with love and reverence to the Lotus Feet of Bhagavan Sri Sathya Sai Baba and to the sacred memory of Sree Ananda Mayee Ma

INVOCATION

To the Masters who constantly guide and illumine our path

"Om. We meditate upon the glorious splendour of the Vivifier divine. May he himself illumine our minds. Om". — RV III, 62, 10.

We offer our everlasting gratitude to the Masters who gave us their spiritual blessings and direct teachings. With our book, we should like to share their blessings with all our fellow seekers on the path of Yoga.

To the memory of Sree Sree Ananda Mayee Ma of Kankhal, Himalayas

To the memory of Sri Swami Sivananda of Rishikesh, Himalayas

To the memory His Holiness the Senior Shankaracharya of Kanchipuram

To the memory of Master Charan Singh Maharaj of Radha Saomi Satsangh, Beas

To the memory of Professor Gaurinath Shastri, Calcutta

To the memory of Swami Gitananda of Ananda Ashram, Pondicherry

To His Holiness the fourteenth Dalai Lama Tenzin Gyaṭso

To worshipful Swami Chidananda Maharaj of the Divine Life, Rishikesh, Himalayas

To worshipful Swami Satyananda Paramahamsa, Rikhia.

We also owe a debt of gratitude to the Masters in whose Ashrams we resided after their physical departure from this earth. They have guided us with their spiritual presence and the teachings in their books.
Our reverence to the memory of Sri Aurobindo and the Mother, to Paramahamsa Sri Ramakrishna and Sree Sarada Devi and Swami Vivekananda, to Sri Ramana Maharishi and to Swami Muktananda.

We offer our sincere prayers to the 'Rishis', the Universal Spirits who always enlighten our planet earth and whose guidance was felt by us in their holy places of worship.
The Himalayas and Ladhak, Benares on the Ganges,
the holy shrines of South India, the temples in Mount Abu,
the holy shrine of Nizamuddin in New Delhi, the Sun temple of Konarak,
the Zen temples of Kyoto, the Buddha Viharas of Sri Lanka,
Lumbini, Bodh Gaya and Sarnath,
Assisi, Rome, Padova, Mariazell, Lourdes and Fatima.

We feel blessed that we could put the final touches to our book during the Marian Year consecrated by his Holiness Pope John Paul II to the Holy Mother of the Christians. May the Cosmic Divine Mother, the Adi Para Shakti, always protect all Her children on earth.

— Cap Saint Hospice, France, 2nd March 2004

CONTENTS

PART – II

LIST OF PHOTOGRAPHS, TABLES AND ILLUSTRATIONS

Photographs

*For photographs 1, 2, 3 and 9, we acknowledge the courtesy of the Archaeological Survey of India in permitting the American Institute of Indian Studies to photograph centrally protected monuments. We likewise thank the American Institute of Indian Studies in Varanasi for having supplied us with some of their archive photographs to illustrate our book Solar Yoga.

Tables

Illustrations

Note : For illustrations of the asanas, please refer to the relevant indications in the table of contents.

FOREWORD

First, some thoughts on Religion and Science.

As a practising Muslim, I believe in the spiritual message of the Holy Koran. As a scientist, I believe in the truth of the manifestations of nature. The Holy Koran emphasises the necessity for reflection on the laws of nature, with examples drawn from cosmology, physics and biology. I recall the words of Einstein, the most famous scientist of our century: "The most beautiful experience we can have is of the mysterious. It is the fundamental emotion, which stands at the cradle of true science. Whoever does not know it, and can no longer wonder, no longer marvel, is as good as dead, and his eyes are dimmed. It was the experience of mystery, even if mixed with fear, that engendered religion."

The Abrahamic religions claim to provide a meaning to the mystery of life and death. These religions speak of a Lord, who not only created natural law and the universe in His glory, but also created us, the human beings in His own image, endowing them not only with speech but also with spiritual life and spiritual longings. The second aspect is of the Lord who answers prayers, when one turns to Him in distress. The third is of the Lord who, in the eyes of the mystic and the Sufi, personifies eternal beauty and is to be adored for this. The fourth is of the Lord who endows some humans, the prophets, and His chosen saints, with divinely inspired knowledge through revelations. The sages and mystics had revelations of the divine truths.

Second, some thoughts about the authors of this book whom I know personally.

Sri Janakiraman is known to me not only as a person with a scientific and technological background, but also as a spiritual being who has excelled in the art of teaching Yoga in a true spirit of sharing his knowledge with ardent seekers. And, his soul finds an even more intense expression when he can dedicate himself to devotional singing in praise of the divine.

Caroline Rosso Cicogna, who has created the Aditya International Yoga Centre along with Sri Janakiraman in Trieste, is a freelance simultaneous interpreter at the United Nations. She is a knowledgeable and sensitive Yoga teacher who has spent many years of her life in India, studying the cultural and philosophical background of the yogic practices.

I give my hearty and sincere good wishes to the authors and to their Aditya Yoga Centre.

Trieste
12th December, 1988

— Muhammad Abdus Salam
Nobel Prize for Physics

PREFACE

Salutations and adorations to Surya Narayana, the Sun God. The sun is a visible manifestation of the Divine. It is the sustainer of life. It is the giver of life. There wouldn't be any form of life on this earth planet without the sun. The sun is the source of all forms of life on this earth.

My salutations to Lord Shiva, the all-auspicious one who is the expounder of Surya Yoga.

Every man or woman in this world wants happiness. Nobody wants pain. No one needs to teach anyone to seek happiness. It is the innate, inherent Svabhava (nature) of everyone to seek happiness. Ananda (Bliss) is the embodiment of one's own nature.

Fulfilment of desires cannot bring true peace of mind. Just as fuel when poured over the fire aggravates it, so also worldly enjoyment intensifies desires and makes the mind all the more restless. Fulfilment of desires will only bring disappointment. Disappointment comes because the object of one's imagination, when obtained, always falls short of all possible expectations.

Yoga teaches the way to withdraw the mind from the objects of the world and to remove desire from the mind. But, before commencing the higher practices of Yoga, it is very important that one should have a sound body and mind. Without health, one cannot achieve anything in this world. Therefore, health is an essential factor for all achievements in this world whether they are secular or spiritual.

The book SOLAR YOGA is the combined effort of Yogacharya Janakiraman and Sister Caroline. The book is divided in three sections. The first section contains a complete description of the essence, the history and the practices of Solar Yoga. The second section offers a detailed study of twenty-five classical Asanas or Yoga postures. The third section presents a thorough discussion of the practice of Pranayama or the art of breathing.

Each subject is dealt with in great detail. It is a handbook for every Yoga seeker. The entire book makes very interesting study. The explanations are given in such a way that even a lay student can easily understand and practice on his own.

Seekers in the West who are interested in Yogic practices naturally start reading every type of book on Hatha Yoga and similar subjects. Sometimes these books are confusing and can even be unintelligible. More often, they have been written by persons whose aim would be only to show off their learning rather than teach real Yoga. At times, some of the books have nothing to do with Yoga.

The difference between such books and SOLAR YOGA is that its authors, Sri Janakiraman and Sister Caroline are themselves first-rate seekers. Whatever they have dealt with in their book is the result of their years of practice of Yoga and application in teaching. They themselves found immense benefit and they were not content to have the benefit for themselves alone. They sought to share their experience and knowledge with fellow seekers. It is with this aim that this book has been written.

In it, Sister Caroline has taken great care in giving detailed and illustrated instructions regarding the technique of the postures so that the reader may follow them with great ease.

I have known Sister Caroline for many years. She herself is a genuine seeker in the path of Yoga. She came in contact with great saints and sages of India and is spiritually bound to Sree Ananda Mayee Ma of sacred and hallowed memory. I am sure that many will be benefited by the study of this book and I hope that it will enjoy a wide circulation.

May God bless you all with radiant health, long life, happiness and contentment.

Swami Chidananda

Rishikesh
27th April, 1988

— SWAMI CHIDANANDA
President of the Divine Life Society

ACKNOWLEDGEMENTS

The preparation of our book Solar Yoga has been a real labour of love and I have been helped in more ways than I can recall. My grateful thanks are due to all those who contributed in a way or the other to this work.

I would like to place on record my special gratitude to the friends who collaborated more closely with Yogacharya Janakiraman and myself.

I would first thank my friend and colleague, Amadeo Solé Léris, author of important books on Theravada Buddhism, for his valuable advice and kind assistance.

I am most indebted to Dennis Craig who read the first draft of the book and encouraged me to proceed in my endeavour.

I am very grateful also to Armando Palma who introduced me to the world of computers and dedicated so much of his very precious time to guide my first steps in this discipline, which was entirely new and fascinating for me.

Aldo Poduie and his staff in APS were of great help in revising the format of the present edition: I acknowledge my gratitude for his suggestions and for the precision of his work.

We are obliged to our dear friend Suzan Katzmann for editing with meticulous care the last proofs sent to the press and bringing to our notice many faults in the wording of the text.

Our close friend Ennio Geromin has laid us under a deep obligation by taking care of all the organization needed to reach the final result: he never refused a favour and always acted with good humour and a smile. Last but not least, the artist who kindly accepted to illustrate this book, our friend Carmelo Vranich, deserves our heartfelt thanks.

The American Institute of Indian Studies in Varanasi, India has given us the permission to publish some of their archive photos, for which we are grateful. Our friend Lauredana Tolloi whom we thank wholeheartedly has taken the photos of the asanas and our friends Charles and Josette Lénars have taken the photos of Sri Janakiraman in later years.

I take it as a matter of great privilege to have had the guidance of Professor Gaurinath Sastri, then Vice-chancellor of the Benares Sanskrit University, throughout my five-year stay in India. I am forever beholden to him for constant spiritual inspiration and scholarly encouragement.

To three books I would acknowledge special indebtedness, they are *Pranayama* by Dr. Swami Gitananda of Ananda Ashram in Pondicherry, *Vedic Experience* by Dr. Raimundo Panikkar and *Light on Pranayama* by B.K.S. Iyengar.

At the time I am preparing this new edition, I feel particularly grateful to pursue ever-new aspects of the yogic sadhana with the precious guidance of Swami Gangadharananda whose presence in my life is felt as a direct blessing from the Divine Mother.

Finally, the words fail to express my loving gratitude to my husband Giorgio Rosso Cicogna who contributed in his beautiful yogic way, relieving me of other tasks so that I could carry on the research needed for writing the book.

PROLOGUE

Homage to Yogacharya Janakiraman

"Flee unto Him for shelter with all thy being, O Arjuna By His grace shalt thou obtain supreme peace and eternal abode." (S.M. Gita, XVIII, 62)

The first English edition of Solar Yoga was published in 1989 when our service to the Yoga community had reached a high point. Yogacharya Janakiraman was then well settled in Trieste, Italy where we had founded the Aditya International Yoga Association together.

In 1990, an Italian edition came on the market, followed the same year by the first Indian edition in English and, in 1992, by a Spanish edition.

From 1996, Yogacharaya Janakiraman chose a more retired life and we resided part of the time in Nice, France. He kept in touch with a few selected students only and with the devotees of the Hindu community in Vienna where I still occasionally worked as a free-lance interpreter at the United Nations. This life of quiet contemplation allowed him to practise his sadhana in an undisturbed manner, devoting his time to singing, mantra and meditation until his last conscious day on earth.

This third English edition, soon to be followed by the first French edition, marks the third anniversary of the passing away of Yogacharya Janakiraman who left his body on the second Tuesday of September 2001, which, incidentally, is celebrated each year as the International Day of World Peace. Sri Janakiraman always believed in living the peace within him rather than preaching it outside. In that way, he was faithful to his great Vedic tradition of non-violence, truth and self-awareness and he sustained his faith in these lofty ideals by his constant practice of Yoga, his devotional singing and his unswerving love for the Divine Mother.

He also believed in sharing his knowledge and experience of the Vedic truths with others through his teaching mission and the publication of our joint book " Solar Yoga" which reached the four corners of the planet.

During the last three days of his life on earth, he kept me by his side for hours and he transmitted to me the essence of his teachings, which he fondly called " the fruits of his entire sadhana".

As the seers of Vedic times, he gleefully worshipped the Sun as the living symbol of the Ancient Spiritual Being. As he always felt this authentic tradition should be perpetuated into our modern way of life, "Solar Yoga" came into being as our humble labour of love and it was blessed by Bhagavan Sathya Sai Baba. It is only natural that the one remaining "at this end of the rainbow" should do her best to serve the " One at the other end" through a new edition, thanks to the kind initiative of New Age Books Publishers.

I also feel it my duty to show how his life as a spiritual seeker and his day-to-day existence were intimately linked.

Born in Madras in 1921 in an orthodox Mylapore Brahmin family, Sri Janakiraman practised yoga as a child and studied the Vedas and Sanskrit in a traditional way along with his normal schooling. Although he chose scientific studies and an engineering career, the first formative years of his life were to leave a deep imprint on his soul with the regular visits to his father's home of Sri Swami Chandrashekara Sarasvati, the Senior Shankaracharya of Kanchipuram Mutt. But it is only much later in life, when he had absolved a great part of his householder's duties that he reverted to his first love, Yoga.

In 1941 he graduated in Physics from the Madras University and then moved to Bangalore where he served as a Senior Aeronautical Quality Control Engineer at Hindustan Aeronautics Limited until his retirement in 1979. Nevertheless, throughout his professional career, he dedicated his entire free time to the pursuit of the inner quest. Already in the early fifties, he travelled to the Himalayas and came in the presence of the great Swami Shivananda, founder of the Divine Life Society, Rishikesh. He would regularly go on pilgrimages to the sacred temples of the South and had the darshan and blessings of saints and sadgurus.

In 1965, providence took him to the Puttaparthi ashram of Bhagavan Sathya Sai Baba where at once the divine effulgence of Sri Sathya Sai Baba struck him. Those were the blessed days when Sai Baba used to go to the homes of his first devotees in Bangalore and when the huge crowds had not yet gathered around him. Some of these homes belonged to friends of Sri Janakiraman and thus he was allowed to be in very close proximity of Sai Baba and he participated in some of the activities of the Sai Organization. But these outer forms of devotion did not give him the inner peace he was longing for. His spiritual intuition, undoubtedly favoured by his early training in the Vedas, coupled with a scientific bent of mind, led him to intensify his search for the Truth by trying and testing several paths, relying on his own efforts but without ever overshadowing his total devotion for the Divine whom he saw incarnated in Sri Sathya Sai Baba.

In the late sixties and early seventies, Sri Janakiraman received initiation in different yogic sadhanas, which he practised rigorously, never sparing himself until he experienced the Light. In Madras, he was initiated by Sri Vaidyanathan into Sri Vidya Upasana (1). He also received initiation from Radha Soami Satsang of Beas in Suret Shabda Yoga (2) and in Atma Vidya from Sad Guru Omkar (3).

All these practices never clashed with his traditional way, the way of the twice born, the path of the Sun, embodied in the Gayatri mantra. On the contrary, these yogic practices reinforced his bhakti by revealing to him the esoteric aspects of the worship of the Divine Mother.

From 1967, he simultaneously pursued a strict and intensive sadhana in Hatha Yoga and he went to Pondicherry to undergo training in the therapeutic aspects of Yoga with Swami Gitananda, a medical doctor by profession and a consummate Hatha Yogi.

In the mid seventies he was encouraged to teach Hatha Yoga but he was so deeply anchored in Bhakti Yoga that he gradually developed his own particular blend of practices into an integrated approach that culminated in Solar Yoga. From his early days of teaching he had indeed realized what a deep impact Yoga had on students when combined with mantra and singing. His deep love for people and his motivation to help others inspired him to "engineer" Yoga sessions which invariably lead his students to a state of inner tranquillity and helped his patients to regain an inner equilibrium, the pre-condition to health.

Those were the years when he became known especially for his gift at yoga therapy as he achieved remarkable results with patients suffering from chronic ailments. He was called as a consultant in two hospitals in Madras and he introduced yoga therapy in the Ayurvedic Hospital in Bangalore. It is during that period that he made several teaching tours to Europe and particularly, in Italy where he was invited by Śri Apa Pant, then Ambassador of India in Rome, himself an ardent practitioner of " Surya Namaskar", the Salutation to the Sun. It is interesting to note that his father, Raja Bhawanarao of Aundh had made this practice popular in a publication in 1929, reedited by Sri Apa Pant himself in 1969.

Soon the home of Sri Janakiraman, where his elderly, devout mother also resided, was brimming with activity in an ashram-like fashion. By then, Janakiraman's daily routine had become completely and intrinsically yogic. He pursued no other activity. The first students would come in the early hours of the morning before Janakiraman set off to work. On the way to his office, he would share a car with three other officers whom he trained to recite a different chapter of the Bhagavad Gita on each journey that would last about forty minutes.

Off duty in the evening, he would attend to his patients and provide them with yoga therapy. This was followed by his own Yoga practices and it was only around midnight that he would sing bhajans on his veena. On certain nights he would be inspired to compose bhajans in classical ragas. Thanks to the innate musical gift in him, his bhakti could soar high and he became an accomplished devotional singer. He gave a number of devotional concerts, the last one being in Trieste at an International Conference for Women Scientists of the Third World hosted by Nobel Prize laureate, Professor Abdus Salam.

In 1979 when Janakiraman retired from active professional life, he had all the time to intensify his inner search. He followed the path of Nada Yoga and Mantra Yoga. His scientific mind and his talent for music were his best helpers. He was endowed with a profound faith in the Divine, but his was not a blind faith. For him, spirituality was also a science, but a higher science of exploration of the transcendental reality, which could be reached through the realm of the known. This, he always claimed, required constant effort, repeated inner experiences and discipline of body and mind. In other words, it is the practice of Yoga in the real sense of the word, which is to be united to God and feel the divine presence in all our day-to-day activities.

That same year, during a pilgrimage to the temples of Tamil Nadu, he experienced an inner awakening in the Shiva Nataraja temple of Chidambaram that totally transformed his outlook on life. He immortalised it in the bhajan "Pranamayi" that flowed spontaneously out of him in adoration for Sai Baba as the Mother Divine who guides our prana. From that time on, he would experiment with the wide range of subtle vibrations, experience their inner effects and observe their impact on body and mind during the practice of asanas and pranayama.

It was also in 1979 that I was blessed to have the first darshan of Sree Ananda Mayee Ma since my husband was appointed to the Italian Embassy in New Delhi for what became a memorable five-year stay in India.

While Sri Janakiraman was intensifying his inner practices of Devi Upasana (worship of the Divine Mother) and Aditya Yoga (Solar Yoga), my destiny was taking a definite spiritual turn. I spent more time in the presence of Sree Ananda Mayee Ma and received initiation directly from Her in 1981. I engaged in the study of the Bhagavad Gita, the Upanishads and practised the Yoga of Light under the guidance of Sri Gaurinath Sastri, a long time devotee of Sree Ananda Mayee Ma and disciple of Sri Gopinath Kaviraj.

But it was not until 1985 when Janakiraman came to Italy again upon the invitation of the Italian Yoga Federation that our two paths crossed. Free from his worldly ties, Sri Janakiraman decided to settle in Italy where he continued to pursue a Yogic life, stronger than ever before. Thus began a close and deep spiritual connection which was to last until he left his body.

At our Yoga Association in Trieste, our main activity was geared to guiding individual students in their inner quest through meditation, mantra and music. Yoga therapy also occupied a great part of our time at the centre while periodical seminars were dedicated to a more general dissemination of Yoga in Italy and in other European countries. Sri Janakiraman was particularly successful in training Western Yoga teachers because his early traditional yogic background and the modern scientific approach he acquired in his professional life enabled him to transmit the teaching of this secular yogic science in a practical, clear and efficient manner. In this process, I was privileged to receive Sri Janakiraman's direct teaching on a daily basis, either by assisting him in his classes or by undergoing personal training. This collaboration culminated in our book "Solar Yoga" which was also an expression of this learning process.

Sri Janakiraman continued to contribute articles to several leading Yoga magazines in Italy, England and Australia, as he had done for the Deccan Herald when he was teaching in Bangalore. He was a full member of the International Yoga Teachers Association (Australia), the British Wheel of Yoga, the Italian Yoga Association, the International and Professional Yoga Teachers Federation (Uruguay) and the Viswa Yoga Samaj (India).

The years at the AYIA were marked by the rhythm of the Hindu festivals, which he celebrated with total devotion and the days were dedicated to teaching and to sadhana.

During his fifteen years in the West, we continued the holy practice of going on pilgrimages to shrines all over Europe and especially to sanctuaries consecrated to Mother Mary, for whom he had a particular devotion. His heart was universal and his mind was open and therefore he left a deep impression on everyone who came into contact with him. Often, words were not even necessary because his inner peace would be felt in his shining eyes, in his calm composure and in his compassionate touch.

In his spiritual will, Yogacharya Janakiraman stated that I had radiated nothing but love and sunshine in his life and that he would like that Source that radiated it from within to protect me and bless me for all times to come.

In offering to the reader this third English-language edition of "Solar Yoga", which was so dear to him that he never moved without a copy of the book, I feel that I have returned in a very small measure the love that flowed incessantly from him. No words can describe the depth and intensity of the love he showered on me, a love that was so divine that no matter what I did I could never reciprocate it in full. In the same spirit, I have chosen to reproduce hereafter some expressions of encouragement and appreciation we received after the publication of the first English-language edition of "Solar Yoga".

"The three years of your steady labour has borne fruit ultimately. Your work will help numerous seekers of Yoga and they will derive immense benefit. This is a noble service, which will bring many positive results to people who study and practice your book Solar Yoga."

Swami Chidananda, President of the Divine Life Society, Rishikesh.

"Jai Ma. Solar Yoga was offered at Sree Ananda Mayee Ma's Samadhi at Kankhal to invoke Her blessings. You have taken up the right path to lead the people of your country by preaching the lessons and teachings about Yoga."

Swami Swarupananda, the then General Secretary of the Sree Ananda Mayee Ma Sangha.

"The book is truly a gem! The information is clearly organised and the illustration is excellent. It will provide much light to Hatha Yoga around the world."

Swami Satchidananda, Founder of Satchidananda Ashram, Yogaville.

"Solar Yoga, a giant volume revisiting some ancient practices in classical Yoga, is a very fine book from cover to cover, but the authors are more important than the book.

The authors develop the concept of Asanas and generously go into the role and purpose of many Asanas. Pranayama is featured along with the glorification of the Pranava AUM and its transcendental consciousness state. This is one of the better explanations of the cosmic Pranava in print."

Swami Gitananda, Ananda Ashram, Pondicherry.

"In Solar Yoga, Yogacharya Janakiraman and Caroline Rosso Cicogna have adopted an approach, which clearly demonstrates that Hatha Yoga is, much more than a set of mere physical activities. I hope that the book will provide to new students a sound introduction to

Yoga and to current practitioners greater insight into this ancient discipline."
R. Venkataraman, the then President of the Republic of India.

"Thank you for the book "Solar Yoga". It is very well brought out."
Sonia Gandhi

"Solar Yoga would most certainly prove to be not only an excellent guide to all those who seek to join themselves with the eternal Energy system, but also a great inspiration. My most sincere congratulations."
Ambassador Apa Pant, author of " Surya Namaskar"

"It is most heartening to learn that your great work of helping humanity is receiving added support with Solar Yoga."
P.R.S. Mani, former Indian Ambassador

"When an eminent scholar and Yogin like Swami Chidananda has blessed your book Solar Yoga, one does not have anything to add."
Vimala Thakar, Mount Abu

"Many thanks for your wonderful book. Congratulations. We did not meet but are united in the Ideal."
Professor R. Panikkar, University of California

"A splendid book! Which I am now reading with all the attention it deserves."
Amadeo Solé Léris, author of " Tranquillity and Insight"

"Solar Yoga is an outstanding book which deals with a carefully selected group of classical Yoga practices in a novel manner, and is suitable not only as a reference manual for the Yoga teacher, but as a guide for the student's practice."
Moina Bower, President of the International Yoga Teachers Association, Australia

(1) Elaborate Tantric sadhana of worship of the Divine Mother.
(2) Sadhana based on the concentration on the sound and the meaning of AUM.
(3) Sadhana is based on the relationship of the individual soul to the cosmic soul.

1

2

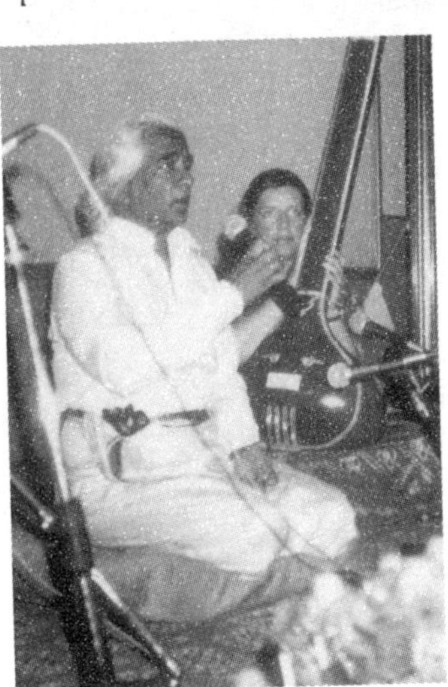
3

4

The Devotee

1. Sathya Sai Baba blesses "Solar Yoga" presented by Sri Janakiraman, Whitefield, 1990.
2. Sri Janakiraman and his mother in Madras, 1990.
3. Sri Janakiraman and Caroline Rosso Cicogna singing bhajans at International Sai Conference, Assisi, 1990.
4. Sri Janakiraman performing puja, Bangalore, 1969.

1

2

3

The Yogacharya

1. With Andre Van Lysbeth in Belgium in 1976.
2. With Dr. Bhole of Lonavla Yoga Institute, Trieste, 1986.
3. With a group of students at Kanya Kumari, India, 1979.

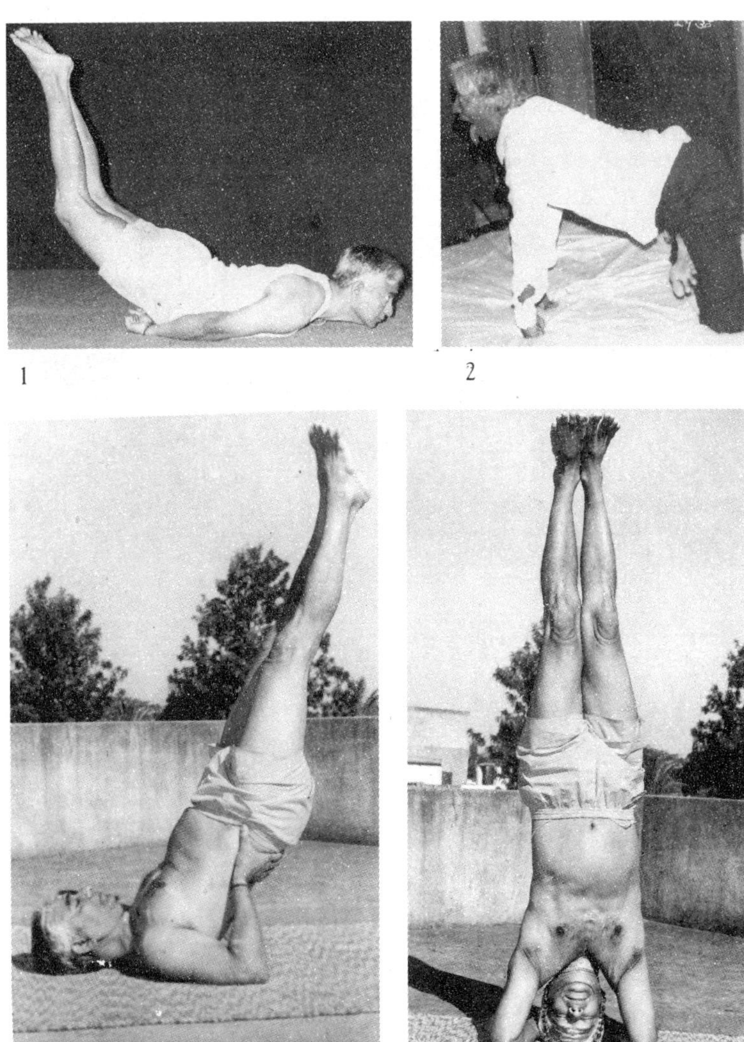

1 2 3 4

The Hatha Yogi

1. Shalabhasana, locust pose, Bangalore, 1972.
2. Simhasana, lion pose, Rome, 1976.
3. Viparitakaranimudra, inverted pose, 1978.
4. Shirshasana, headstand, Bangalore, 1978.

The later years in Nice, 1996 to 2001

1. Pranayama - Vitality
2. Ganesha Mudra - Surrender
3. Yoni Mudra - Inner Awareness
4. Namaskar - Peace and Surrender

INTRODUCTION

In every human heart there is a metaphysical quest to discover what lies behind appearances. Each one, in his or her own way, tries to pierce the mystery of life. And what led to the writing of this book is somehow the story of such an existential quest. It is the genesis of this book that I should like to recount briefly in the introduction, with a feeling of overwhelming gratitude to the great beings who are constantly guiding us in the process of unfolding.

The quest starOted during my five-year stay in India where I was to visit some of the ancient holy places of the land that gave birth to Yoga and to come in contact with some of the great living masters of our century. In those days, when I visited the shrines and temples or when I spent some time in the presence of an enlightened being, I would always have the same experience: I would feel different, more joyful and much lighter and have a greater and easier propensity to meditate. At first, I did not pay too much attention to this phenomenon but, as time went by, I became more and more attracted by these energy-laden places and I attributed this feeling of inner harmony to my happiness to be in surroundings, which, in a way, allowed me to dedicate myself totally to the study of Yoga that I had started some years before when I was still in Europe.

It is at that time that I was brought into the presence of Sree Ananda Mayee Ma, on Holi Purnima, in Brindavan, the holy town of Krishna, on the banks of the Jamuna River. This blessed encounter changed my entire outlook and this darshan of an enlightened being was to be the first of a long series of meetings with the great saint of Bengal. Rarely did I put questions to Ma, as I intuitively felt that the moments in Her presence were so sacred and were such a rare experience in a lifetime that they were best savoured in a state of silent communion with this beautiful incarnation of the Divine Mother. Moreover, the first darshan is like the Sa note of the Indian musical scale. All the following darshans are but permutations and combinations of the notes. One practises one's sadhana like a musical scale, invariably coming back to the fundamental note. And no two scales are ever the same. It was in Brindavan again that two years later, again on Holi Purnima, I was initiated directly by Her. As Sree Ananda Mayee Ma followed the ancient tradition of the Hindu itinerant monks, She would never stay in any one holy place for long but would travel all over the Indian sub-continent, guided by Her inner intuition. By the time I was blessed to meet Her, more than twenty 'ashrams' or places of retreat had been built in the most sacred places of Hinduism, as Kurukshetra, Brindavan, Benares, Haridwar, Pune or Almora to receive Her and Her devotees.

During my frequent visits to Her, I started to feel a great sense of harmony in and around me. It was as if Her being and the atmosphere surrounding it would create a vibratory field of such intensity that Her devotees would easily be attracted and elevated to a higher plane when they found themselves in Her physical presence. Gradually, I realized that this inner experience, which would come to me spontaneously in the presence of Ma, could also be felt, although with lesser intensity, in ancient temples, by a sacred river, in the Himalayas or in some places of pilgrimage. Could it be that the special vibrations of sacred spots and the devotion of the hundreds of thousands of pilgrims who visited these places had left something in the atmosphere, thereby contributing to the creation of an invisible presence?

With that question in my mind and more, an interesting experience happened when I was invited to take part in a pilgrimage to Kedarnath. At first sight, Kedarnath is an almost inaccessible hamlet in a narrow Himalayan valley close to the border of Tibet. For a spiritual seeker, however, Kedarnath is hallowed by the aura of its famous Shiva temple. My expectations were high because I had heard that the temple was one of the most powerful places of worship in northern India and well worth the hard eight-hour-long climb on foot or on horseback. So, I was greatly disappointed when the feeling of inner harmony I had experienced in the temples in the plains did not manifest itself here. I therefore resigned myself to leaving the barren, lunar landscape of Kedarnath without having been fulfilled by one of my cherished experiences. It was to happen later, though, at a few hours' distance from the Shiva shrine, when on a pony's back I was calmly returning to the lush and inviting slopes of the Himalayan foothills. As the first green bushes and lovely wild flowers started to appear on the mountain path, I suddenly felt the 'vibration of Shiva' spreading like a very slender cobweb from my heart throughout my body to my immediate surroundings, to the mountains encircling me, then, to the deep valley waiting in the distance and beyond.

To experience the ether enveloping the earth was a feeling of total bliss. It was an extraordinary moment of truth: its extreme subtlety was its great power and I realized that it had in a way transformed me. From that time on, I knew an entirely fascinating world was opening up for me, the world of cosmic and telluric vibrations which can be directly experienced by all human beings in special circumstances: we have the possibility, in certain privileged places and at some chosen moments, to disentangle ourselves from our standardized, programmed cerebral worlds and to be absorbed in a powerful supramental current which is felt in highly charged spiritual places or in the presence of spiritually evolved beings.

At that time, I was also blessed to be studying the Bhagavad-Gita and some of the major Upanishads under the guidance of Professor Gaurinath Shastri who was then the Vice-Chancellor of the Benares Sanskrit University and was an ardent devotee of Sree Ananda Mayee Ma. His duties would often take him to some of the remotest, oldest and most authentic places of Hindu India and sometimes I accompanied him, which enabled me to continue my silent and discreet quest. I now started realizing that the vibrations differed from one holy place to another. Each holy place had its own colour, its own quality and intensity of vibration. Moreover, the particular nature of the vibration would also manifest itself in the shape and the geometrical configuration of the temple and in the emotions expressed in the sculptures of the deities. This vibration, with its particular colour and intensity, could even be noticed in the facial expression of the assembled devotees and in the tone and modulation of the priests' chanting.

But, whether it was the shattering vibration of Shiva as a destroyer in the Mahakala temple at Ujjain or the vibration of Krishna as the benevolent sustainer of creation in Brindavan or, still, the many-faceted vibrations of the Mother Goddess in the Shakti shrines I visited, the effect was almost invariably the same: the vibrations produced an inner transformation followed by a profound state of harmony. Undoubtedly, the ancients had chosen certain particular places for their spiritual practices because they had a clear understanding of the relationship between our earth and the cosmos and they had experienced in themselves the kind of inner transformation such privileged places could produce in them.

As I was progressing in my quest, I was reminded of what I read years ago in some Yoga books: that a state of psychophysical balance was obtained through regulated breathing, concentration of the mind and devotion of the heart. Could it be possible that in some privileged places, the cosmic and telluric energy configurations were such that we were spontaneously and effortlessly in harmony with the universe and with ourselves even for a very brief moment only?

The time had come for me to intensify the inner aspects of the quest and to delve deeper in the yogic practices. There is a profound truth in the saying 'one does not soar alone'. On my return from India, I was to meet Yogacharya Janakiraman in Rome. Thenceforth, I continued on my yogic journey, under his instructions: what was to become a strong and abiding relationship until he left his body. Sri Janakiraman had been a long-time devotee of Bhagavan Sathya Sai Baba and I, too, had felt the transforming touch of Bhagavan. Our providential encounter was to become the starting point of this book.

With his wealth of knowledge and experience in the different branches of Yoga, his scientific bend of mind, his enlightened vision and his total devotion to the Divine, Sri Janakiraman patiently guided me further in the sadhana of the Yoga of Light. The more I practised, the more I realized how the inner power of Yoga became apparent and effective when the three planes of energy, the physical, psychic and spiritual, were harmoniously integrated. The book SOLAR YOGA is the expression of this learning process. It has been written with the intention of introducing newcomers to Solar Yoga and of helping persons who already practise Yoga to apply the solar vibrations gradually and scientifically to their daily yogic session and ultimately experience a state of peace and harmony.

The book has been written on the assumption that the practice of Yoga should form a part of our daily lives with profound implications for the world in which we live. Yoga is a universal technique that enables us to acquire an insight into the true nature of things by direct experience. Like any other science, Yoga has an experimental basis and has been practised in India for many centuries for maintaining good health and achieving inner balance and enlightenment. Yoga provides an answer to the problems of today and may become the way of life of tomorrow, provided the practical application of the yogic techniques accompanies the knowledge of their philosophical background in a manner that is suited to the environment in which we live. This fundamental principle is reflected in the two parts of the book.

Part One is of a conceptual nature and sets out the methodological principles on which the yogic practices of Part Two are based. Chapter One gives a description of the essence, antiquity and authenticity of Solar Yoga. It also explains how this ancient discipline has been adapted to the needs of our lives. Chapter Two studies the 'asanas' or basic postures, placing particular emphasis on the different sheaths of energy and the spiritual aspect of the postures. The section on the method Yogacharya Janakiraman and I have developed is of particular importance to understanding all the interrelated elements of the practice of Solar Yoga. Chapter Three gives a detailed background to the conscious-breathing techniques or 'pranayamas' and includes a study of the physiology of breathing followed by a description of the main features of the body's energy pattern. Chapter Four is based on a thorough study of the solar vibrations or 'mantras' according to original Sanskrit texts.

Part Two is of a practical nature and describes a selected number of classical Yoga practices (asanas, pranayamas, bandhas, kriyas, mudras and mantras) in a novel manner, integrating the use of solar sound vibrations with that of postures and breathing and energy techniques at the physical, psychic and spiritual levels. It is divided into four chapters. The first chapter is introduced by a presentation of the eight joint release method and goes on to deal with a carefully selected number of classical asanas. It concludes with a twelve-week program and a brief outline of the Salutation to the Sun. The second chapter is dedicated to the study of different types of pranayama, highlighting some important features of each practice.

The third chapter concerns a selection of bandhas, kriyas and mudras. In the present edition, a fourth chapter has been added on solar meditation. This is, in a very concise form, the outcome of some higher practices of Solar Yoga I had already initiated under the guidance of Professor Gaurinath Sastri, in the days I was living in Benares. Aware that the search for the inner Light is an unending process until one reaches total enlightenment, I pursued this sadhana during my fifteen-year long spiritual collaboration with Yogacharya Janakiraman. After his demise, the Divine Mother who never forsakes Her children, put on my path Swami Gangadharananda, an intiated disciple of Sri Swami Satyananda Saraswati, founder of the Bihar School of Yoga.

With him, I could benefit from the invaluable teachings and revolutionary insights of his master thus giving yet more depth to the glimpses of an inner Reality I had gathered intuitively some twenty years earlier. But all Yogic practices serve only to purify oneself so that the Divine grace may totally flood our inner being. Without devotion; grace will not flow. Devotion is the small lamp we light in our hearts and divine grace is the effulgent sun of consciousness. Another name for this sun is love. Sathya Sai Baba and Sree Ananda Mayee Ma constantly radiate this powerful Light on their devotees. In their Divine Love, I wish to dedicate Solar Yoga to the reader.

Everyone can enjoy this book because it describes practices of Solar Yoga that give vitality, logevity, mental peace and spiritual upliftment. It is the fervent hope of the authors, therefore, that it will not simply adorn bookshelves, but will be fully used by the readers for their daily practice of Yoga.

Cap de Nice
8th January, 2004

Premamayee
Caroline Rosso Cicogna

PART I

"jyotisam api taj jyotih tamasah param ucyate
jnanam jneyam jnanagamyam hrdi sarvasya visthitam"

S.B. Gita, XIII-17

"That, the Light of all lights, is said to be beyond darkness.
It is knowledge, the object of knowledge and the goal of knowledge,
seated in the hearts of all."

Photo 1. Sun Temple of Modhera (Gujarat, India) - ca AD 1027. Built in stone in the Maru Gurjara style. General view from northeast. By courtesy of the American Institute of Indian Studies (A.I.I.S.)

CHAPTER 1

SOLAR YOGA

Whatever ideal human beings may hold in life, be it trivial or sublime, it possesses an intrinsic value for it inspires them to harness all their energies towards giving a concrete shape to a hitherto formless reality. In striving to realize an ideal they allow a particular facet of the great unknown to manifest itself on the human plane. They thus become a syntropic medium of exchange between the unmanifest, transcendent Light and the relative plane of matter.

Since life appeared on earth, it has constantly been the play between entropy, a mechanical causality that characterizes the physical world and syntropy, a fundamentally unifying principle of finality, which introduces an indispensable element of spontaneity into the animate kingdom. All living forms truly tend towards a goal with a mission to fulfil. The higher, the vaster and remoter the aim, the more complex and diversified the structures and means to reach this ideal are. This is clearly seen in the differentiation from unicellular to complex organisms in the course of time. The human being, who is only a ring in the evolutionary chain, is endowed with a nature that also follows this dual movement of causality and finality.

That which in human nature tends towards a harmonious unity or a spiritual dimension of being, in which growth is spontaneously following the dictates of a deep, hidden essential nature, can be considered to have a finality and be syntropic. That which on the contrary keeps human nature inexorably tied down to a mechanistic law of cause and effect, which ends up in disintegration, belongs to the world of causality and is essentially entropic. This can be seen, by way of example, at the organic level: when all the body cells collaborate normally towards the higher goal of human health, they are following the natural course of life or syntropy. When, however, some cells follow an independent, erratic development, separated from the main structure, they will tend to get caught in the chain of causality and they will proliferate abnormally and produce disease. In other words, syntropy creates order, entropy leads to chaos and both phenomena characterize life on earth.

To strike the right balance between these two principles is one of the aims of Yoga. This Sanskrit word comes from the root 'yug' which means to unite and it represents both the process of unification and the state of unity. The state of Yoga is the culmination of syntropy: it is a state devoid of the limitations of time and space, a state which transcends matter and energy and which cannot be qualified by any attribute. This reality of pure Consciousness has been recognized by all thinkers, spiritualists or materialists, as the fundamental axiom of life from which intelligence, volition, love and thought emanate.

When Yoga is seen as a process, it refers to any set of practices or techniques which will help one to free oneself from the entropic law of cause and effect which keeps a person in a condition of illusory identification with the psycho-physical world only. In this gradual unification process, the different aspects of human personality are harmonized and life is made to unfold as a powerful manifestation of pure Consciousness.

Seen in this perspective a human life is but a brief passage on earth in which the highest ideal should be to discover the transcendental, unitary Consciousness and manifest it through thought, will and action. To become aware of this higher dimension of life on earth corresponds to the process of Yoga whereas the state of Yoga is to live permanently in the awareness of a supreme, intelligent Consciousness guiding the universe.

So long as a human ideal is shaped by social conventions, influenced by educational standards or inspired by cultural trends, which are all exogenous factors, it is destined to disappear. This kind of ideal is as ephemeral as the morning dew. It gives human life the strength it needs to withstand the difficulties of existence, but it does not serve as a springboard from which to transcend the boundaries of circumscribed personality. When, on the contrary, an ideal surges from the core of being as an answer to a deep inner call, it may survive an individual's existence and may serve to strengthen the link between human and cosmic consciousness. It may also reinforce the bond of unity between human beings. An ideal of this nature is the expression of a search for the centre and essence of life, for the Light of lights, for the supreme Consciousness from which all living forms emanate. When one begins to realize that striving for what one holds to be one's personal ideal is nothing but the manifestation of a greater movement impelling one to return to the source of one's being, one gradually starts to discover one's own true nature. When, moreover, one strives to subordinate one's lesser ideals to the one, universal quest — the transformation of human nature into a state of pure Light — one penetrates into the world of Yoga, which is the common heritage of mankind.

THE TRADITIONAL BRANCHES OF YOGA

Classical Yoga is considered to be one of the six main schools of philosophy of Hindu India. With time, different forms of identification with the absolute reality appeared as ways to render manifest the latent potential of human beings according to their diversified temperaments and personalities, and as attempts to respond to their needs and aspirations.

Karma Yoga or the Yoga of selfless action

The practice of this form of Yoga is to discover through conscious, purpose-oriented and selfless action the true meaning of human life. The action is concentrated mainly on the entropic aspect of life: it aims at interrupting the chain of causality so that the inner spiritual nature of man may fulfil itself through action. This form of Yoga is suited to active, altruistic, energetic persons who are interested in the concrete, outward world. This Yoga is highlighted in the Bhagavad Gita.

Jnana Yoga or the Yoga of discriminating knowledge

This form of Yoga tends towards the unfolding of a detached, impartial, witnessing attitude on the part of the practitioners towards the events of life and through this, the attempt to discover the truth of every lived experience. This Yoga acts more on the syntropic side of life.

Discrimination helps to discard what is temporal, unreal and useless in a given situation, allowing the moving force of finality to act. This form of Yoga is suited to reflective, intellectual, adaptable and non-materialistic persons who are interested in the workings of the inner self rather than in the fluctuating movements of the outer world. This sense of discrimination is enlightened by a sharp and pure intellect and is not impaired by a flawed, logical mind.

This is the Yoga of the Upanishads, of the Vedanta line and of the great Shankaracharya.

Bhakti Yoga or the Yoga of devotion

This Yoga is practised through the cultivation of a humble, devoted service with overflowing love to a higher cause in order to try and break the limitations of the ego and experience the unity of all living creatures.

This form of Yoga combines the principles of syntropy and entropy. It consists mainly in surrendering the lower human nature to a higher principle in an act of selfless love. This Yoga is adapted to self-assertive, dominating, emotional persons who find it difficult to open up to their fellow beings. It is the Yoga of Jayadeva and the great Hindu mystics.

Mantra Yoga or the Yoga of vibrations

In this rigorous discipline with vibrations the intention is to overcome the memory traces left in the brain and in the nervous system by past events, which create conditioned thinking. In this manner, the mantra yogi tries to experience the joyful, perfect inner silence that is an immediate manifestation of Consciousness. This form of Yoga acts at a subtle psychic level by breaking the entropic chain of psychic impressions and enhancing the syntropic insight into the spiritual nature of a human being. This Yoga is suited to persons who are either not independent enough and therefore caught up in their own thoughts and concepts or who remain excessively linked to the authority of religious persons or to scriptures. This ancient Yoga finds its origin in the Vedas.

Tantra Yoga or the Yoga of ordered expansion

This branch of Yoga seeks, through well-defined methods and rituals, to expand the power of human imagination and visualization in order to break the individualistic, illusory world and to discover the unlimited power of cosmic ideation and creation. This Yoga acts both on entropy and syntropy seen as Shiva and Shakti or the male and female cosmic principles. Its aim is to remove the separation of these energies in a human being so that the cosmic union may become a direct, intuitive experience.

This Yoga is suited to creative, daring persons who are self-controlled, intellectually lucid and who are not preys to drives or noxious living habits. This Yoga is found in the Tantra and Agama literature.

Hatha Yoga or the Yoga of psychophysical self-training

By physical practices of movements and breathing, by psychic practices of pranayama, the hatha yogi endeavours to pierce through the cyclical movement of life, its moments of brightness and confusion, its ups and downs with a view to discovering the underlying calm and wisdom. In other words, hatha yogis try to transcend the opposites of human nature and to live with singleness of purpose and action so that they may always be guided by their true nature. This Yoga is suited to persons who are active and resolute and who aspire to develop their personality in an integrated and harmonious manner. This Yoga is described in texts such as Hatha Yoga Pradipika or Gheranda Samhita.

Raja Yoga or the Royal Yoga

This Yoga, also known as Ashtanga Yoga, is based on a very rigorous practice in eight graduated steps, which requires great concentration and inner guidance. It is an integral way of life that involves the entire range of the human personality. It traces the way to supreme identity with the cosmic Consciousness in a world of constant change. This all-embracing Yoga suits contemplative, sensitive, dedicated and independent persons. It is the Yoga of the Yoga Sutra of Patanjali.

SURYA YOGA OR SOLAR YOGA

Solar Yoga crowns all the traditional forms of Yoga as a brilliant synthesis of these different approaches, which highlights in an unmistakable fashion the profound heliocentric character of human nature. Moreover, Solar Yoga fuses into a single practical structure the basic principles of the two fundamental Hindu schools of thought and spiritual practice, the Vedic and the Tantric. This integral and dynamic method consists of a course of physical, psychic and spiritual processes. Its aim is to unfold the vibrant consciousness of life and the all-pervasive cosmic power in day-to-day existence. Contrary to common belief, human beings do not constitute the centre of the universe. The genuine source of life on earth is to be found in the sun and in the cosmic Light from which it draws its undying energy. This mysterious Light has been the subject of speculation since the remotest time of human history and has always been revered as a reality of infinite creation and regeneration of which the sun, in its multidimensional nature, remains till this day the striking symbol. What exists on earth first existed in the sun in an etheric form. By a process of gradual materialization, the elements that constitute the universe left the cosmic centre and developed an apparently independent life. In reality there are no discreet units of life in the universe, but everything is united in an immense ocean of vibrations. So, at a very subtle level, sun and earth are in a constant state of fusion and the same energy that is constantly renewed in the sun vibrates also as an infinitesimal spark of light hidden in the deepest core of human nature.

The practices of Solar Yoga are geared towards the rediscovery of this state of union or fusion through a sustained discipline of concentration on pure Light and on the emanations of Light as vibration, energy, breath and movement. These different dimensions of Light are powerfully concentrated in the sun, which is taken as the main object of concentration in Solar Yoga. In the solar practices, the light and the energy emanating from the sun are experienced on three different planes. At the physical level, the movement and pattern of the sun are felt as simple, reproducible and energizing phenomena. At the psychic level, the sun becomes the inner eye of individual consciousness that enlightens the subtle bioenergetic field of the human system. At the spiritual level, the sun becomes the gateway to a greater existence: it becomes a radiant core of Light, which has to be pierced before individual consciousness can itself become the infinity of Light. By following the graduated steps of the integral solar discipline, one begins to realize that one is built upon the same structure as the sun: a vibrant core of self-renewed energy, which emits rays of consciousness that supply life to the different planes.

The active personal search into one's own nature prompted by the solar method awakens the power of intuition and leads towards a total unification of the different planes of experience through an inner vision of the creative sun. One realizes then that the three-dimensional nature of the universe and human beings resolves itself into a single, harmonious and greater dimension: a world of Light where all opposites merge. It is only when this transcendental sun is discovered through cosmic insight that the divine power can freely operate in a human being as a constant flow of life, energy, intelligence and joy. In the same way that the sun does not spread out its rays on a circumscribed part of the earth, but pours out its light cyclically on the entire surface of the planet, regenerated human beings introduce the renewed spiritual dimension into their lives. They follow a regular course of practices aimed at enhancing awareness of the link that unites them to the cosmic intelligence that guides the universe through the powerful manifestation of the sun.

THE ANTIQUITY OF SOLAR YOGA

From time immemorial Light has been recognized as a universal principle and the adoration of the sun was one of the first mystical feelings of human beings out of which religions grew. Solar Yoga is of great antiquity and corresponds to a remote period of history when human beings still possessed an integrated and unified nature of body, mind and spirit.

This concept of the perpetual renewal of light through light has been the object of continuous interest in ancient cultures. At the agricultural stage of human society, when the sun's influence over crops was discovered, humans attributed the sun with divine powers, as a source of order and measurement. Being intuitively aware of the sun's creative might and destructive power they showed extreme reverence towards the ruler of the universe, invoking his blessings in a myriad of ways.

The sun made a deep impact on the human psyche and its apotheosis became manifest in the mythology of the ancient solar cultures. Light is at the basis of millenary Egypt, from the Osiris rites to the vision of Hermes Trismegiste. The Eye of Horus is the symbol of purifying light appearing on all the monuments of the time. The Egyptian Book of the Dead states that when the god Nourr sprang out of the primeval waters he was holding the solar boat where one could see the scarab carrying the new sun.

In ancient Greek initiation myths, light represents salvation as one of the greatest aspects of the informal world. It was light that presided over the mysteries of Eleusis. In the orphic tradition, the initiate was brought from the darkness of the temple through symbolic purification rites to discover the sun and to start his inner search for the subtle light hidden to the physical eyes.

But it is principally in Persia that the old mythological sun gave way to the new sun, a sun of moral light where the central idea of Zoroastrian religion highlighted the individuality of the human being and his responsibility towards the universe.

In biblical times, the light of the verb appeared as the foundation of Jewish and Christian religions. It is well known that light has an important role to play in Jewish mysticism and the Kabala is a Book of Lights where the seven spirits of the Throne correspond to the seven gradings of light and the seven notes of music, whereas nine great lights preside over the creation of the universe. To this day, the Hebrew tradition has maintained a great worship of lights in synagogues.

In the Bible, light is likewise a sign of salvation. In all the books the hidden light of the Spirit is exalted whether in the hymns of Isaiah, the psalms of king David, the exaltations of the prophets or the Book of Wisdom of king Solomon. All form a bright chain extending from the ancient Moses who received the lights on Mount Sinai and who was guided by light throughout his life, to the greatest of spiritual solar figures, Christ himself, whose words recorded in the gospels were all carriers of spiritual light. Each gospel speaks of a light that pierces darkness. On one hand, the transfiguration of Christ, evoking that of Moses descending from Mount Sinai, seals the biblical continuity and the succession of prophets until Jesus. On the other hand it gives a divine confirmation of Christ's transcendental role as redeemer of man.

The Koran is yet another book of light and the Sufi tradition has brought forth a number of enlightened souls who have scrutinized the depths of reality.

In Buddhism, the principle of enlightenment is striking. Gautama Sakyamuni, the Buddha, who lived more than 2000 years ago, obtained enlightenment through a powerful mental mutation. The physical tree in Bodh Gaya, India, under which he attained self-realization, was to fuse later with the symbolic tree of Tao in China where Buddhism spread in the first century A.D. And in Taoism itself, the doctrine of LaoTseu taught that in order to become immortal, man should unite with the fundamental energy, which is light.

In Mahayana Buddhism, the highest Tantric initiation is based on light and the origin of the universe is represented as a triangle of light, creating the worlds uninterruptedly.

In Zen Buddhism, the satri is like a psychic revolution of light through which one acquires a new vision of life by relinquishing the dualism of subject and object.

Although the origins of solar revelation are lost in a dim past, this revelation appears for the first time in scriptural form in the Vedas. The Vedas mark the historical birth of the Indo-Aryan civilization, which flourished around 2000 B.C. in the Indo-Gangetic valley. In its broader sense, the term covers the entire body of Vedic literature, from the four Vedas — Rigveda, Yajurveda, Samaveda and Atharvaveda — to the Upanishads of the Vedanta school and the later epic works, like the Ramayana and the Mahabharata of which the Bhagavad Gita is a part. But the deeper meaning of Veda relates to the totality of knowledge, which can be experienced with regard to the manifest and unmanifest aspects of reality. In this sense, Veda is a revelation of a universal and permanent nature, which goes beyond religions, dogmas and philosophical speculations. The medium of expression of these sacred scriptures was Sanskrit: a scientifically and mathematically precise language in which sound vibrations have remained pure and intact, each word revealing its own meaning like a formula.

In the Vedas, the sun of self-awareness, the inner spiritual sun, forms the central theme of the Vedic hymns. It is one of the greatest aspects of the sun seen as the core and source of all forms of existence and considered to be an interface between the transcendental reality and its relative manifestations on earth. In the early Vedic period, the seer had a fundamentally heliocentric attitude towards life that led him to invoke the powers of the divine light and surrender to the greatest amongst them, the sun, which he adored in numerous forms. The seer's spiritual realization was based on pure monism or a deep feeling of unity of the entire creation.

In the Rigveda, the seer invoked and praised the multifarious aspects of cosmic Consciousness. In the Samaveda, he sang the melody of the universe. In the Yajurveda, from which the solar mantras studied in this book originate, he spelled out the divine powers of the cosmic Consciousness and in the Atharvaveda, he tried to transfer these powers to his mundane existence. So the Vedic knowledge, the true Veda, like a tree unfolding its branches, grew out of a single seed, the monistic consciousness and carried its invisible sap, the solar revelation, throughout the centuries.

When the Vedantic times began, this sap was still flowing with all its power and vitality and it found an excellent expression in the Upanishads, which can be considered as the most representative texts of that philosophical school of thought. In Vedanta, which means the end or the culmination of the Vedas, the Vedic universal message is experienced in a new light. In the Vedas, it was felt that the entire universe was permeated by light, that nothing existed but light, that even the darkest night would be removed by light. In the Upanishads, this cosmic light became the unseen, inner light, which impelled the sage to search for it deeply in his own nature by a process of untiring discrimination. The Upanishads were the outer poetic expression of this inner quest as the Vedas were the hymns of praise to the all-pervasive nature of the divine light.

Today, the Vedic corpus of mantras, together with the data and practices recorded in the Tantra and Agama literature, remains one of the rare keys to experience the spiritual light, which dawned in the conscience of the Vedic seers, and it is on these ancient revelations that Solar Yoga rests. The method presented in this book is an original attempt to fuse into a single practical approach the search for the spiritual sun found in the two main branches of Hindu Yoga sadhana, the Vedic and the Tantric lines, which have existed for millennia in India, developing in parallel with other main schools of Hindu philosophy.

Inspired by their practical experience of Hatha Yoga and Raja

Yoga and guided by their intuition, the authors studied a great number of texts, often in their original Sanskrit version, searching for a common denominator, a basic pattern which would reflect this quest for the spiritual light in a simple, reproducible and energizing way and, at the same time, be suited to the modern way of life. This pattern is highlighted in the mantras dedicated to the sun. These solar mantras, which are studied in chapter four, find their origin in the section of the Yajurveda dedicated to the worship of the spiritual sun and attributed to sage Praskanna. In the later Vedic literature, namely, in some of the Upanishads, the power and healing qualities of the solar sound vibrations are emphasized. The solar revelation is found again in the later epic period of Sanskrit literature, in the Ramayana, where sage Agastya initiates Rama, the hero of the Mahabharata, into the solar mantras. In the entire stream of Vedic literature, the texts show that the seers worked with the sun, light and nature in order to discover the inner resonance of the cosmic laws in their individual consciousness, which they used as a medium of reflection for the universal Consciousness.

For the Yoga seekers of today, the sun can likewise become a great source of inspiration. The physical sun should not only be an object of scientific research or a dispenser of energy and light; but it should also impel the seekers to search beyond the physical sun for the infinite, divine source of energy out of which it was itself created. As scientific knowledge increasingly expands, a return to one of the furthest shores of spiritual knowledge, the Solar Yoga, seems justified in order to recover this Light.

THE METHOD OF THE SOLAR YOGA

The primary manifestations of Consciousness are infinite light and endless sound. This eternal light is extremely subtle and invisible to the physical eyes but it illuminates the entire creation. It corresponds to a state of complete unity and harmony. The immeasurable space cannot be limited or fragmented since it is the ethereal support of all the vibrations which shape and condition life. The radiant sun, which shines in the immense celestial vault, is the most powerful and natural concentration of the vibrant light spreading its rays of energy through the vastness of cosmic space.

In Solar Yoga the sun is chosen as a mandala or an icon of

meditation with which a complete state of identification is sought. The solar reality has to be experienced on three different planes before the energies of the sun can be made to transform human nature in a positive manner. These are the physical sun, with the processes of visible light, heat and movement; the psychic sun, with the phenomenon of energy and breath; and the spiritual sun, with the dynamic inner awareness of pervading consciousness. The yogic practice consists in attracting the light and the energy of the sun in order to achieve a constant purification and regeneration of the body, the mind and the spirit. Therefore, a scientifically designed set of techniques and exercises are prescribed in this book to achieve a gradual and partial identification with the sun, which should eventually develop into a total identification of human consciousness with the supra cosmic origin of the solar light and energy, or, in other words, with pure Consciousness.

This form of Yoga is dynamic and integral and has to be practised on the three planes simultaneously but in a graduated manner. The aim is to find the genuine centre of individual consciousness and to re-establish the link between it and cosmic Consciousness through a method of concentration on the multi-dimensional solar reality. This state of full self-awareness will then imprint a new direction onto all the cells of the human psychophysical system until they will be in a condition to vibrate in unison with the universal, cosmic rhythm. This should bring health to the body, peace to the mind and pure light to the spirit. The solar triad should, indeed, inspire those who practise this form of Yoga to work towards greater ideals by refining physical sensations and mental processes and by heightening the faculties of insight into, and the understanding of human condition and cosmic love.

The Solar Yoga method follows the basic principles and divisions of the traditional forms of Yoga while giving a major emphasis to the process of identification with Light. When this sense of identification is limited to the physical plane, the aspect of movement is stressed and the practices are concentrated on the body and the lower mind as well as on breath, the unifying instrument between them. The aim is then to prepare body and mind by a regulated course of asanas or body postures and breathing techniques in order to create harmony and peace on this plane.

When the sense of identification is extended to the psychic plane, the aspect of energy is emphasized and the techniques will focus on the higher aspects of breathing and the energy processes or pranayama. Through these exercises practitioners learn to nourish the brain and the deep-seated spinal centres with subtle energy, or prana, so as to awaken the latent spiritual faculties. So, after physical and mental purification, the solar spark, which vibrates in the subtlest level of the mind, can be experienced as a source of constantly renewable energy.

When, finally, the sense of identification reaches the spiritual plane, the aspect of pure light is underlined and the processes are based on the gross and subtle production of vibrations or mantras. The subtle energies of the spiritual sun are to be assimilated by specific vibrational exercises, which help to extract the essence of the solar light and energy and to store them in the different subtle spinal centres. Through vibrations or mantras, the contact of the physical and psychic planes of being with the spiritual essence of life is rendered conscious and the subtle centres of the brain are made receptive to the descent of a superior form of energy.

In Solar Yoga body movements, breath, vital energy, lower and higher mind and vibrations, are all experienced as secondary manifestations of supreme Consciousness whereas light represents its first and foremost expression. By a gradual identification with light, practitioners learn to isolate body and mind from lower and grosser forms of vibrations and to attract progressively subtler vibrations until they experience a state of full identification with the eternal light. They will ultimately discover that there is no real separation between their individual consciousness and the all-embracing cosmic Consciousness.

Through the process of Solar Yoga the state of Yoga or unity is obtained. The whole personality becomes loving, compassionate, energetic, harmonious and bright, like the sun, which projects its radiant rays outwardly, but inwardly absorbs the subtle energies of the invisible, perennial light.

Photo 2. Sun Temple of Konarak (Orissa, India). View from the south. Detail of wheel on 'Jagati'. Mid 13th century. Kalinga style. Sandstone. By courtesy of A.I.I.S.

CHAPTER 2

ASANAS

THE CONCEPT OF ASANA OR POSTURE

In Solar Yoga the practice of asanas or postures has an important role to play provided it is not considered as an end in itself but rather as a means towards a greater goal. In this book, twenty-five of the main classical asanas have been presented in a way which tries to suit the scientific frame of mind of a modern seeker while remaining faithful to the spirit of the classical Yoga texts. This has been possible owing to the particular nature of Solar Yoga, which attempts to blend in a harmonious, clear and practical way the Raja Yoga precepts with the Hatha Yoga techniques. While the former approach requires a great power of concentration to discover the true essence of human existence, the latter approach is closer to a psycho-physical discipline which aims at an integrated system of personal development. When these two approaches are blended into a spiritual and scientific method they constitute a way of life, which involves the whole spectrum of human personality and cosmic reality: the purpose of Solar Yoga.

In the Yoga Sutras of Patanjali, one of the most important classical texts on Raja Yoga, which unfolds the entire path of Yoga in eight graduated stages, the practice of asanas constitutes the third step. In the relatively limited number of aphorisms dedicated to the study of an asana, the author describes it as a steady and easy posture to be practised after mastering the first two stages of the Yoga path, the yamas and niyamas, or codes of behaviour. In this context a yogasana is considered a steady posture which can be comfortably kept by the practitioners for a period of time long enough to enter into communion with the divine essence of human life. This state of communion is the goal of the Yoga practice and philosophy, which Patanjali has admirably condensed in about two hundred Sutras or aphorisms. In this classical text the evolutionary work of Yoga is described in a universal yet concrete manner. By a progressive practice divided into eight stages practitioners are led to discover their true nature through a discriminatory awareness of what is permanent and what remains transitory in life. In this discovery, which requires a total concentration of the senses, the organs of action, the mind and the inner intuition, the body can become a source of disturbance when it has not been trained to be still and relaxed. In Raja Yoga, the evolutionary work is carried out simultaneously on the physical, the psychic and the spiritual planes, but the changes of consciousness come mainly from an acquired control of the mind. Patanjali has therefore dedicated only a few aphorisms to the asanas, which are practised essentially to calm the body in order to remove any obstruction that may disturb the inner search of the mind.

By contrast, in the classical texts on Hatha Yoga, like the Hatha Yoga Pradipika by Yogi Swatmarama or the Gheranda Samhita by Sage Gheranda, the practice of asanas is treated in a more detailed and scientific manner and is focused on the body and the energy. According to this school of thought a correct and sustained practice of asanas should produce movements of subtle energy in the body, which, in turn, would lead to the changes of Consciousness needed to reveal the true nature of human existence. Whatever the approach chosen may be, the practice of asanas seems to be the bedrock of the entire process since no work of evolution can truly start without the foundation of a healthy body. This realization led the ancient yogis to devise an entirely scientific series of postures giving greater stability and resistance to the psychophysical system.

This stability and firmness of the body and mind depend strongly on the inner attention and silent awareness, which are brought about by breath regulation.

It will be easily understood that asanas are not mere physical exercises, but they constitute a field of multiple experiences for the practitioners. They are performed to balance the incessant activity of the body and the mind. Harmony comes from a proper relationship of the different planes of being whereas disorder results from unfulfilled desires on any of the three planes, which create obstructions to the free flow of energy. In other words harmony sets in when a true sense of identity with the eternal spiritual nature of the human being arises whereas disorder, with its consequent psychosomatic tensions, stems from an erroneous identification with the impermanent nature of physical life.

When the asanas are properly executed they can support an infinite variety of psychic experiences, which create a stronger unity between body and mind. Finally, when the asana ceases to be the field of psychophysical sensations only, it becomes the instrument of an inner experience and the asana becomes a meditation posture or a true yogasana.

This triune concept of body, mind and spirit finds a further justification in the ancient philosophical approach to the constitution of the human system. According to the classical schools of Hindu philosophy like the Samkhya, Yoga or Vedanta systems, a human being is considered as a centre of Consciousness that irradiates energy or prana, on five main planes of manifestation known as the *koshas* or sheaths of energy. These sheaths are seen as specific configurations of matter and energy, which interpenetrate one another and are kept in harmonious functioning by the power of prana, the subtle cosmic energy. Through a constant practice of asanas and pranayamas, the practitioners become a better exchange medium between the cosmic, universal energy and the individual, differentiated forms of energy, which activate each of the five planes. The koshas are thus to be understood as planes of consciousness and they represent concrete stages of the inner experience which, with practice, unfold before the practitioners'consciousness acting as a witness.

The yogic work of evolution consists in bringing the effulgence of the inner core to each sheath, thereby rendering it fully conscious and alive with the Divinity that is the essence of being. The practice thus consists in working from the physical sheath, the annamayakosha, up to the subtlest, the anandamayakosha, through which the inner core of Divinity can be experienced.

THE CONCEPT OF KOSHAS OR ENERGY SHEATHS

In Solar Yoga the five sheaths constitute the three main planes of experience for the practice of asanas and pranayamas.

Koshas or sheaths	Asanas	Purification methods
Annamayakosha	Body plane	Asanas, Cleansing processes
Pranamayakosha Manomayakosha	Energy plane	Bandhas, Kriyas, Pranayamas, Mudras
Vijnanamayakosha Anandamayakosha	Divinity plane	Concentration, Mantras, Meditation

Table 1. The Concept of Koshas or Energy Sheaths

On the physical plane, the effects of the asanas and the pranayama practices are mainly felt in the endocrine and nervous systems, which direct the main organic functions of the body. The neurochemical effects produced by the postures help to restore the biological rhythms of the tissues by removing tensions, which are built up in different parts of the organism. These tensions may have their origin in the physical, the mental or the spiritual plane but they are normally revealed in the execution of the postures as blocks to the movement of energy. The removal of these tensions brings organic regeneration and health.

On the energy plane, breath is the guiding factor and its regulation and control produce changes in the bio-energy potential of the human system. In this sense, the asana can be experienced as an interface between the subtle psychic plane and the nervous system.

On the divinity plane, the asana becomes an attitude of meditative adoration: the body becomes the temple of the Divine. Vibrations or mantras are practised to enhance the link between the individual centre of energy and the cosmic source of energy according to specific energy patterns created in the different asanas.

Body Plane

Annamayakosha corresponds to the body plane. Its gross nature is made of the chemical constituents of the organism and it is sustained by solid and liquid food as well as by the denser element of air, the oxygen.

Energy Plane

Pranamayakosha corresponds to the energy plane. It is of a subtle nature and it is composed of a vast and intricate network of energy conductors and synthesizers, the nadis and the chakras, which channel the subtle cosmic energy, the prana, throughout the physical body so that it may be a healthy support for the mind. This sheath is sustained by the bio-energy of solid and liquid food and by the subtle bio electromagnetic force of the atmosphere, which is absorbed into the human system during the act of breathing. There exists an intimate connection between these first two planes. And, while the pranamayakosha is essentially an energy plane, it still has a strong physical component that can be influenced by the yogic breathing techniques. But, this sheath also owes its sustenance to more subtle planes and this is done, in the form of sound vibrations, thought forces or intuitive states. In this sense the pranamayakosha can be considered as a plane of energy which serves as a support for the divinity plane, constituted by the fifth subtlest sheath.

The Hatha Yoga techniques apply mainly to these two planes while the Raja Yoga method concentrates more on the subtler planes of Consciousness. In Solar Yoga an attempt has been made to blend these two classical approaches and give the practitioners a practical and simple method to develop their inner awareness and obtain a greater psychophysical harmony.

Manomayakosha or the mental plane is the receptacle of all the sensory impressions created by past experiences, be they gross or subtle, individual or collective, external or internal. It has a strong genetic component and the mental and psychic processes, which constantly stir it into action, sustain it. The objective of the Patanjali Yoga Sutras is to still this plane so that it may become a transparent medium of reflection for the two higher planes. Since this is an extremely subtle and dynamic plane, great vigilance and perseverance are required to discover its functioning and master it. When this plane is pacified, the inner light of the next plane can shine.

Divinity Plane

Vijnanamayakosha is the fourth sheath, the plane of evolution. It is the intuitive faculty of higher discrimination which is not influenced by the energies emitted from the three lower planes but which is in constant, intimate union with the fifth sheath. Unquestionable knowledge is derived from it in the form of pure Light and pure Sound. In this state the practitioners' entire lives are guided by their intuition that allows them to discriminate between what is true and false. It is also the plane of revelation on which truth is transmitted directly in silence by the enlightened beings to their closest disciples.

Anandamayakosha is the last subtle field of energy enveloping the inner core of the five sheaths. To discover this core and manifest its beauty, the entire work of Yoga graduated in seven steps on the previous planes is performed. It is the constant awareness of the inner Divinity in total surrender of the individuality. It is the truth experienced by the great spiritual masters who were not influenced by dogmas or rules but who followed the dictates of the inner voice. On this plane the universal cosmic law of truth operates beyond body, energy, senses, mind and intellect. It is a state in which all these human components fuse into a blissful unity. It is the state of liberation. Anandamayakosha or the blissful experience is the state described by all the great world religions as the Divinity living in the innermost recess of the human heart. The discovery of this state is the ultimate aim of Yoga and it can only be realized by a process of inner awareness, a return to the source of being.

THE ROLE AND PURPOSE OF ASANAS

According to the classical Yoga texts the number of asanas defies imagination. In more realistic terms about one hundred asanas can be retained as practicable and, out of these, twenty-five are considered to be important for the present phase of human evolution.

Traditionally, asanas were classified by names, which evoked different aspects of life, from the mineral to the human plane. Asanas could thus represent objects like Dhanurasana, Halasana, minerals like Vajrasana, Parvatasana, vegetals like Vrikshasana, Padmasana, animals like Matsyasana, Ushtrasana or archetypes like Hanumanasana. This was not a haphazard classification since the regular practice of the particular asanas was intended to develop the power potential corresponding to that particular class of inanimate and animate beings. By concentrating on the qualities or attitudes of these different classes of living creatures the yogis could develop certain energy patterns, which conferred on them the power inherent in these beings. This realization was derived from a close and intimate study of nature performed by the ancient yogis who experimented with the energy patterns on themselves and devised a code of practice known as Hatha Yoga.

In the true spirit of a Yogasana, practitioners are led to experience the tremendous energy that lies dormant inside their system, as the culmination of millennia of planetary evolution. They are required to control and master these different forms of energy in order to fuse them into the divine energy, which resides in the core of their being and consciously recover their link with the cosmic intelligence. In other words, the supracosmic intelligence manifests itself on the cosmic plane and it is revealed in silence to the spiritual masters in the form of mantras or vibrations, which they, in turn, transmit to their disciples who energize their mind and body with these powerful divine vibrations with the help of asanas and pranayamas. This is the reason why the Yoga practice is progressive and is normally performed under the guidance of a master. It is then easily understood that an asana is not an end in itself, but only a means to reach the highest goal of Yoga or the state of communion with the inner Divinity.

The asana is meant to play a stabilizing role for the physical organs, the nervous system and the mind in order to harmonize the inner energy movements with the breath. This process can take place because the performance of asanas has a direct effect on the nervous system. The central nervous system is graphically a tube that expands to form a number of ventricles in the centre of the brain. Like a tree growing upside down its trunk develops as the spinal cord inside the vertebral column from which the nerves of the autonomous nervous system branch off to the vital organs of the body.

The ancient yogis, through their keen inner awareness, discovered the link between cosmic and individual consciousness as well as the flow of inner energy, which they described as a tree with its roots in the air and its branches to the ground. By an attentive observation of the laws of nature these ancient sages realized that the main axis and roots of the tree had to be preserved from any risk of damage if the tree was to survive. This realization led them to devise, by analogy, a series of postures to strengthen the vertebral column by making it flexible and resistant. This would reinforce the nervous system and influence favourably the energy movements inside the psycho-physiological system. They encountered obstacles to the perfect execution of the postures and to the complete calming of the mind in the form of energy blocks in the different parts of the organism. They then had recourse to the powerful instrument represented by their breath and, as is explained in the chapter on Pranayama, they experimented with various forms of breathing techniques and recorded the effects on their organisms. They then coded these various methods according to the desired results. This became the science of pranayama transmitted from masters to disciples.

In substance, for the energy to move freely, all the joints of the body have to be properly released and the vertebral column energized in all its sections by a series of postures and counter postures. Following this, the entire psycho-physiological system must be properly relaxed before any pranayama practice can be undertaken. When the asana is properly executed it helps practitioners to withdraw from the outer world and to start the inner discovery of the various planes of consciousness, described earlier as koshas, going from the grossest to the most subtle level of inner experience.

Because of an uninterrupted line of transmission between masters and disciples, asanas to this day still fulfil this role. They have been designed primarily to maintain the flexibility and stability of the vertebral column, which constitutes the vital axis of the body, to eliminate the blocks that build up in the joints due to an accumulation of toxins and to remove any obstruction to the flow of energy in the psychophysical system. In this way the mobility of the vertebral structures is maintained while the possible degeneration of the four natural physiological curves of the spine are prevented. In the execution of asanas, this is achieved by the combined effects of breathing and the action of anterior, lateral and posterior muscles of the trunk while the arms and legs are used as a lever mechanism in the dynamic phases of the postures.

Every asana described in Part Two produces specific effects on the physiological curves of the spine. The spine is composed of four main physiological curves. The lowest curve is a concave rigid structure made of five vertebrae, which have joined into the sacral bone. The second curve is convex and it is made of the lumbar vertebrae. This area of the spine tends to be affected by a phenomenon of hyperlordosis caused by an excessive contraction of the back muscles and an exaggerated weakness of the abdominal muscles. Asanas, such as Padahastasana, Paschimottanasana, Setubandhasana, Ushtrasana, Pavanamuktasana, Shalabhasana, which help to relax the posterior muscles and tone the anterior muscles, will have a beneficial effect on the sacrolumbar section of the spine.

The third physiological curve of the spine corresponds to the dorsal vertebrae, which act as junction points for the ribs and the intercostal muscles. These muscles tend to be stiff and their lack of elasticity increases the back cifosis and depresses the thoracic girdle, thereby reducing the breathing capacity. Asanas, like Gomukhasana, Ardhamatsyendrasana, Ardhachandrasana, Parvatasana, Dhanurasana, Trikonasana, Halasana, Matsyasana and Bhujangasana, which help to reinforce the posterior muscles and to relax the thoracic girdle, will have a positive effect on the thoracic section of the spine.

The last curve made of the cervical vertebrae is the most mobile and delicate one and the group of muscles in this section of the spine tend to contract easily, thereby producing a cervical hyperlordosis. Asanas, such as Vyaghrasana, Matsyasana, Gomukhasana, Shirshasana, Bhujangasana, which help to relax and strengthen the neck muscles while toning the anterior and lateral muscles of the same area, will have a favourable effect on this section of the vertebral column.

Other asanas, such as Trikonasana or Ardhamatsyendrasana, which turn and tilt the vertebral column, will have a torsion effect on the back muscles while asanas, such as Vrikshasana, Shirshasana and Vyaghrasana, produce a stretching and balancing effect on the entire spine.

The vertebral column will become more flexible and the nervous system properly toned when the execution of asanas provides for an alternate elongation and arching of the entire back. This is achieved by a combination of forward bending postures and backward bending postures. The forward bending postures such as Padahastasana,

Paschimottanasana, Halasana, Pavanamuktasana and Dharmikasana produce a posterior elongation and an abdominal compression on a slow, deep and conscious breathing rhythm. The backward bending postures such as Bhujangasana, Shalabhasana, Matsyasana, Dhanurasana, Ushtrasana or Hanumanasana cause an arching of the middle back with an expansion of the rib-cage, thanks to the elongation of the anterior part of the body.

Another class of asanas, the inverted postures in which the navel is higher than the throat, have a deep effect on the energy currents: they are Shirshasana, Sarvangasana, Viparitakaranimudra or in a limited way Padahasthasana, Setubandhasana or Parvathasana.

All the asanas should be executed according to a precise method in which the movements should be mechanically correct, effected with a minimum waste of energy and effort, and aided by the correct breathing sequence. A relaxation interval should be provided between the asanas to allow natural reactions to occur. When asanas are performed according to the method described later in this chapter, they help to remove all the obstructions to the free flow of energy, which can then radiate in the body and in the mind.

All asanas should be practised gradually with concentration on, and awareness of, the inner movements of energy, which are linked to the breathing rhythm. This, in turn, has a calming and balancing effect on the mental energy, which can then tune into the subtle cosmic energy.

At a more advanced stage of practice, certain asanas can become pure meditation postures in which the breathing becomes completely subtle and spontaneous. These postures are the true yogasanas in which the body is kept steady and motionless and the mind is concentrated effortlessly on the subtle inner vibrations.

THE METHOD

The Solar Yoga method is an original blending of ancient yogic practices adapted to today's needs and way of life with a view to helping and guiding practitioners in their search for an inner harmony based on physical well-being, mental peace and spiritual illumination. In the following pages of this chapter, a description is given of the main elements that come into play in the study and practice of asanas.

Owing to the importance of the joints in the practice of asanas, a series of movements, called ashta sandhi vimochana kriya or the eight-joint-release-method, is also described in this chapter and the practical applications thereof are developed in Part Two.

Ashta sandhi vimochana kriya or the eight-joint-release-method

In a sedentary life the human body tends to become stiff, and unless the joints are properly exercised and the various muscles correctly trained, the flexibility needed to render the posture easy and steady cannot be summoned. This is the reason for introducing the chapter on asanas by a section dealing with the opening of the main joints.

The structure of joints in the human body gives it flexibility and motion as well as the possibility of keeping verticality and balance. These joints are fragile components of a perfectly well designed anatomical architecture, which have to support the weight of the bones and muscles attached to them. It is therefore important to protect and reinforce them by proper movements.

The easy movement of the joints and the flexibility of the muscles are interdependent. Moreover, the main joints are placed strategically in the human body to articulate the trunk, which contains the vital organs, the spine and the spinal cord, with the limbs and the head containing the brain, the motor of existence. These joints, namely neck, shoulder-joints and hip joints are composed of a number of bones, cartilages and ligaments, which serve to protect the vertebral column. These serve as a first barrier in case of danger and their degree of efficiency will depend on the extent of their flexibility. At no time should the body be forced into difficult postures.

From the physiological point of view, the joints are also crossroad areas where certain nerves, veins, arteries and lymph glands are grouped for the organism to function systemically. So these areas are likely to become congested with an accumulation of toxins blocking the free flow of energy. The practices to open the joints help to alleviate this congestion. On the energy level, the position of the joints in the body corresponds to very important pranic energy circuits, which liberate energy when the higher yogic practices are performed. Therefore, it is essential that there should be a maximum flexibility of the joints on the body plane to allow the free flow of energy.

Asanas

The methodology applied to the study of the asanas presented in Part Two is briefly described here. As can be easily understood, the features of each asana have been described on three levels: the body, the energy and the divinity planes. Illustrations are also given for easy reference during the practice.

BODY PLANE

Definition and concept

The meaning of the Sanskrit name of the posture is given along with a presentation of the corresponding concept of the asana. This should help practitioners to understand the spirit underlying the practice of a particular posture.

Execution

This section describes the asana in its final form. It describes the goal of the practice for each asana with a minimum of detail and with extreme clarity. It is understood that when practitioners have reached this level of training, they no longer need to refer to a lengthy description but should rather be careful to remember the main features of the classical posture and try to experience the asana within their own system. In this context the main features of the classical posture have been given in each case.

1. The order of execution of the five stages of an asana is as follows: starting position, taking the posture, obtaining the posture, remaining in the posture and dynamic return movement to the initial position. These phases succeed each other harmoniously without any hasty or jerky movements.
2. The breathing cycle is the main element, which gives harmony to the execution of the asana. The breathing phases to be followed are given in capital letters in the text. In principle, exhalation accompanies a movement of the trunk with thoracic contraction as in the case of lateral and forward bending or rotations of the trunk. Inhalation is generally performed during a movement of

the trunk with thoracic expansion such as back bending and arm movements. In the case of breath retention, the specific indications are given for each asana. When there is no retention of breath, the posture is kept for at least half a minute and breathing should be done in a regular way.

3. The timing of the execution and holding of the asana is usually left to the practitioners' judgement and should result from the gradual practice of the asana. In case of time limits, which should not be exceeded without proper guidance, a word of caution is given with precise mention of the time. It should be remembered in this respect that the ancient yogis fixed an ideal duration of four and a half hours as a sign of perfect mastery over a particular asana: this is known as asanasiddhi in Sanskrit or the excellence in a posture. This is neither realistic nor desirable for ordinary practitioners.

Preparatory movements

The experience of the body plane should start with simple and easy movements. The asana is separated into various elements so as to reduce the difficulties, which may be encountered in the practice of the entire asana. This concept of preparatory movements fulfils a double purpose: firstly to liberate the energy by a maximum opening of the joints before performing the full asana; secondly to allow persons who are not able to perform the full asana to obtain the pranic effects associated with a partial execution of the posture. In the early stages of Hatha Yoga these preparatory movements should be practised to the exclusion of the full asana. They help the body to familiarize itself with the final asana and to overcome the energy blocks with a minimum of strain and risks. The body has its own intelligence and should never be forced.

In the intermediate stages practitioners who wish to study a particular asana in more detail can also perform these preparatory movements. At a more advanced stage practitioners should resort to this series of movements in the case of a lengthy interruption of the Hatha Yoga practice, which requires a progressive readaptation to the execution of asanas.

Counter postures

Kept for a certain period of time, an asana subjects certain parts of the body to more pressure than others. In order to eliminate any exaggerated effect created by an asana, the asana that follows in the sequence will be chosen with a view to balancing the pressures that may have been created by the previous asana and to adjust the energy movement in the body. This is the principle of a counter posture in which the general body movement usually goes in the opposite direction of the previous posture.

Contra-indications

For each asana, a warning is given to persons who may be affected by certain disabilities. They should refrain from practising that particular asana without proper guidance.

Sequence of asanas

This is the logical unfolding of certain movements and postures intended to produce a given result known in Sanskrit as vinyasa. For each asana, a complete vinyasa has been given in a graphic illustration. Any vinyasa can be built around a posture provided it takes into account the basic principles of Hatha Yoga.

Main benefits of the Asana

Under this heading a general idea is given of the main effects an asana may produce on the physical and psychic planes. The benefits listed are the most common and obvious ones. Nevertheless their appearance cannot be construed as an automatic and systematic phenomenon but will be determined by a whole series of factors ranging from age, sex, morphology, state of health, mental attitude, breathing capacity, to such aspects of the practice as environment, duration, progression, frequency, tenacity, inner awareness and devotion.

ENERGY PLANE

The scientific and philosophical background to the energy plane is given in chapter three on pranayama. It is important to remember that the yogic approach to psycho-physiological well-being is based on a process of continuous cleansing and purification of the body and the mind. In such a state the cosmic energy can flow harmoniously through the network of subtle nerve channels, the nadis, which form the pranic body or pranamayakosha. When the psycho-physical system is constantly purified it allows for a better absorption of the energy from outer sources, such as sun, moon, cosmos and earth and provides an even distribution of the individual's own pranic energy. The breath is the main element of the asana, which will be used to reinforce, direct and distribute the flow of energy.

For each asana, a specific energy pattern has been given as well as the centre of energy or chakra mainly involved. This description is complemented by an indicative list of pranayamas, kriyas, bandhas and mudras given both as a preparation to the asana and as a feature of the asana itself. If they are practised as a preparation for the asana, they render the body more pervious to the flow of prana, which will find its optimum configuration in the energy frame delineated by the asana itself. If they are practised during the asana, they reinforce the particular energy pattern formed during the execution of the posture. These techniques that are described in the Pranayama chapter of Part Two are advanced forms of practice: they should be learned first under proper guidance in the context of a pranayama programme and only later be integrated into a full asana program of a more advanced type.

Mudras are practices, which help to create certain energy configurations: they intensify the energy movement already created by the posture and the breathing. Kriyas are techniques, which promote powerful localised energy movements. Bandhas are muscular locks that seal the energy in clearly defined parts of the body in order to intensify its flow in a reduced area. Pranayamas are all the breath regulation and energy management techniques.

DIVINITY PLANE

This refers to the Divinity present in every human being. In order to understand the background to this aspect of the asana practice an attentive reading of chapter four on Mantras is essential. On the divinity plane, the asana acquires its real meaning of yogasana or, in other words, a posture intended to free practitioners from any kind of psycho-physical limitations and allow them first to discover, then concentrate on, and finally identify with that Divinity which is the essence of life.

This is a contemplative attitude, which can be brought into the execution of the asanas at a higher stage of practice. This meditation in action helps practitioners to realize that life on earth becomes truly spiritual when each action, each movement and each thought is invested with a feeling of adoration, devotion and surrender to the higher principle of life. This is known in Sanskrit as bhavana, which is the ultimate state of the asana experience. It is a state that can be felt once the body has become pliable, obedient and relaxed, the mind alert, clear and vigilant, the nervous system calm and purified of all toxins and the breathing regulated, harmonious and spontaneous. Mantras or sound vibrations are used during the execution of the asanas in order to achieve these particular conditions.

In Solar Yoga, seven important sound-patterns have been chosen because of their particular connection with solar emanations. Each of the seven mantras displays a sound pattern directly related to a specific chakra. When these solar mantras are repeated in the order prescribed, their effect on the subtle spinal centres becomes very powerful. During the holding of the asana, the inner awareness links the particular mantra to the corresponding chakra and the entire concentration is centred on an infinitesimal point of the physical field of the asana. By a sustained concentration on this particular point the energy enclosed in that deep-seated spinal centre is released and distributed within the energy configuration created by the particular posture. These mantric patterns can be applied in a dynamic or a static way. In the former case the inner awareness is always directed in an ascending movement from the lower subtle spinal centres towards the higher ones. In the latter case the inner awareness is focused on the subtle spinal centre, which is mainly activated by the execution of a particular asana. This is an experience of silent observation.

When the three interrelated levels of energy — physical, psychic and spiritual — are properly integrated, the posture becomes an authentic yogasana : the three planes of being are totally identified with the solar mantras which irradiate their divine light and power in all the pranic channels and in all the cells of the body. The practitioners' consciousness becomes identified with cosmic Consciousness and the bhavana of the asana is experienced with all its concomitant beneficial effects on the three planes of yogic experience. In this state, the mind becomes calm and transparent and the higher Consciousness invests the brain and the nervous system and, through them, regenerates the physical body.

CHAPTER 3

PRANAYAMA

THE TRIUNE CONCEPT: PRANAVA, PRANA, PRANAYAMA

In Yoga as in any holistic approach to life, human nature is seen as a complex system of interrelated levels of energy. This global vision of the human being is enshrined in the three concepts of pranava, prana and pranayama. Breath, the support of life, is the common link between these energy levels and is intimately related to the universal, cosmic energy. Whether this relationship is viewed in its authentic, traditional and holistic context or reduced to a modern and scientific demonstration of the energy phenomenon, the fact remains that breath is the foremost manifestation of life. When a child is born, it emits its first cry with a breath and when life is ebbing out of the mortal frame, it does so with the last breath. This thread of life is a divine gift; its origin resides in the transcendental Consciousness manifested by the cosmic vibration ***Aum***, also called pranava. This God given breath is the vitality of both body and mind and the carrier of prana, the subtle cosmic energy that lies at the core of vibratory cell life and sustains all the vital functions of the organisms living on earth.

In the animate kingdom human beings are in a particularly privileged position as they are endowed with a mind presenting an elective affinity with prana. The powers of reflection, introspection, memory and intuition are all higher manifestations of prana, which, if properly used with the techniques of pranayama, help the mind to concentrate and allow the inner divine energy to manifest itself. Human beings are thus given the rare privilege of being able to return to the source of their own being and to manifest the Divinity on the plane of matter. The relationship between these three concepts is given unequivocally in the following Yoga Sutras of sage Patanjali.

'The Divine manifests in Pranava' I, 27

'The mind may also be calmed by the inward and outward movement of prana' I, 34

'After mastering postures, one must practise control of the prana -pranayama- by stopping the motion of inhalation and exhalation.' II, 49

'As the result of this, the covering of the Inner Light is removed and the mind gains the power of concentration.' II 52, 53

The three Sanskrit words pranava, prana and pranayama come from the same Sanskrit root 'pran' that represents the life force, the universal energy. These three concepts and the realities they represent form a continuum in which human beings are indissolubly linked to the divine source of cosmic energy.

Pranava

This is the original cosmic sound, the primeval vibration that constituted the beginning of the created universe. In the spiritual traditions of the world, it is referred to as the Word, the Logos or the First Breath of the Almighty. In the Hindu tradition, which is the frame of reference of Yoga, it is symbolized by the sound ***Om*** or ***Aum,*** which is considered to be the first manifestation of the divine or the origin of the entire creation. The divine, ultimate reality is beyond time, space and causation but it can be experienced through its prime manifestations, pure Light and pure Sound or ***Om***. The divine Consciousness is unlimited but it reveals itself through self-imposed limitations. Its first and greatest limitation is its union with energy out of which emanated the cosmic vibration ***Om***. This vibration shapes the unseen rhythm and harmony of creation. It is one and indivisible like the universal Consciousness out of which it was projected. In this light, it is said to be the Word through which all the words were created, the root of all languages and the goal of all forms of knowledge. ***Om*** is the beginning and the end of creation, as well as the expression of the eternal support of this creation. The graphic representation of ***Om*** consists of four curves: the first three curves represent the three states of manifestation and the fourth curve symbolizes the transcendental nature of ***Om***.

Since the cosmic vibration *Om* originated from the union of Consciousness with energy, it will last as long as this union exists, or, in other words, it will coexist with creation until the final dissolution. Although *Om* is an infinitely subtle vibration, it is nevertheless made up of all the vibratory manifestations into which it expanded after its initial projection out of Consciousness.

When energy is transformed into matter, *Om* becomes *Aum*: it is then experienced in its differentiated state and it divides itself into three audible parts *A, U, M* and a fourth inaudible part pointing to eternity. These three sound symbols or sound archetypes represent the three-dimensional structure of any manifested reality, which is in constant movement and transformation.

A represents the waking state of the universe and of all living beings. It stands for the evolution of matter, the phase of expiration in breathing and it symbolises creation.

U represents the dream state in living beings and the Light of the universe. It stands for the maintenance of matter and the phase of retention in the breathing process. It symbolises preservation.

M represents the state of deep sleep into which all experiences are unified. It stands for the involution of matter and the phase of expiration in breathing. It symbolises the state of dissolution.

This entire process of manifestation is present also in the cellular structure of the human embryo. From an initial cell, the first mitosis took place and caused a fast multiplication of cells into three main groups, which in turn constituted the ectoderm (skin and nervous system), the mesoderm (skeleton, muscles, vessels and blood) and the endoderm (breathing and digestive systems). The fourth group of cells developed at a slower rhythm into the reproductive system, the nexus between the human species and the higher states of consciousness. This group is formed by the reserve cells of immortality, which give the human being the potential to further the human species and to sublimate individual consciousness into cosmic Consciousness.

Om can thus be regarded as a powerful instrument of communication with life and its manifestations in a myriad of forms and with the divine support of life in its formless reality. In ordinary perception, the constant change called life is construed by the mind and the senses as a firm reality. But in yogic experience, this constant transformation is unreal: it becomes an illusion compared with the constant formless energy which supports it. The purpose of Yoga is to discover this subtle vibratory energy and to concentrate the entire inner strength on its development and mastery.

By concentration on Pranava, the latent Divinity is stirred into manifestation. When body, breath, senses, mind and intellect are unified, *Om* reveals itself. When all the preliminary stages of Yoga have been mastered, the power of the cosmic vibration *Om* can be felt and experienced in the depth of meditation as a very subtle wave without any resting point. Through identification with this endless vibration individual consciousness willingly and purposefully integrates itself into the endless cosmic process of creation, preservation and dissolution and thereby becomes master of its own destiny.

Prana

In the science and practice of Yoga, prana, a manifestation of pranava, is considered to be the universal subtle energy that animates matter. The entire physical universe is immersed in an ocean of prana, which constitutes the all-pervasive basis of all life forms.

The word prana thus represents the subtle energy, which permeates the universe at all levels as the prime manifestation of universal Consciousness, the supreme support and the sole and hidden cause of all manifestations. This metaphysical approach to prana is found mainly in the Upanishads, the basic texts of the Vedanta philosophy, where prana is seen as the life flow springing from the core of Being and manifesting itself according to the vibratory rate of the material bodies, dense and subtle, that it permeates.

The phenomena of gravity, magnetism and electricity are only outer manifestations of this subtle prana. All bioelectrical phenomena in the body are also governed by this subtle prana since this force determines the electrical mechanisms of cellular life.

Without wanting to reduce the concept of prana to a purely bio-electrical phenomenon, it can nevertheless be said that the vital prana required for sustaining life on earth is mainly found in the atmospheric air in the form of negative ions and in the fresh food that is consumed. These ions create a pranic field in the atmosphere, which has a direct influence on the human system through the nervous system and the subtle pranic channels. This bio-energy circulates in the human psycho-physiological system according to a very precise pranic pattern and it is accompanied by electrical manifestations such as ionic exchanges, modifications of the electrical potential and important bioelectrical charges in the organism.

In the act of breathing, the body is recharging itself with these negative ions, which are vital to the growth and the reproduction of the billions of cells in the body. The intricate mechanisms of absorption, distribution and evacuation of these ions can literally be experienced as subtle psycho-physiological currents needing constant recharge. In the ultimate analysis, it would seem that health, vitality and longevity would depend on the harmonious distribution of these currents throughout life.

In his excellent treatise on pranayama, a living Indian master of Hatha Yoga compares the activity of prana in the human organism to that of electrical energy: *'The generation and distribution of prana in the human system may be compared to that of electrical energy. The energy of falling water or rising steam is made to rotate turbines within a magnetic field to generate electricity. The electricity is then stored in accumulators and the power is stepped up or down by transformers which regulate the voltage or current. Prana is like the falling water or rising steam. The thoracic area is the magnetic field. The breathing processes act like the turbines, while the chakras represent the accumulators and transformers'.*[1]

The word prana can also denote the potential reserve energy in every human being. It is then divided into five major and five minor pranas according to the functions they fulfil in creating, preserving and transforming life. In this case, the word prana is usually accompanied by the word "vayu" which means current or air. Prana vayu thus means a current of subtle energy.

These five main prana vayus or five different types of vital energy perform all psycho-physiological functions. These five pranas act through the five subsidiary nerve centres in the brain and in the spinal cord. Amongst the main classical texts referring to prana, the Sangita Ratnakara of Sarngadeva gives in the second section entitled "Genesis of the human embodiment" the ten modifications

1. 'Light on Pranayama' B.K.S. Iyengar.

of air with a richness of details about the location, the function and the modes of operation of these ten pranas. The Gheranda Samhita of sage Gheranda gives the ten prana vayus and their description in the fifth lesson of the sage to his disciple Chanda Kapali.

1. ***Prana*** moves from the root of the navel into the thoracic region. This energy controls the breathing process and the verbalization function. Its field of action extends from the navel to the mouth and nose. Prana governs the verbal mechanism and the vocal apparatus, the respiratory muscles and the movement of the gullet through the cervical portion of the autonomic nervous system. In pranayama, prana activates the inhalation process.
2. ***Apana*** moves from the root of the navel into the lower abdominal region and it controls the function of elimination. Its field of action extends from navel to feet. Apana mostly controls the autonomic actions of the excretory apparatus of the body through the lumbar portion of the autonomic system. In pranayama, apana activates the exhalation process.
3. ***Samana*** is the power behind digestion. It is the gastric fire, which extracts the pranic essence from solid and liquid food, and it maintains the health of the abdominal organs. It also has an integrating action on the entire physical body. It operates through the nerve channels and is responsible for metabolic processes. Its main field of action is from the heart to the navel and in the nervous system. Samana controls the digestive secretions through the sympathetic portion of the autonomic system in the thoracic region. In pranayama, samana activates the process of digestion needed for proper breathing.
4. ***Udana*** is an uplifting power and it controls the vocal chords and the assimilation of air and food. It is also the last breath at the moment of death. Its main field of action is in the throat and in speech organs. Udana functions above the larynx and controls all the automatic functions that come under the cephalic divisions of the autonomic system. It also functions as a psychic force that separates the pranic from the physical body at the time of death. In pranayama, udana activates the fire energy from the lower spine to the brain.
5. ***Vyana*** plays the role of energy distribution. It assimilates the energy from food and air through the circulatory and nervous

systems. Its field of action covers the entire body through the cardiovascular system. Vyana controls the voluntary and involuntary movements of muscles, joints and associated structures. In pranayama, vyana activates the transfer of energy from prana into apana and inversely.

There are also five minor pranas called upapranas:

Naga	or relief of the abdominal pressure by belching.
Kurma	or regulation of the intensity of light for the eyes by winking.
Krikara	or elimination of obstructions to breathing by sneezing or coughing.
Devadatta	or inducement to sleep by yawning.
Dhananjaya	or conservation of the substance remaining in the body after death.

Pranayama

Prana, the subtle life force, is maintained at the biological level by the twin processes of internal and external breathing. External breathing is activated by the complementary actions of the nervous system, which picks up the subtle movement of prana and triggers the breathing mechanism, the pumping action of the heart and its distribution of oxygenated blood through the circulatory system to all the organs of the body. Internal breathing takes place at the cellular level and consists of various metabolic processes of which oxydoreduction is the most important.

The act of breathing is one of the most obvious and tangible manifestations of prana and it constitutes the tool and the object of experimentation in the science of pranayama.

The ancient yogis concentrated their attention on their own breathing mechanisms, experimented with and discovered the cosmic laws that united them to the cosmic power. A methodical regulation of breath allowed them to enter the plane of subtle energy and to draw from it the vitality and power needed to give health and longevity to their physical frame. This ancient science of breathing and control of the subtle energies is known as pranayama, a Sanskrit word composed of the terms 'prana', the energy and 'yama', its extension, expansion and control. One of the main purposes of pranayama is to control and equalize the energy that is pulsating through the body and the mind. When this mastery is gained with the appropriate asanas and breathing techniques and when all parts of the organism are working in harmony, a power greater than the physical energy can manifest itself in humans. Moreover, the science of pranayama allows practitioners to discover their fundamental divine vibration, attune it to the cosmic vibration and find a resonance with all the vibratory rhythms of the universe.

To achieve this goal, pranayama techniques have been devised to intensify the rate of absorption of energy by the physical body. These techniques use the nervous system as a communication mechanism capable of increasing, reducing or modifying the energy potential in an individual. Moreover, these pranayama techniques have a profound effect on the mind, helping it to concentrate through the regulation of breath. And finally, pranayama is used as a spiritual discipline for the higher forms of Yoga, by attuning the breath to subtle vibrations known as mantras.

Pranayama allows practitioners to draw prana from its main sources, the atmosphere, the sun, the cosmic and telluric radiations, to store this prana in subtle energy centres situated along the spine, to move the prana in a harmonious and rhythmic manner along the pranic pathways and finally to remain in constant harmony and union with the universal energy.

Thus, pranayama covers a vast range of practices from the physiology of breathing, the different types of breathing, breath management, to the purification of the respiratory organs and the mastery over the subtle energy pathways and centres.

THE PHYSIOLOGY OF BREATHING

The basic physiological needs of the human body are predominantly met by the supply of oxygen and glucose. Whereas oxygen has an elimination function through the oxidation of waste matter, glucose mainly carries out the function of supplying energy to the cells. The respiratory organs in the act of breathing perform this process. The main function of these organs is to take the oxygen from the air, to transform it and to make it available to the cells as well as to expel the carbon dioxide accumulated in them. Ordinary breathing is thus a self-regulated mechanism of gas exchange. This self-regulation determines the rate and intensity of breathing through a control mechanism of the respiratory centres in the central nervous system, which integrates the information from mechanical and chemical receptors. When the carbon dioxide level in the arterial blood increases, the proportion of hydrogen ions in the cerebro-spinal fluid is changed. This, in turn, influences the respiratory centres in the medulla oblongata, which send impulses to the respiratory muscles and to the phrenic and vagus nerves and trigger the movement of the diaphragm and the rib-cage. When the muscular, nervous and skeletal structures surrounding the lungs start operating, the breathing mechanism starts working. This happens when a newborn child emits its first cry and produces its first breath: the breathing process begins to function and it will continue throughout life in a twin movement of inspiration and expiration.

In ordinary breathing, the lungs will inflate and deflate about sixteen times a minute and the heart will pump the blood through the body at an average rate of seventy times per minute. This kind of breathing depends on the automatic co-ordination of the nervous system, heart, lungs and circulatory system coupled to the smooth movements of the rib cage and the respiratory muscles.

Inspiration consists of an active expansion of the chest, which allows the soft and spongy lungs to be filled with fresh air richly charged with oxygen. This takes place when the rib cage expands and the diaphragm is lowered causing a reduction of pressure inside the lungs with a concomitant drawing in of air from the atmosphere. The oxygen from the atmosphere penetrates into the alveolar sacs of the lungs and diffuses into the blood stream through the capillaries surrounding the outer walls of the alveoli.

Expiration consists of passive recoil of the elastic rib cage, which pumps the vitiated air out of the lungs. This recoil takes place when the respiratory muscles are relaxed and when the surface tension inside the lungs keeps them contracted. At that moment, the pressure inside the lungs is greater than the atmospheric pressure and the air is driven out of the lungs through the respiratory tract. The expiration phase is completed when the abdominal muscles push the abdominal organs against the relaxed diaphragm and the residual air in the lungs is thereby expelled.

A retention phase separates the inspiration from the expiration: a pause at the end of each breathing phase in which the heart muscle is allowed to relax and the heartbeat is reduced.

The respiratory organs and their purification

Oxygen is vital to life. The intracellular metabolic processes that use oxygen for their sustenance also produce carbon dioxide, a waste product. In simple single-celled creatures, this gaseous diffusion occurs according to pressure gradients whereas in a complex system, like the human one, an elaborate blood circulation system activated by an even more refined system, the nervous system, carries out the transport function to and from the bodily tissues.

The gaseous exchange constituting the act of breathing takes place in paired specialized structures, the lungs, which are connected to the outside air by a breathing tube, the respiratory tract, composed of the nose, the pharynx, the larynx, the trachea and the bronchi. This respiratory tract is supplied with a great number of nerves and blood vessels, which play an important role in the breathing process. Finally a number of respiratory muscles come into play in the breathing process.

The nose

In its external portion, the nose is delineated by bony borders that carry the flexible cartilaginous attachments. This visible part of the nose only represents a small section of the organ. Its most important part is situated inside the head, above the hard palate, which forms a part of the roof of the mouth. It is made up of two cavities, the nasal cavities, which continue backward and open into the throat. Each of these cavities has a floor, a roof and walls covered by a mucous membrane.

Two functionally distinct areas appear on this mucous membrane: one corresponding to the lower two thirds of the nasal cavities, the respiratory area, the other corresponding to the upper one third, the olfactory region. In this upper region, very fine brush-like nerve filaments appear on the septum and on the lateral walls. From here, they are connected through the ethmoid bone to the olfactory bulb, which is joined to the base of the brain through the olfactory tract. In ordinary breathing, the two lower parts are mainly used for the passage of air during inhalation and exhalation and, in conscious breathing; the upper third is utilized also. This distinction acquires a particular relevance in the practice of pranayama as it is in the upper part of the nasal cavities that the separation occurs between the gross element in the air, oxygen, which goes to the respiratory tract and the finer element, prana, the bioelectrical impulse as it were, which is sent directly to the brain. The olfactory mucous membrane is softer and more delicate than the respiratory mucous membrane, which is not only thicker and more resistant but also marked by a greater vascularity which warms up and moistens the external air which is breathed into the lungs through the nose.

The pharynx

The pharynx is the portion of the respiratory tract, which starts from the backward openings of the nasal cavities and ends at the lower openings leading to the oesophagus and the larynx. It is divided into three parts: nasal, oral and laryngeal. It is equipped with seven openings: nose, mouth, oesophagus, larynx and ears.

In the act of breathing, the soft palate allows for a free movement of air by keeping a sufficient opening between it and the back wall of the pharynx whereas the oesophagus and the Eustachian tubes remain closed. The mucous membrane, which covers the nose, likewise lines the pharynx and all the passages leading there from. This is one of the reasons for insisting on purification techniques in pranayama.

The larynx

The larynx occupies the anterior portion of the neck from the base of the tongue to the cervical vertebrae (third to sixth). This part of the respiratory tract always remains open except in the case of swallowing and it is responsible for the human voice: Here, the mucous membrane after taking the shape of very thin folds, the true and false vocal chords, extends into the trachea into which the larynx opens. During normal breathing, the folds stand apart and the passage of air is smooth and noiseless and, in the act of speaking and singing, the folds are brought closer to each other and start vibrating due to the passage of air through the glottis. The air thus made to undulate produces the sound that is heard by the ears. In pranayama, there are certain techniques, which chiefly concern this area of the respiratory tract.

The trachea

The trachea is a membranous tube buttressed by cartilaginous rings enclosed in a fibrous membrane. The mucous membrane, which lines the inner surface of the trachea, contains a large number of mucous glands and is covered by a ciliated epithelium. Inhaled foreign particles are wafted by ciliary action towards the pharynx for expulsion by coughing. The trachea descends through the superior mediastinum of the thorax before dividing into two main bronchi.

The bronchial tubes

The bronchial tubes appear where the trachea divides into two sections at the level of the fifth thoracic vertebra. The left and right bronchi, one for each lung root, divide in turn into lobar and sequential bronchi, then into progressively smaller bronchioles, which terminate in the alveolar sacs of the lungs. Except for the last finest branches of the bronchi, these tubes are made of cartilaginous rings held by a very elastic tissue, permitting a permanently open state of the bronchi for the passage of air. This part of the inner mucous membrane is likewise lined with ciliated epithelium.

The lungs

The lungs consist of two spongy sacs made up of the alveoli, which are grouped into lobules themselves forming the lobes. The right lung has three such lobes and the left one has only two. These innumerable thin-walled alveoli, although compressed into a relatively small volume, provide a surface area for gas exchange that is thirty times greater than the body's surface area. This oxygen/carbon dioxide exchange is greatly facilitated by the pulmonary capillary network covering the air cells and the network of nerves inside the lungs. Since the endothelium of the capillaries is very thin, there is practically no barrier between the air contained in the alveoli and the very fine currents of blood streaming through the capillaries. This allows for a very rapid exchange of oxygen and carbon dioxide, the red cells spending less than a second in the pulmonary capillaries before returning to the left side of the heart for systemic distribution. Two layers; the pleurae consisting of a serous membrane, separated by the pleural cavity, cover the lungs. The lungs are shorter in front (sixth rib) than in the back (eleventh rib) owing to the position of the diaphragm, which forms the floor of the thorax, and they extend beyond the clavicles.

The respiratory muscles

All the respiratory muscles of the throat, the neck, the torso and the spine as well as the intercostal muscles and the diaphragm come into play in the breathing process. Amongst these, the diaphragm assumes a particularly important part in yogic breathing, especially when its movement is aided by the control of the abdominal belt.

The diaphragm is a large dome-shaped muscle, which constitutes the floor of the thorax: it separates the thoracic cavity from the abdominal one. It is attached in front to the cartilage of the breastbone, on the sides to the lower ribs and at the back to the lumbar vertebrae.

During inspiration, the diaphragm lowers itself from its normal resting arched shape and compresses the digestive organs situated below it.

During the automatic expiration, the diaphragm moves up again and allows the venous circulation from the abdomen to the thorax to be activated.

The diaphragm is a powerful muscle, which moves about eighteen times per minute, and it has been called the second heart because of its beneficial effects on the circulation.

Many breathing difficulties can be caused by an excessive rigidity of the diaphragm. Therefore, it has to be activated by pranayama techniques such as adhama pranayama or bhastrika that help to tone this important muscle. The abdominal muscles play an important part in forced expiration whereas the neck muscles become active during the practice of powerful pranayamas and during breath retention.

Good breathing is one of the first and basic aims of pranayama. The breathing control, as has been explained earlier, is of an involuntary chemical nature and it depends on muscular health, digestive ability, quality and quantity of blood supply, nervous vitality, a good elimination system and a proper mental attitude. Since the breathing process acts as a continuous recharging process of the entire organism aided by the unimpaired working of all its components, it is of the utmost importance to protect its integrity by removing all the obstructions to a smooth and efficient passage of air through the respiratory tract. Any respiratory impairment may have a physical, a nervous or a mental origin and, in each case, purification techniques are prescribed for the proper cleansing of the respiratory organs.

In the case of obstructions to the upper respiratory tract, nose, sinus, pharynx, larynx, due to chronic inflammation, mucous deposits, irritation and allergies, the techniques recommended for practice are:

- Jala Neti (Outer cleansing of the nose with water)
- Anunasika Pranayama
- Wall Posture
- Dhouti Pranayama
- Parvatasana

When the obstruction is due to a weakness of the diaphragm or to abdominal congestion, the techniques advised for practice are:

- Shvana Pranayama
- Breathing in Ushtrasana
- Breathing in Shashasana

When the obstruction is of a nervous origin, the techniques prescribed for practice are:

- Nadi Shodhana
- Nadi Shuddhi

When the impairment is of a mental origin the technique recommended for practice is:

- Pranava Pranayama

THE MANAGEMENT OF BREATH

Breathing is absolutely natural for a living being but it is usually performed under capacity and can be greatly improved. By a gradual awareness of the respiratory process, practitioners can bring the involuntary breathing act under their conscious control. This is done by a progressive discovery and regulation of the periodicity and rhythm involved in the breathing process during the practice of asanas, pranayamas and mantras. The regulation of the four phases of breathing: inspiration, full lung retention, expiration and empty lung retention, is needed to maintain the energy balance in the organism at a positive level. From the pranic standpoint, breathing represents the mechanical action and prana the electromagnetic force. So, energy spent in daily routine activities is automatically compensated for through conscious breathing and the organism is continuously recharged with pranic energy. In ordinary breathing, the quantity of oxygen substituted for carbon dioxide is greater than the quantity of the latter by 0,60% because the former is also used for physiological functions other than breathing. In conscious breathing, the emphasis is different: the carbon dioxide has to be expelled efficiently (rather than inhaling more oxygen) so as to allow the remaining portion of oxygen in the lung to carry the prana to the different organs of the body and induce an adequate cellular or internal breathing. This is achieved by the regulation of the four phases of breathing, the practice of the four types of breathing and by other pranayama techniques, which train the respiratory organs to function intensely, rhythmically and consciously.

The four phases of breathing

Inhalation or puraka is the act of receiving the cosmic energy through the air that is breathed into the lungs.

Exhalation or rechaka is the act of giving the individual energy to the cosmic energy through the impure air and the carbon dioxide that are expelled from the lungs. During inhalation, the pranic energy is stored in the brain and the central nervous system and during exhalation, the pranic energy unites with the mind and the soul and dissolves itself in the cosmic prana.

Retention or kumbhaka is the act of retaining the breath in the lungs between inspiration and the following expiration or retaining the breathless condition between an expiration and the successive inspiration. It is called antara kumbhaka and bahya kumbhaka, respectively.

During antara kumbhaka, or full lung retention, the cosmic energy is merged with the individual energy and the senses and mind are stilled.

During bahya kumbhaka, or empty lung retention, the individual energy is surrendered to the cosmic energy and the sense of ego tends to disappear at that moment. Since breath is the common link between the body, the energy and the divinity planes, it is of the utmost importance to start any pranayama practice by experiencing, directing and mastering the four phases of breathing.

This disciplined breathing known as sukha pranayama produces subtle chemical changes in the organism, brings the functions of the autonomic nervous system under control and calms the mind. This introduces harmonious and positive changes in the psycho-physiological complex while improving the rate, rhythm, intensity and quality of breathing. It is recommended that the practice should concentrate first on the inhalation and exhalation phases and, later, on the full lung retention followed by the empty lung retention phase. To achieve mastery over the four phases of breathing, practitioners should perform this breathing for fifteen minutes twice a day for a period of four to six weeks.

The four types of breathing

Apart from a temporal experience of breathing, practitioners should also become aware of the spatial dimension of breathing by practising regularly the four types of breathing:

Diaphragmatic, abdominal breathing or 'adham pranayama'

The lower lobes of the lungs are activated while the upper sections of the lungs remain less active. This is accomplished by specifically directing the awareness to that portion of the abdominal wall just above the pelvis. On inspiration, the anterior and lateral abdominal muscles contract and, since these muscles are attached to the rib cage and to the pelvis, their action lowers the diaphragm and increases the thoracic capacity. On expiration, the diaphragm moves up again and, by elastic recoil, the lower lobes are emptied of their residual air.

Intercostal, thoracic breathing or 'madhyam pranayama'

The right middle lobe and the left angular region of the lungs are mainly activated in this type of breathing. On inspiration, the lower rib cage expands in an ascending movement through the full activity of the intercostal muscles while the diaphragm and the abdominal anterior walls remain contracted. On expiration, the intercostal muscles relax, the rib-cage narrows and the lungs are emptied of the vitiated air.

Upper chest, clavicular breathing or 'adhyam pranayama'

The upper lobes are chiefly activated. On inspiration, the higher intercostal muscles and the muscles connecting the upper ribs, sternum and clavicles to the neck and skull are contracted and the rib cage expands to its fullest capacity. On expiration, the entire rib cage deflates as the diaphragm returns to its natural position.

Full yogic breathing or 'mahat yoga pranayama'

The three sections of the lungs are operating at full capacity by successive movements of the muscles of the abdomen, chest and neck in which each series of movements prepares the way for the next series of movements. This enables the lungs to be filled at maximum capacity and the gaseous exchange to be performed efficiently. When the first three types of breathing are practised in stages, they constitute vibhaga pranayama or sectional breathing. When they are practised in direct succession, they become mahat yoga pranayama or full yogic breath. When the vibration Om accompanies this latter type of breathing, it becomes pranava pranayama or the cosmic breath.

Since all life is sustained by the joint action of the external and internal breathing processes, the former taking place in the cells, and the latter in the respiratory tract, the major responsibility for Solar Yoga practitioners is to maintain the integrity of their breathing systems. This is achieved by the practice of asanas which will help them to train and discipline their lungs, diaphragm and intercostal muscles so that their breath may move rhythmically. Moreover, the regular practice of breathing techniques will give them a mastery over their breathing process, nervous system and mind. In the Yoga tradition, there are said to be more than seventy thousand pranayama practices. This is to be understood as meaning that a wide range of techniques exists, from the simplest to the most advanced, to meet practitioners' individual needs.

THE CHAKRA SYSTEM

In the previous chapters, the emphasis was on the physical aspects such as the physiology of breathing, the different types of breathing or the purification of the respiratory organs. A correct understanding of these principles coupled with a constant and rigorous practice of the asanas and the pranayama techniques will allow practitioners to gain a control over their physical body. The practice of asanas and simple breathing techniques helps to remove the obstructions to the flow of prana throughout the physical body whereas elementary pranayama techniques regulate the flow of prana in the body, calm the nervous system, positively balance the endocrine system with the result that the mind is able to concentrate and the will-power is strongly reinforced.

When this stage of development is reached, practitioners will be able to discover the higher aspects of pranayama, which will be briefly described in the present chapter. The practice of more advanced techniques of pranayama results in the control and harmonization of the subtle energy patterns that constitute the pranamayakosha or energy sheath, the second of the five sheaths described in the chapter on asanas. These advanced techniques are generally practised under the guidance of a Yoga master and they require great constancy on the part of the practitioners as well as a certain adaptation of their living habits, diet and environment and cannot, therefore, be considered in detail here. But an overview of the vast field of pranayama would not be complete if the main points of the pranic anatomy were omitted. This chapter gives therefore a descriptive presentation of the energy dimension of the yogic experience, which by its very nature is intuitive and subjective. It only gives an introduction to this very complex subject intended for those who are still in the early stages of the Solar Yoga practice. The more advanced practitioners may directly apply the instructions given in the sections entitled 'Energy Plane' and 'Divinity Plane' of the asanas in Part Two of the book.

According to most of the authoritative Yoga and Tantra texts, human beings are composed of five energy sheaths or koshas acting on one another through the power of prana. Although this subtle energy can be directed at will to any of the five koshas, it is best experienced as a well-defined energy structure in the pranamayakosha or subtle energy sheath. This energy anatomy can only be discovered by a keen and time-consuming inner perception of the movement of energy inside the human system.

In other words, the pranic body can be likened to a vibrating bio-electromagnetic system, which is the seat of constant exchanges between telluric, cosmic and divine energies. This field, which is structured according to a definite pattern, surrounds the embryo in the prenatal stage, accompanies the human body throughout its earthly life and survives the physical frame after death. It has been stated earlier that the entire universe is bathed in an ocean of prana, which is of a vibratory nature. Any living organism on the surface of earth draws its vital rhythm from prana according to a general principle of resonance. This world of vibrating energy acts like a universe of music where each octave is in resonance with the lower and higher ones. The ancient yogis discovered this cosmic law in their arduous and penetrating work of self-discovery and they laid out the chakra system, which can be considered as the archetypal form of manifested life in the universe.

In human beings, the chakra structure is built along a central axis, the sushumna, with seven main chakras or centres of energy, which are surrounded by two criss-crossing energy lines leading from the lowest to the sixth chakra. The pingala line starting from the right of the axis carries a positive energy. The ida line starting from the left of the axis carries a negative energy. Ida, pingala and sushumna are the three main subtle channels of the nadi network that spreads throughout the pranic body. The word nadi comes from the Sanskrit root 'nad' which means sound, resonance, vibration and it represents a subtle channel of cosmic, vital, seminal or other forms of energy.

In the pranic anatomy, the network of nadis has two main points of origin. One centre is located in the heart, as the seat of consciousness: about one hundred nadis emanate from that centre and their main function is to unite mind and heart. These nadis are either a medium of manifestation for emotions and mental formations or they are receptors for the manifestation of higher consciousness. The other centre is located immediately below the navel: it is the point of origin of more than seventy thousand nadis. Their role is to transmit the subtle part of the digested food, the vital energy in breath, water and blood to the main organs. Some of these nadis are the subtle counter-parts of arteries, veins, nerves or lymph tracts and all nadis are conductors of energy in one form or the other. Fourteen of these nadis play an important part in balancing the pranas and the koshas.

Sushumna, the central axis of the chakra structure is the link between two poles: the first and the seventh chakras. According to the law of resonance, this portion of the axis represents only one fraction of reality. This seven-element structure is in resonance with the structure immediately below it, corresponding to the subconscious plane, and the one immediately above it, corresponding to the seven planes of higher consciousness. The figure seven constitutes an octave and, in most esoteric traditions, this number has been chosen as the symbol of full manifestation, the beginning and the end of a cycle. From microcosm to macrocosm, at the atomic, cellular or planetary level, this number governs the rhythm of creation. In the energy sheath of the human system, the pranamayakosha, this structure is reflected in the seven chakras found along the sushumna axis, from the base of the spine to the crown of the head. Their Sanskrit names are muladhara, svadhishthana, manipura, anahata, vishuddhi, ajna and sahasrara.

These seven main chakras, which are situated along the sushumna, play an important role as interfaces between the three interrelated energy planes, namely physical, psychic and spiritual. The lowest pole of the axis is located at the base of the spine, in the sacral region, and it constitutes the pole of the human species. This is the muladhara chakra in which the kundalini or the divine cosmic energy is stored and sealed in the body at the base of the spine. This potential energy can be tapped, by yogic practices, and channelled towards the highest pole of the axis, the sahasrara chakra, which is the seventh centre located at the crown of the head. When the kundalini energy rises along the central axis, the sushumna, it activates specific energies in the chakras, which have a reflection on the psychic and the physical planes.

These centres of radiating energy pick up the cosmic vibrations transmitted along the sushumna nadi and distribute them in the form of prana along the nadis. The chakras also receive the solar energy through the pingala nadi and the lunar energy through the ida nadi. In other words, these energy vortices are synthesizers of different types of vibrations, which give life and vitality to the psycho-physiological human system. The chakras are multidimensional structures exhibiting different energy patterns. Each chakra has its specific pattern, which is highly responsive to rhythmic breathing and to the repetition of sound patterns like mantras, or mental patterns such as different forms of concentration. In the average human being, each chakra works in an autonomous fashion and regulates the psycho-physical area under its control. In this case, the chakra acts exclusively as a self-regulated energy junction and its basic harmonious relation with the nadis and prana vayus, on the energy plane, is almost automatic. This natural harmony is reflected on the physical plane in adjustments of the energy flow effected by the nervous and endocrine systems in the vital organic systems, such as the urogenital, digestive, respiratory and circulatory systems. When the energy flows rhythmically, the different systems are in proper balance and the body is healthy. Moreover, any minor or temporary disturbance of the energy flow is automatically recorded at the chakra level of the particular organic system and the needed energy readjustment will take place. If the energy imbalance is of a more permanent nature, disease breaks out. Chakras are mainly interfaces between the pranic and the physical bodies, the pranamayakosha and the annamayakosha. They work as autonomous centres of energy regulation to ensure the integrity of the organic systems they command, like in any fail-safe system.

For practitioners, however, chakras have a more important role to play. From centres of energy, they have to be transformed into centres of consciousness. Yoga is a work of evolution in which cosmic Consciousness transforms the mind and through it the brain and the nervous system. The kundalini energy, which is the latent power in the human nervous system, is stirred into action through the influence of cosmic Consciousness and it arises along the sushumna, piercing the core of each of the seven chakras. In other words, the central core of the chakras, which is deeply embedded in the sushumna, opens up under the influence of the rising kundalini and allows the cosmic energy to fuse with the fiery energy. This fusion transforms all the energies, which have hitherto created the vortex known as chakra into a unique, extremely powerful, divine energy, which takes over the command of the entire system. This flow of a new form of energy in the five sheaths creates a mutation, a step in evolution. The classical Yoga texts have described this stage of evolution in different allegorical ways: the flowering of the lotuses, the piercing of the chakras, the awakening of kundalini or the arousal of the Serpent Fire. This stage can be reached only when the three energy knots or granthis, which separated the chakras and the koshas, are severed.

The first knot separates the muladhara and svadhishthana chakras from the manipura chakra. This knot seals the physical plane of being. The second knot separates the manipura and anahata chakras from the vishuddhi chakra. This knot seals the psychic plane of being. The third knot separates the five lower chakras from the two higher ones and marks the division between the two lower planes of being and the divinity plane. Ordinarily the lower koshas have a strong grip on the mind or, at best, these two koshas are so intimately linked that they continuously influence each other. This is because the two higher energy seals are still closed. In the case of an evolved human being, the higher koshas dictate the behaviour of the lower ones because the intermediary seal has been released.

And, finally, in the case of an enlightened human being, who has reached the ultimate step of yogic practices, the last kosha, the anandamayakosha, acts directly on the other four koshas since the third knot has been severed as well, thus allowing the divine energy to flow unimpeded through the five sheaths. The koshas are then integrated into one single unit and the three planes of being fuse in harmony. The aim of Yoga practices is thus achieved. This represents the highest state a human being can reach in this phase of planetary evolution: it is the Divinity manifested on the plane of matter, the end of the homo sapiens octave and the beginning of the homo intuitens octave.

By virtue of the resonance principle, each pranic feature such as a nadi or a chakra has a physical counterpart under its control and through which it operates. The different interrelated energies meet in the third ventricle of the brain. There, the cerebro-spinal fluid is influenced by the earth's electromagnetism, which, in turn, is affected by solar and cosmic events. From there, the cerebro-spinal fluid moves slowly through the ventricles of the brain down into the cerebro-spinal canal, lodged in the spinal cord, where it is processed by the nervous system. Through a network of pathways the nervous system works in co-ordination with the endocrine system to direct all the vital functions in the human system. The former acts as a synthesizer of information between the outer and the inner worlds and the latter operates like a modulator of the inner environment through a system of ductless glands, which secrete hormones that circulate freely in the bloodstream. These two systems are the physical counterparts of the pranic structure of nadis and chakras and they are organized according to the same principles. The central nervous system, with the brain contained inside the skull and the spinal cord enclosed in the vertebral column, corresponds to sushumna. The central nervous system is connected to the skin through the sensory peripheral nervous system and to the rest of the body through the autonomic nervous system.

The spinal cord is composed of a grey portion corresponding to the chitra nadi, a white area corresponding to the vajra nadi and in the centre of the grey area, a small orifice corresponding to the brahma nadi.

Thirty-one pairs of nerves emerge from the spinal cord to form the autonomic nervous system. It is divided into the thoracic and lumbar sympathetic system with an adrenergic activity of a more voluntary nature, which corresponds to the pingala nadi and into the cranial and sacral parasympathetic system of a more receptive, cholinergic nature that controls the vegetative functions and corresponds to the ida nadi. The vertebral column is divided into five sections corresponding to the organic areas governed by the five lower chakras through important nerve plexuses and groups of endocrine glands. The two upper chakras correspond to the pituitary and pineal glands respectively.

	Chakra	Spinal Section	Endocrine Glands	Organic Systems
1.	Muladhara	Coccygeal	Gonads	Urogenital
2.	Svadhishthana	Sacral	Adrenals	Urogenital
3.	Manipura	Lumbar	Pancreas	Digestive
4.	Anahata	Thoracic	Thymus	Circulatory
5.	Vishuddhi	Cervical	Thyroid	Respiratory
6.	Ajna	Brain	Pituitary	Mental
7.	Sahasrara	Brain	Pineal	Mental

Table 2. Correspondence between Chakra System and Anatomy

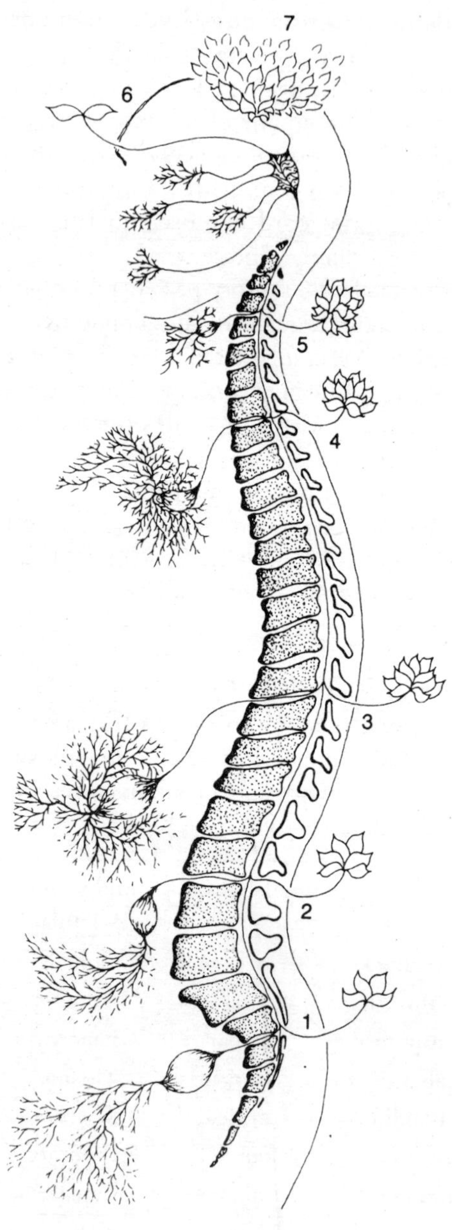

Illus. 1: Graphic representation of the Chakra system.

1. ***Muladhara*** is the root chakra located at the base of the spine. It is the nexus between the human species and the individual. It constitutes the starting point of the three main nadis; ida, pingala and sushumna. Its corresponding plexus is the sacral plexus for which the pranic control centre is situated at the junction of the fourth and fifth sacral vertebrae. It governs apana vayu in its balancing action with prana vayu during the breathing process. It is represented by the geometric figure of a yellow square, which represents the earth element, and its colour is yellow. When this chakra is transformed into a centre of consciousness, practitioners are ready to sublimate their physical nature. This chakra is the foundation of annamayakosha.
2. ***Svadhishthana*** is the seat of kundalini and is intimately linked to the muladhara chakra. This centre stores the impressions left by past actions and thoughts as well as the seeds of future actions in accordance with the law of causation. Its corresponding plexus is the hypogastric plexus for which the pranic control is situated at the level of the first lumbar vertebra. It governs the elimination function of apana vayu. It is represented by the figure of a silvery grey crescent, which symbolises the water element. When this chakra is transformed into a centre of consciousness, it confers the mastery over apana to the practitioners.
3. ***Manipura*** is the solar centre of the pranic body. It is the point of convergence of most of the nadis and it is an important connection between annamayakosha and pranamayakosha. A good co-ordination is required between this chakra and the preceding one in order to ensure a proper harmony between the energy of inhalation and that of exhalation. Its corresponding plexus is known as the solar plexus: a group of vegetative ganglia, which are densest in the abdominal region. The control centre is located at the level of the eighth thoracic vertebra. It is represented by the geometrical figure of a red triangle, which is connected with the fire element. When this chakra is transformed, it confers compassion and freedom from disease and fatigue. Together with svadhisthana, it constitutes the foundation of pranamayakosha.

4. ***Anahata***, the mystical heart, is the seat of emotion, creativity and imagination. It is manifested through the rhythmic beating of the physical heart which is directly associated with the ego. Its corresponding plexus is the cardiac plexus and its centre of control is located at the level of the seventh cervical vertebra. It is represented by a grey hexagon, which represents the air element. When this chakra is transformed into a centre of consciousness, it favours devotion and knowledge. It opens the spiritual path and liberates practitioners from sensual pleasures. It is the foundation of manomayakosha.
5. ***Vishuddhi*** is the important nexus between cosmic and individual consciousness. Its mastery opens the way to the divinity plane in the human being. Its corresponding plexus is the pharyngeal plexus and its centre of control is located at the level of the third cervical vertebra. It governs udana vayu. It is represented by a white circle, which represents the ether element. When this chakra is transformed into a centre of consciousness, it confers the power of understanding and true speech. It is the foundation of vijnanamayakosha.
6. ***Ajna*** is the meeting point of the three main nadis; ida, pingala and sushumna, and it is a strategic point for the generation and distribution of prana. Here, the divinity plane influences the functions of the lower planes. When this chakra is transformed into a centre of consciousness, it confers intuition and control over the body-mind complex. This chakra is the foundation of anandamayakosha.
7. ***Sahasrara*** is the opposite pole of muladhara. Its physical counterpart is the pineal gland. It is the culmination of anandamayakosha and the integration of the four lower koshas with the higher one. By continuous concentration on these two poles, control is gained over all the intermediary chakras. This centre governs the two brain hemispheres, the left hemisphere associated with analytical, logical thinking, corresponding to the solar energy, and the right hemisphere associated with a holistic, artistic and mystical tendency, corresponding to the lunar energy. When these two aspects are fully harmonized at the level of the cerebral cortex, the physical and psychic planes are in proper balance and can then be united to the spiritual plane.

CHAPTER 4

MANTRAS

Solar Yoga blends elements of various branches of traditional Yoga and effects a balanced harmonization of Hatha Yoga and Raja Yoga. But what singles out Solar Yoga is its important component of vibration techniques pertaining to the age-old tradition of Shabda and Mantra Yoga. In ancient India the power of vibrations manifesting as sounds and the energy of mental images expressed as thoughts was fully recognized and experienced on both the scientific and esoteric planes. A detailed study of these phenomena is beyond the scope of this book but some general principles can be given for the advanced stages of practice in Solar Yoga.

To reflect on the origin of any phenomenon constitutes an ideal way of discovering its essence. All philosophical schools have devoted a particular importance to the phenomenon of creation from which the entire universe and life in all its forms emanate. In Shabda Yoga, the Yoga of sound, the creation of the universe is seen as the union of shabda, sound, and artha, meaning. Pure sound is eternal, unstruck and subtle but it acquires a transient character when it is produced as audible sound by the striking of air with the vocal organs. It becomes a material manifestation in response to a thought movement, which seeks outward expression by the working of the will. The different stages of manifestation of this pure sound have been classified in the following manner in Shabda Yoga.

The unmanifest, primeval sound, is known as parashabda or supreme speech or logos. This state precedes creation: its nature is transcendental and it cannot be perceived by the mind or the senses. This is the causal state in which sound and light are identified and are expressed in the hidden power of pranava or *Om*.

When this subtle power is seen as the source of all vibrations it is known as pashyanti or the effulgence that accompanies a non-particularized movement towards ideation. It becomes an all-pervading vibration, which supports the entire creation. This is the state of unstruck sound when *Om* is experienced as the endless energy current of the universe. In this state lies the mystery of the harmonious and precise movement of planets, galaxies, stars and cells. This extremely subtle vibration can only be experienced in a state of deep meditation. At this stage, there is no differentiation between the object and its sound form or name. In other words, shabda and artha are in a merging state in which the mind plays the role of perceiver without being influenced by mental impressions or formations. The mind is thus in a state of perfect calm which renders it truly creative.

At the next stage, the mind comes into action stirred by the multiplicity of vibrations, which were enclosed in the original cosmic vibration *Om*. This is the madhyama state in which the mind acts both as the perceiver and the object perceived. The mind is involved in a constant process of conveying a meaning to the subtle impressions it receives: a movement of intuitive identification has begun while the inner and outer manifestations of sound remain fused at the inaudible level. This state can be experienced during concentration practices: the mind withdraws from the senses and recognizes impressions by naming them while remaining at the same time the object of its own cognition.

This is followed by a last stage in which the outer stream of verbal expressions dissociates itself from the inner current of subtle sounds giving utterance to the spoken word. This is the vaikhari state where sound becomes a language, a means of expression, a connection between the material world of objects and the subtle realm of vibrations. This is the state in which the spiritual dimension of life can easily be lost. When the association between the spoken word and the object it evokes becomes too strong or when the vibrational basis which is common to both the spoken expression and the object expressed is ignored, the mind falls into a condition of illusion in which it experiences a feeling of separation from its own inner source of pure light and sound. The mind is trapped in a world of multiplicity and forgets its quintessential nature of unity. This is what has been described as the state of maya or illusion in

Vedanta and as the original fall in the Bible. The ancient yogis experienced this cosmic movement of consciousness in their own psycho-physiological system and designed the principles and practices to be followed in order to rediscover the original state of identification with universal Consciousness. Their research forms the core of Mantra Yoga.

It is by a principle of resonance that the ancient yogis discovered the cosmic laws and applied them. Their inner realization found its expression in sound formulae, known as mantras, which contained in a seed form the subtle power or energy of their experience. Masters gave these mantras to disciples as coded transmission systems of the original vibration experience. These systems had to remain coded and in a certain way secret because the ancient yogis had discovered that a tremendous production and exchange of energy could take place, by a phenomenon of resonance, between systems vibrating at the same frequency. In meditation, the yogis could tune themselves to the cosmic vibration, and through resonance, they could transmit the power of the cosmic vibration to their mind, senses, organs, tissues and cells, so as to maintain them in a state of harmony and health. By an act of will, they could also transmit this power to worthy disciples: this was done by the ancient seers and is still practised by the living masters with extreme caution owing to the tremendous energy contained in a mantra which should only be used in a positive and spiritual manner.

THE CONCEPT OF MANTRA

A mantra is not an ordinary word made of a succession of syllables but it is a facet of cosmic Consciousness manifested as a sound vibration in the individual consciousness of a yogi. It consists of a subtle ideation movement and a gross uttered sound. Through a constant repetition of this sound vibration the mind is gradually sundered from the constantly changing flow of expressed and subtle sounds and gradually focuses on itself as the instrument of cognition of all these expressions. When the mind becomes its own object of cognition, it moves to a higher stage of evolution known as mantric consciousness or intuitive, causal consciousness.

In this way subtle energies can be made to resonate in the individual consciousness as emanations from the cosmos and directed to vitalize the mind, the senses and all the organic functions. When these subtle energies are focused, by an act of will and through the repetition of a mantra, on the individual consciousness itself, they will produce a gradual expansion until it becomes totally identified with cosmic Consciousness. This is known in Yoga as the state of enlightenment in which the individual consciousness loses all sense of separation and merges into the supreme Consciousness. It is the highest state in Yoga, the culmination of all the efforts dedicated to a regular practice of asanas, pranayamas, mantras, concentration and meditation.

The body energy has to be regulated by asanas and kriyas, the breath and the mind have to be controlled and harmonized through pranayamas. The psychic energies have to be unblocked by concentration and meditation in order to bring about the awareness of the pranic energy. Then the subtle mind is free to be constantly engaged in the repetition of sound vibrations. From the diversity of vibrations, the mental activity is focused in a single direction on a unique vibration. It acquires the strength to transcend itself and merge into supreme Consciousness. These Yoga practices gradually lead to a state of solar Consciousness or awareness of the spiritual dimension of human nature through the independent repetition of mantras or the combined execution of asanas, pranayamas and mantras. One of the main purposes of Solar Yoga is to discover the subtle vibratory energy that acts as the invisible support of all forms of life and to concentrate all the inner strength on its development. This is achieved by harmonizing the body, the breath and the mind with the subtle vibrations of the mantras in the same way a musician would tune his instrument. In fact a human body acts like a bio-cosmic set of resonance forks, which are made to vibrate at different levels of frequency. Some sounds can disturb the psychophysical harmony whereas other sounds can promote the entire well-being, health and balance of the system. Moreover the body has its own cycles, periods, and frequencies for the different organic functions: different parts of the body will respond to specific ranges of vibrations. The body, in turn, is linked to the mind through the breath, which can be made to vibrate at different frequencies. And the mind itself has its own bio-rhythm, which strongly influences all the organic functions, by a process of harmonic resonance, through the nervous system. Sound vibrations, as is made abundantly clear in modern scientific research, can have a very powerful effect on the electromagnetic envelope of the body or pranamayakosha.

When the vibrations are harmonious and musical they will produce a positive reordering of the energy fields; when they are noisy and jerky they will induce a state of stress and imbalance in the same fields. When the body is made to vibrate in phase with itself, as in the former case, it produces relaxation of the nervous system and the mind is free to concentrate on the inner reality. In the latter case however, the body and the mind are locked in negative vibrations and the union with the inner reality is prevented. When the vibrations are produced in the form of mantras, they will reach certain centres of subtle energy located on the main axis of the electromagnetic envelope of the body and will enhance their natural harmonic vibrations. The mantras act as a reference axis. Their repetition brings what tends to deviate back into axis, be it at the subtle level of thoughts, at the physical level of organic functions or even at the biological level of the cells. By constant concentration on a particular vibration, the mind absorbs the energy of that vibration and transfers it through the subtle nerves and the physical nervous system to the different organs of the body. With time and practice, the subtle nerve channels and the main subtle centres are purified and become receptive to the influx of spiritual energy transmitted by the mantras.

In Solar Yoga, practitioners work at their own spiritual evolution by trying to obtain a harmonious blending of the solar energies from the sun with the seven main spinal centres or chakras, which are in constant rotary vibration at different frequencies. There is indeed a very strong elective affinity between mantras and chakras, both being of a subtle vibrational nature. The seven chakras have a precise location along the main axis of the pranamayakosha but their extremely subtle nature makes it difficult to discover and experience them.

Moreover in a human being who does not practise Yoga, the rate of vibration of the chakras will be very low and the subtle nerves, not having been purified by yogic techniques, will not be sensitive enough to pick up these vibrations. In this case there will be a lack of subtle communication between the higher planes of consciousness and the lower states of awareness and the state of identification of individual with cosmic Consciousness, the goal of Yoga, may not be realized.

THE SOLAR MANTRAS

In Solar Yoga, practitioners work on their own spiritual evolution by trying to obtain a harmonious blending of the solar energy with their individual energy. This process takes place along the main axis already described, the sushumna, with the seven chakras acting as energy accumulators and the seven mantras as energy conductors. The practitioners' aspiration to fulfil their spiritual nature acts like an upward moving energy of a fiery, psychic and composite nature whereas the subtle solar emanations transmitted through the mantras follow a downward current of a pure, divine and calming nature.

In Part Two of the book, an entire set of asana and pranayama practices is recommended in order to facilitate the union of these two energies. These techniques can only help in providing a good equilibrium to the psychophysical system but they cannot by themselves produce the desired result. Asanas and pranayamas can help practitioners to progress in their work of refining their psychic instrument but the union of the two main energies depends essentially on divine grace and on the faith, the devotion and the purity of heart experienced by practitioners. With the execution of asanas and mudras, joints are made flexible, muscles are relaxed and, with pranayamas, breathing is regulated, and an awareness of the location of the chakras is made possible.

With the practice of bandhas and kriyas, the spine is kept in an erect position and the rotary vibrations of the chakras are facilitated. With the repetition of mantras, the mind is freed from thoughts and impressions: a deep and sustained concentration on the chakras is made possible and the subtle vibrations of mantras are made to resonate in the chakras and to refine their natural vibrations. This entire process is based on a very ancient method of harmonics.

It does not however lie within the scope of this book to unfold all the stages of these spiritual practices since they should be performed under the personal guidance of a spiritual master who initiates practitioners with a mantra corresponding to their natural vibration: this becomes a personal mantra invested with the spiritual energy of the master which will allow them to progress fully protected on the spiritual path. Nevertheless some basic ideas can be given about this ancient system of harmonics and about the solar mantras used in the method.

The seven mantras correspond to the seven chakras:

Muladhara	*Hram*
Svadhishthana	*Hrim*
Manipura	*Hrum*
Anahata	*Hraim*
Vishuddhi	*Hraum*
Ajna	*Hraha*
Sahasrara	*Om*

According to the mantric science each sound of the Sanskrit alphabet possesses a subtle energy, which vibrates at a specific frequency that can be picked up by the subtle nerve centres and currents of the human bio-magnetic sheath. These sounds acquire more power when they are scientifically assembled into sound-formulae known as seed vibrations or bij mantras. This type of mantras does not present any outward intelligible form but possesses an intrinsic power, which gradually manifests itself in the practitioners' individual consciousness. These bij mantras, of which a great number are recorded in the classical Yoga texts, are thus given to the practitioners according to their own potential and limitations and the particular result to be achieved. The solar mantras given here are bij mantras constructed in a manner, which allows the necessary faculties of the practitioners to develop naturally so as to attract, store and radiate the subtle solar energies.

General pattern of the seven solar mantras

The common root of the first six mantras is *Hr* from the sound forms Ha and Ra. In the mantric code, *Ha* corresponds to one of the energies of the ajna chakra, and *Ham* is the bij mantra of the vishuddhi chakra. The sound *Ha* corresponds to the spiritual plane and represents the luminosity aspect of the Sun. ***Ra*** corresponds to one of the energies of the svadhishthana chakra, and ***Ram*** is the bij mantra of the manipura chakra. The sound *Ra* corresponds to the material plane and represents the heat aspect of the sun.

This common root of the six solar mantras represents the subtle current of energy uniting the six chakras to the highest centre, the sahasrara, manifested by the pranava sound *Om*. This cosmic vibration, as explained in chapter three, is the manifestation of cosmic Consciousness. In Solar Yoga, the different planes of consciousness are always linked to the state of universal Consciousness. In this way the vibration *Om* that is decomposed in the three audible sounds *A*, *U*, *M* and in one inaudible vibration is organically linked to the solar mantras through the vibration *M*, the seed of which is the element of fire.

The sahasrara chakra, with the vibration *Om*, is united to the six lower chakras through the vibration *M* and these six chakras are linked together through the vibration *HaRa* that connects the ajna chakra through the vishuddhi chakra to the svadhishthana chakra through the manipura chakra.

The vocal *A* is the sound vibration, which gives manifestation to the vibrations *H*, *R* and *M*. It is connected to the root chakra, the muladhara, and to the highest of the six chakras, the ajna, while being the first of the three audible vibrations composing the cosmic vibration *Om* at the sahasrara chakra.

The vocals *I*, *U*, *Ai* and *Au* represent specific forms of energy which have to be developed in the different chakras in order to absorb the solar vibrations.

I associated with the svadhishthana chakra constitutes a magnetic force.

U associated with the manipura chakra represents a purifying and liberating power.

Ai associated with the anahata chakra represents a force of cohesion.

Au associated with the vishuddhi chakra constitutes the energy, which controls all disturbing vibrations.

Am associated with the ajna chakra represents an energy which helps to overcome the physical and psychic limitations associated with time and space.

Therefore it will be easily understood that the constant repetition of the solar mantras in an ascending order will produce a double result: it links all the psychic centres of individual consciousness to the plane of cosmic Consciousness and it purifies the psychic centres by enhancing the latent psychic faculties enclosed in them which will then be able to absorb the subtle solar energies.

THE CONCEPT OF YOGASANA

The silent practice of sun mantras during the execution of asanas has been given a particular emphasis in Solar Yoga. When a posture is executed with the attention focused on the physical plane, the field of concentration will encompass the entire body with a particular awareness of the effects produced in certain areas, like the joints, muscles or specific organs. When the same posture is performed with the attention centred on the breathing and the movement of subtle energy, the field of concentration is narrowed down to specific energy configurations that build up around a subtle energy centre, which is usually a deep-seated spinal centre or chakra. Finally if the same posture is accompanied by the repetition of a solar mantra, awareness of the body is reduced and the field of concentration is identified with the vibration of a particular mantra, which enhances the rotary movement of the corresponding chakra. When the human psycho-physiological system resonates in this manner, it produces its own subtle nutriment and creates its own waveform. A posture can then be considered to be a yogasana in which the conscious mind is disconnected from the body and the subconscious mind takes over the purely organic functions. The body remains fixed in the posture without any conscious attention of the mind and the latter is united to the subtle object of concentration constituted by the solar mantra. In this way the individual consciousness is gradually led to radiate a tremendous amount of energy.

In part Two of the book, where the asanas are described from a practical angle, each posture has been presented on three planes, namely physical, psychic and spiritual in order to enable practitioners to progress from the stage of the asana to the experience of a yogasana. In the latter case, a state of meditation is induced by the silent repetition of the solar mantras, which accompany the execution of the asana. The meditation can be dynamic or static. In the static form of meditation, the awareness is focused exclusively on the subtle spinal centre, which is activated in the particular posture, and the silent repetition of the corresponding solar mantra is performed with the mind fully concentrated on that chakra.

In the dynamic meditation, an energy grid is formed by the silent repetition of a number of solar mantras directly associated with the chakra activated in a particular asana. The number of solar mantras as well as the number of consecutive repetitions may vary from one posture to another, the purpose being to create definite energy patterns which enhance the linkages between the various chakras leading ultimately to a better integration of the human personality.

The yogasana itself is to be seen in the broader context of the Solar Yoga sadhana or, in other words, the entire course of Yoga practices aimed at training the mind to discover the inner Divinity.

SOLAR YOGA IN SEVEN STEPS

The solar revelation serves as the foundation of the Solar Yoga sadhana or an integral Yoga method articulated in seven successive steps which are presented here as a general guideline for practitioners. These seven steps have been charted along the lines of the traditional method prescribed by sage Patanjali in Raja Yoga. From the first steps of Solar Yoga, the spiritual awareness should be integrated into all the experiences whether they are asanas, pranayamas or mantras. The consciousness of the spiritual dimension of human existence should in fact enlighten every action, every thought and every word of the practitioners' lives. It is only in this way that the true objective of Yoga can be met: a dedication of the results of all actions to the divine power, which is the essence and support of the entire creation. This noble aim can be pursued whatever a person's belief, creed, religion, age, sex or race may be.

First step

The purpose of the first step is to purify and enhance the potential energy, which is naturally generated in human beings because of their intimate connection with the divine source of creation. This first step is carried out with the help of mudras, bandhas, asanas, kriyas and pranayamas.

Second step

The aim of the second step is to harmonize the flow of prana along the two main nadis, ida and pingala, and thereby to create a balance between the two sides of the brain. This is needed because a state of natural tension usually exists between the chakras and their physical counterparts. This second step is carried out by purification techniques, cleansing pranayamas as well as alternate nostril breathing techniques.

Third step

The goal of the third step is to purify all the nadis so that the prana may be evenly distributed along the main energy pathways. This third step is carried out with certain bandhas, kriyas and pranayamas.

Fourth step

The object of the fourth step is to concentrate on the chakras in order to transform them from centres of energy into centres of consciousness. This will generate the inner fire kundalini, which will uncoil at the root chakra. But the chakras have to be completely transformed before the ascent of this energy is made possible.

This step is carried out by the practice of yogasanas, higher pranayamas like kevala kumbhaka, solar mantras and meditation. Once the nadis and intermediary chakras have been purified, the divine light shining in the higher chakra has to be channelled to the anahata chakra and from there to the muladhara chakra. In this particular process, the descent of light is the moving force that will attract kundalini and make it rise.

In another process, the energy can be concentrated in the three higher chakras allowing them to unite and attract kundalini by their combined power. The descent goes from the plane of intuition to the higher mind and, then, to the lower mind. During its ascent the fiery kundalini will follow a geometrical pattern along and through the deep-seated spinal centres or chakras and will increase their vibratory power. This energy pattern is specific to each individual and will have a profound impact on all the interrelated planes of energy. If, however, the chakras have not been properly purified, they will create obstructions to the flow of kundalini thus producing energy imbalances on either the physical, the psychic or the spiritual plane. Therefore it is highly advisable to practise the advanced techniques leading to the awakening of kundalini under the guidance of a master who has experienced all the subtle energy patterns and movements.

Fifth step

The role of the fifth step is to open the three knots or granthis and to allow the chakras to work harmoniously in a grid formation. It has been stated in all the classical texts that this step can only take place with the master's grace. All the enlightened beings have confirmed this truth in the light of their own experience. No asanas, pranayamas, or any other Yoga techniques can efficiently awaken kundalini and make it rise. All these practices can only prevent the energy from dissipating and they can create the necessary inner conditions of disciplined energy to awake kundalini. The word kundalini comes from the Sanskrit root 'Kund' which means a pit. It is divine energy and it is ***Aum***. The first three letters correspond to the first three coils of the energy in the root chakra and the fourth sign corresponds to the state of samadhi, the last half-coil of the serpent power. Kundalini is also a synonym for the Vedic fire Agni. It is one of the manifestations of the divine energy kept as a reserve potential at the base of the spine in spiritually unawakened humans. The cosmic energy is stored at the other end of the vertebral column in the brain. By virtue of the resonance principle these energies are similar in nature but they operate on different octaves.

Spiritual realization or enlightenment consists in bridging the octave and uniting these two energies. Even from a simple explanation like the one just given of an extremely complex, subtle and sacred process, it can easily be deduced that no human action alone can provoke it. It is only with an attitude of humility, devotion and surrender that practitioners may expect to receive the master's grace and with it the divine power that will untie the subtle knots that keep these two energies from meeting.

Sixth step

The essence of the sixth step is to draw the divine grace now that the three main granthis have been opened. This step is carried out by purifying all the energies from the sense of attachment. To this end, the sexual energy is purified by self-restraint. This activates the root chakra and has an effect on the physical plane. The psychic energy (mental, emotional, and vital) is refined by removing all impurities owing to forms of attachment such as anger, desire, envy, greed, infatuation and pride. This activates the heart chakra and has an effect on the psychic plane. The spiritual energy is enhanced by the practice of mantras and meditation. This activates the network of subtle channels and the higher centres of the pranic body in the crown chakra.

Seventh step

The final purpose of all these steps appears in the seventh step when the physical, the psychic and the spiritual planes are merged in a state of pure Consciousness. It is the state of samadhi in which the individual consciousness is spontaneously removed from the lower planes of being and identifies itself with cosmic Consciousness. This yogic mutation happens when the ascending psychic energy and the descending spiritual energy meet in the highest chakra, the sahasrara. In this state, the higher Consciousness, the spiritual sun of which the physical sun is but a manifestation, enlightens the individual consciousness and produces a transformation of its main instruments: the mind, the brain and the nervous system.

These seven steps are given here as a general guideline for the practice of Solar Yoga. In Part Two, all the practical indications for the execution of the asanas, pranayamas, bandhas, mudras, kriyas and mantras are given in the general context of the Solar Yoga sadhana.

PART II

Photo 3. Sun Temple of Konarak (Orissa, India). View from the east, detail of wall. Mid 13th century. Kalinga style. Sandstone. By courtesy of A.I.I.S.

CHAPTER 1

ASANAS

ASHTA SANDHI VIMOCHANA KRIYA– THE EIGHT JOINT RELEASE METHOD

In the Yoga Sutras of Patanjali, an asana has been described as a steady and comfortable posture in which the flow of prana becomes harmonious. This condition is not easily fulfilled when the body remains stiff and the breathing is shallow. Therefore, in the early stages of practice, it is recommended that some simple movements should be executed which will act on the leg joints, the hips, the waist, the shoulders, the neck and the arm joints.

This series of movements is aimed at rendering the main articulations of the body more flexible before practising asanas and pranayamas.

In this chapter, a set of forward bending movements and abdominal movements have been included as well because of their strengthening effect on the abdominal belt. The muscles, which form this belt, have an important part to play in breathing as well as in maintaining the steadiness of the body in pranayama and meditation postures.

Therefore, it is highly advisable to perform these movements whenever the need for extra flexibility is felt. Some of these movements can act as excellent intermediary steps between various asanas. For this reason, they have also been included in the sequences of postures described in the chapter on asanas.

A. Prasarita Pada Uttanasana, Forward Stretching, Standing

Stand with legs half a meter apart and inhale. Exhale, bend the trunk forward and place the palms of the hands on the ground. Bend the elbows in order to allow the head to touch the ground. Remain in the posture with gentle breathing. This releases the neck, the waist, the shoulders, the hip joints and the knees.

B. Ardha Padahastasana, Half Hand-to-feet Posture

Stand with feet slightly apart. Inhale and lift the arms up, parallel to each other. Exhale and bend the trunk forward, keeping the arms stretched out. Allow the trunk to be parallel to the ground and remain in this posture with gentle breathing. Inhale and return to the standing position. This posture releases the neck, the shoulders, the elbows, the wrists and the waist.

C. Uttanasana, Forward Stretching

Lie on the ground with the legs stretched forward. Inhale and push the trunk forward, keeping the spine erect and the arms stretched and parallel to the legs. Exhale and relax the arms and the legs. This posture releases the shoulders, the waist and the hip joints.

D. Janushirshasana, Head to Knee Posture

Sit on the ground with legs stretched forward. Spread out the legs at an angle of 90 degrees. Inhale, bend the right knee and place the right heel at the junction of the thighs, keeping the left leg stretched. Exhale and bend the trunk forward towards the left leg, allowing the hands to grasp the toes of the left foot and the head to rest on the left knee. Remain in the posture with gentle breathing. Exhale and come back to the initial position. This posture releases the neck, the waist, the hip joints, the knees and the ankles. Repeat the process with the other leg.

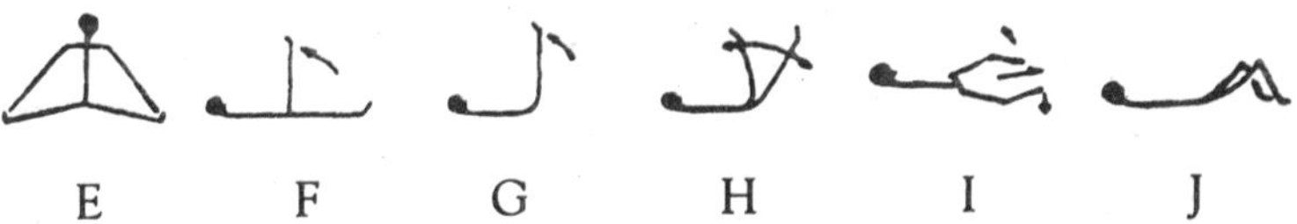

E. Upavishthakonasana, Triangle Posture, Sitting

Sit on the ground and spread the legs at an angle of 120 degrees and inhale. Exhale, stretch out the arms, grasp the toes with the hands and bend the trunk forward, spine erect, until the chin touches the ground. Inhale and return to the initial position. This posture releases the neck, the waist and the hip joints.

F. Eka-pada Uttanasana, Single Leg Lifting

Lie on the back, legs stretched out together on the ground. Inhale and lift one leg vertically. Exhale and bring the leg down. Repeat the same process with the other leg. This releases the hip joints, the knees and the ankles.

G. Dvi-pada Uttanasana or Double Leg Lifting

Lie on the back, legs stretched out together on the ground. Inhale and lift both legs vertically. Exhale and bring the legs down. This releases the hip joints and the waist.

H. Scissor Movements of the Legs

Lie on the back. Lift both legs vertically and perform a scissor movement. Exhale and bring the legs down. This releases the hip joints.

I. Rowing Movement of the Legs

Lie on the back, legs stretched together on the ground. Bend the knees and bring the legs closer to the chest, allowing the toes of the feet to touch each other. With normal breathing, perform a rowing movement with the legs. This releases the waist, the hip, the knees and the ankles.

J. Side Rolling of the Legs

Lie on the back, bend the knees, keep the feet on the ground, and bring the heels near the buttocks. With the back fixed to the ground,

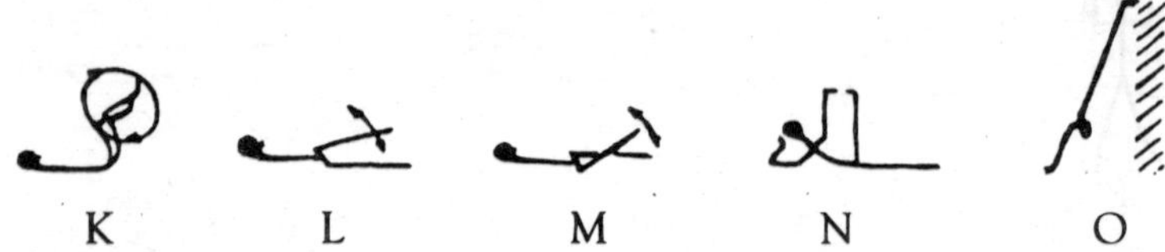

perform a slow rolling movement, with the hips and knees, from one side to the other. This releases the waist, the hip and the knees.

K. Cycling Movement of the Legs

Lie on the back. Lift the legs in the air and perform cycling movements of the legs with bent knees. This releases the waist, the hip joints, the knees and the ankles.

L. Side Sliding of the Legs

Lie on the back, legs stretched out on the ground. Inhale and slide one leg to the side, as far out as possible. Exhale and slide the leg back. Repeat with the other leg. This releases the waist and the hip joints.

M. Cross Sliding of the Legs

Lie on the back, swing one leg over the other without bending the knee. Then, repeat this movement with the other leg. Breathe normally. This releases the hip joints and the knees.

N. Ananthashayanasana, Lateral Stretching of the Leg

Lie on the left side, keeping the body in a straight line from toe to head. Inhale and lift the right leg, knee stretched. Hold the leg with the right hand. Exhale and bring the leg down. Repeat the movement five to ten times. Turn to the right side and repeat the same process with the other leg.

O. Wall Posture

Stand with the back to a wall. Place the hands firmly on the ground near the wall and lift the legs, one after the other, on the wall. Stay in this position with the neck and head totally relaxed. This releases the wrist joints and helps to remove the tensions that build up in the neck.

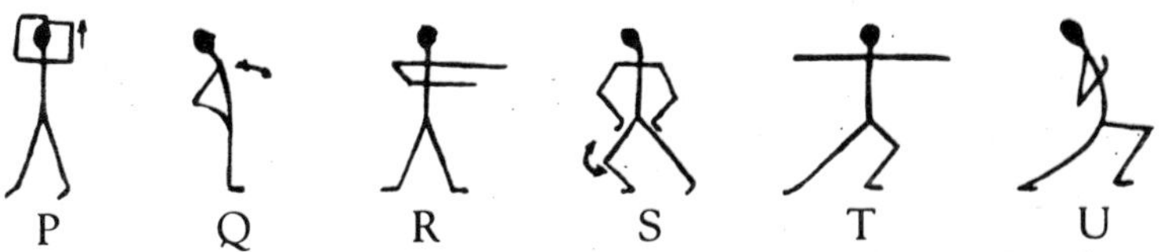

P. Arm Lifting

Stand with feet slightly apart. Place the palms of each hand under the elbows of the opposite arm. Inhale and lift the arms up. Exhale and return to the initial position. Repeat ten times. This releases the elbows, the shoulders and the neck.

Q. Back Bending

Stand with feet slightly apart. Place the palms of the hands in the small of the back. Inhale and bend back. Exhale and return to the initial position. This gives flexibility to the waist.

R. Twisting Movement

Stand with feet slightly apart. Keep the arms stretched horizontally at shoulder level and slightly bent at the elbows. With normal breathing, twist the body from side to side. This releases the shoulders and the waist.

S. Knee Rotation, Standing

Stand with one leg forward and slightly bent at the knee. Perform rotary movements with the hip and the knee in a clockwise and anticlockwise fashion. This releases the hip and the knee joints.

T. Side Swing

Stand with legs apart and arms outstretched to the sides and parallel to the ground. With normal breathing, sway the body from right to left and back with a gentle lateral swing of the knees. Perform this movement twenty to thirty times. This releases the shoulders, the waist, the hip, the knees and the ankles.

U. Ardha Hanumanasana, Single Leg Back Stretching

Stand with one leg, bent at the knee and the other leg stretched backward. Clasp the hands in front of the chest in namaskara mudra.

V

W

X

Y

Perform short stretching movements of the thighs by simultaneously bending the front leg and stretching the back leg. The same position can be repeated with the palms of the hands touching each other above the head. This movement releases the waist, the hip joints, the knees and the ankles.

V. Knee Rotation, Sitting

Sit on the ground. Lift one leg and join the hands under the thigh so as to keep the knee free. Perform rotary movements in a clockwise and anti-clockwise fashion. This releases the knee joints. Repeat with the other leg.

W. Hip Rotation, Sitting

Sit on the ground. Place the hands on the ground behind you and recline the back slightly. Lift one leg and perform rotary movements in a clockwise and anti-clockwise fashion. This releases the hip joints.

X. Hip Release

Sit on the heels and stretch one leg to the side, forming a right angle with the thighs. Keep the hands clasped together on the chest. Stay in this position for one minute and then return to the initial posture. Perform the same movement on the other side. This releases the hip and knee joints.

Y. Butterfly Movement

Sit on the buttocks with the knees touching the ground. Place the soles of the feet against each other and slide the feet as close to the body as possible. Once the posture is obtained, hold the feet with both hands and flap the knees up and down as in the wing movement of a butterfly. Repeat twenty to fifty times. This releases the waist, the hip and knee joints and the ankles.

VAJRASANA
(Kneeling Pose)

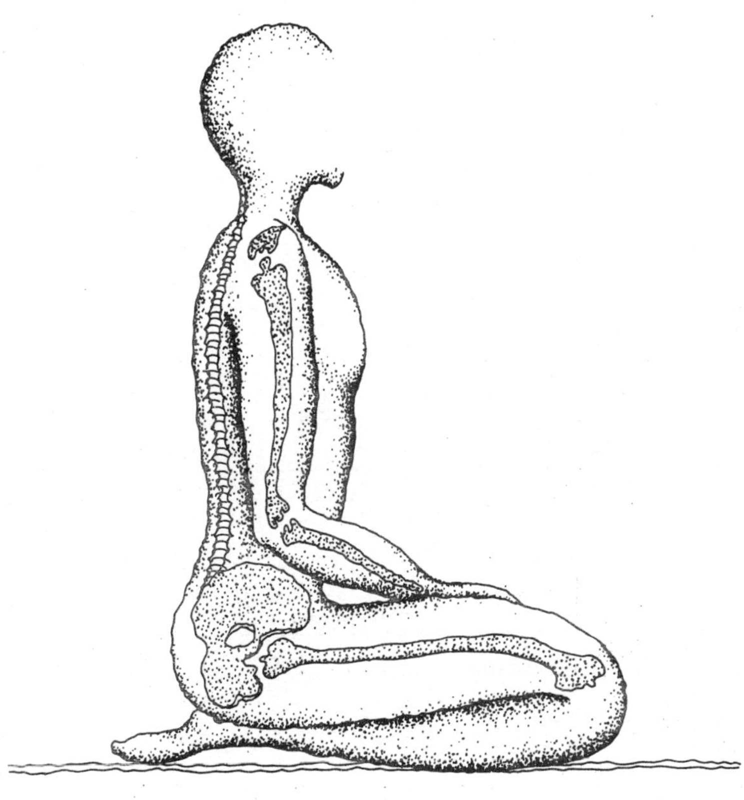

BODY PLANE

Definition and concept

'Vajra' is commonly known as a thunderbolt as it refers to the weapon of the Vedic divinity Indra. But the etymological meaning is 'va', to move, and 'ra', to radiate. So, in this asana, which is known also as the adamantine posture, the energy is allowed to move freely along the spine and to radiate throughout the entire body.

Execution of the Asana

Kneel down with knees and heels together. Sit back on the heels and keep the spine erect. Gently pull the chin in so as to keep the back perfectly straight. Place the hands on the thighs in a relaxed fashion and breathe normally.

Vajrasana in a sequence of Asanas

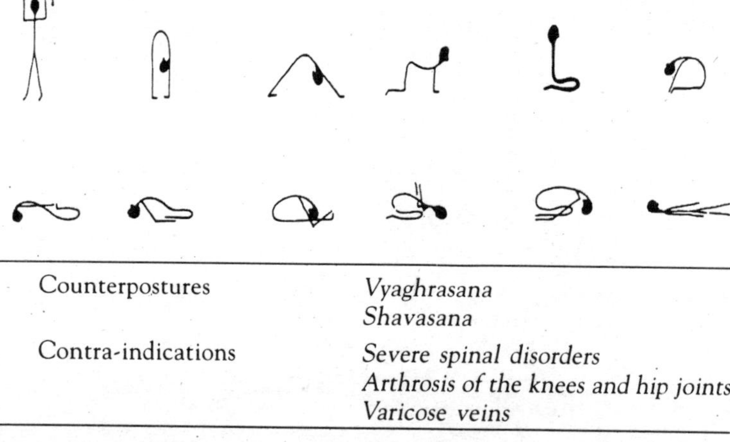

Counterpostures	*Vyaghrasana* *Shavasana*
Contra-indications	*Severe spinal disorders* *Arthrosis of the knees and hip joints* *Varicose veins*

Variations of the Asana

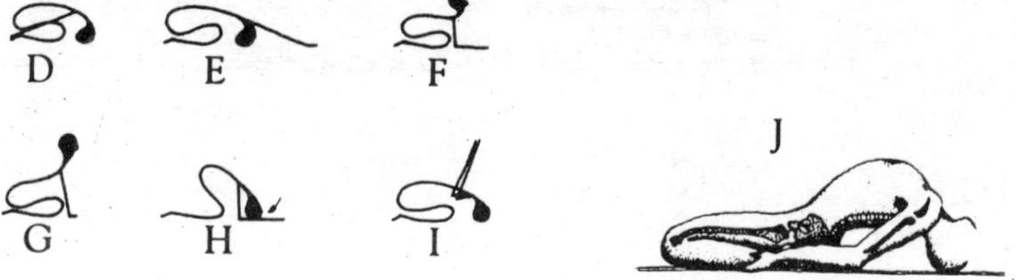

A. **Purna Vajrasana**

Sit in Vajrasana, slide the feet apart and rest the buttocks on the ground.

B. **Ekakin Vajrasana**

Sit in Vajrasana with the feet crossing each other.

C. **Gulpha Vajrasana**

Sit in Vajrasana with the feet crossed at the ankles.

D. **Dharmikasana**

Sit in Vajrasana. Exhale and bring the trunk forward until the forehead touches the ground. Keep the arms to the sides and allow the hands to touch the soles of the feet.

E. **Namaskarasana**

Sit in Vajrasana. Inhale and raise the arms above the head, allowing the palms of the hands to touch each other. Exhale, bend the trunk forward until the forehead touches the ground, arms extended forward on the ground.

F. **Shashasana**

Sit in Vajrasana. Place the elbows and the forearms in front of the knees on the ground and bend the trunk forward. Breathe in lower chest.

G. **Purnashashasana**

Sit in Vajrasana. Place the palms of the hands on the ground in front of the knees and keep the spine erect, with the trunk slightly tilted forward. Breathe in mid chest.

H. **Paripurnashashasana**

Sit in Vajrasana. Place the elbows and the forearms on the ground, in front of the knees. Bend the trunk forward and allow the head to rest on the ground. Then, with normal breathing, gently roll the head backwards and forwards on the ground.

I. **Pranamahamudra**

Sit in Vajrasana. Clasp the hands behind the back and inhale. Exhale and bend the trunk forward, lifting the arms and the clasped hands behind the back. Inhale and return to the initial position.

J. **Suptavajrasana**

Sit in Vajrasana. Inhale and, with the help of the arms and the elbows, lower the trunk until the back of the head touches the ground. Keep the arms alongside the body. Stay in the posture with normal breathing. Exhale and return to the initial position.

K. **Purna Suptavajrasana**

Kneel on the floor with the feet kept apart. Lower the body until the buttocks touch the ground between the heels. Place the hands behind the neck and lower the trunk until the back of the head touches the ground. Stay in the posture with normal breathing. Exhale and return to the initial position.

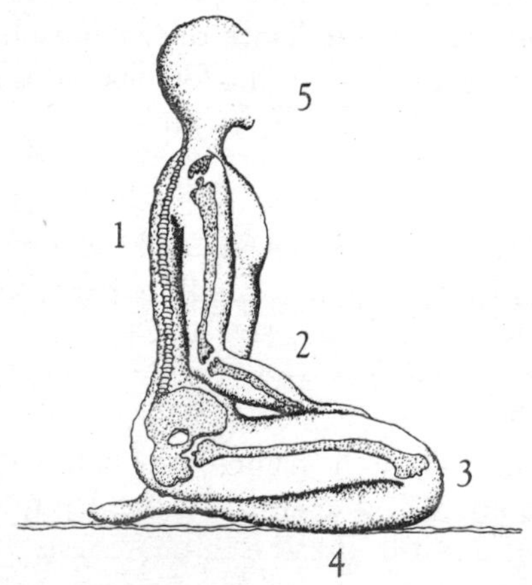

Main benefits of the Asana

1. The spine is naturally erect and free from tension.
2. The breathing function is greatly improved.
3. The hip joints, the knees and the ankles are strengthened and the sciatic nerve is toned.
4. The blood flow is restricted in the legs and is stimulated in the trunk, thereby nourishing the main digestive and respiratory organs.

5. A profound psychic benefit is derived from this posture with a quietening effect on the mind.

ENERGY PLANE

In Vajrasana, the energy is gathered at the base of the spine and prevented from flowing excessively downward because of the position of the legs. Moreover, when the knees are kept together, the abdominal pressure created by the practice of pranayamas and kriyas does not adversely affect the inguinal region but, on the contrary, reinforces the energy of the vajra nadi, the subtle equivalent of the sciatic nerve.

Since the energy is concentrated mainly in the muladhara chakra, this asana is used as a base for the practice of advanced pranayamas and meditation.

In Vajrasana, the sense of well-being and harmony experienced derives from the alignment of all the important joints of the body with the centre of gravity of the body. In the perfect posture, a line can be drawn from the mid-brain point to the base of the spine and passing through the centre of all the important joints: neck, shoulders, elbows, hips and ankles. The following series of pranayamas, kriyas and mudras can be practised.

As A Preparation For The Asana	*Prishta Tadana Kriya* *Pavanamukta Kriya*
During The Asana	*Adhi Mudra* *Chin Mudra* *Chinmaya Mudra* *Brahma Mudra* *Maha Mudra* *Vibhaga Pranayama*

DIVINITY PLANE

Vajrasana is one of the most important postures adopted for meditation. In order to derive the main advantages from the posture, the solar meditation can be performed in a dynamic mode by repeating seven cycles of solar mantras in the appropriate subtle centres.

Muladhara	*Hram*
Svadhishthana	*Hrim*
Manipura	*Hrum*
Anahata	*Hraim*
Vishuddhi	*Hraum*
Ajna	*Hraha*
Sahasrara	*Om*

In the static meditation, the awareness is concentrated in the muladhara chakra with the appropriate mantra for a period lasting from five to twenty-four minutes.

Muladhara	*Hram*

VRIKSHASANA
(Tree Pose)

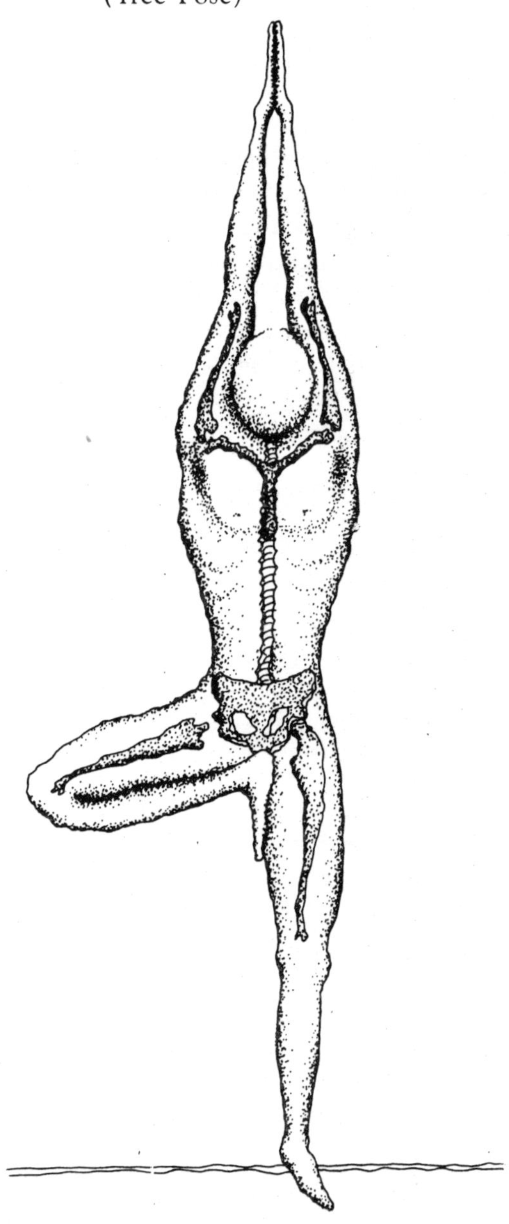

BODY PLANE

Definition and concept

'Vriksha' means tree. This posture evokes the stability of a tree.

Execution

Stand with feet slightly apart. Bend the right leg at the knee and place the right heel at the groin, toes pointing downward.

Inhale, and find the balance on the left leg, raise the arms straight over the head and join the palms of the hands. The junction of the palms, the nose, the navel and the inner left thigh should be in a straight line. Stay in the posture with normal breathing.

Exhale, separate the palms, lower the arms and bring the right leg back to the initial position. Repeat the process with the other leg and stay in the posture with normal breathing.

Preparatory movements

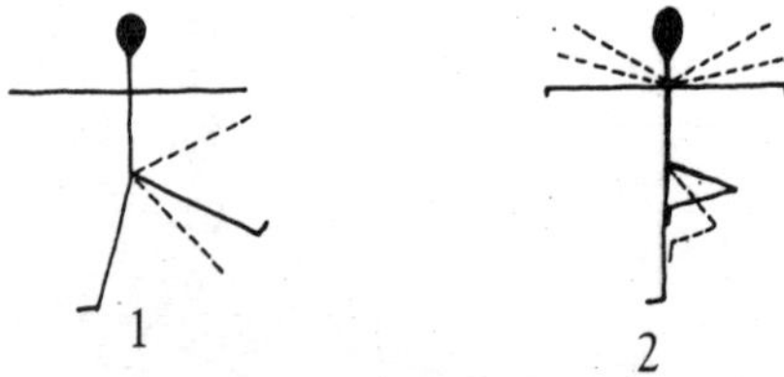

1. Stand with the legs at a sixty-degree angle. Perform swinging movements with each leg alternately, to the sides, to the front and to the back.
2. Try to find the body balance by placing the foot first on the thigh, then near the groin.
3. Try to find the body balance by adjusting the position of the arms.

Counterposture	*None*
Contra-indications	*Severe arthrosis of the knees or shoulders*

Main benefits of the Asana

1. The leg muscles are toned and strengthened.
2. The chest expansion improves the breathing mechanism.
3. The sense of stability and balance is developed.

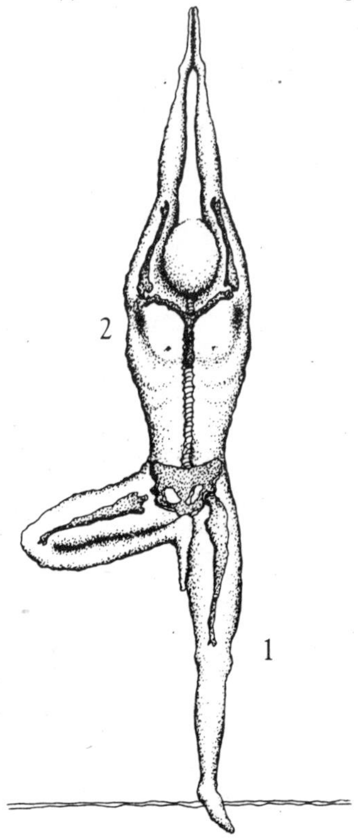

Vrikshasana in a sequence of Asanas

ENERGY PLANE

Vrikshasana is a position of balance, prayer and stability in which the pranic energy is equally distributed between the right and left sides of the spine. Muladhara chakra is activated in this posture and a good exchange of energy takes place between the six minor chakras of the legs and the lower spinal centres, muladhara, svadhishthana and manipura chakras. Pranayamas, bandhas and kriyas are recommended only,

As A Preparation For The Posture	*Govinda Mudra* *Namaskara Mudra* *Mula Bandha* *Adhama Pranayama* *Uddiyana Bandha* *Nadi Shuddhi*

DIVINITY PLANE

In Vrikshasana, the dynamic meditation consists in reciting the solar mantras of the seven subtle centres in an ascending order seven times.

Muladhara	*Hram*
Svadhishthana	*Hrim*
Manipura	*Hrum*
Anahata	*Hraim*
Vishuddhi	*Hraum*
Ajna	*Hraha*
Sahasrara	*Om*

The static meditation is performed for a period of up to two minutes by concentrating on the subtle centre in the crown of the head.

Sahasrara	*Om*

TRIKONASANA
(Triangle Pose)

BODY PLANE

Definition and concept

'Tri' means three and 'kona' means angle. This triangle posture embodies the concept of fixity and stability.

Execution

Stand with the legs spread apart.

Inhale and raise the arms sideways in line with the shoulders, palms down. The arms are parallel to the ground. Turn the right foot sideways to the right and turn the left foot slightly to the right, controlling the extension of the legs by tightening them at the knees.

Exhale and bend the trunk to the right until the right palm rests completely on the floor near the right ankle. Stretch the left arm up, bringing it in line with the right shoulder, extend the trunk and turn the face upward. Remain in this position with gentle breathing.

Inhale and return to the initial position. Execute the posture on the left side, reversing the process.

Trikonasana in a sequence of Asanas

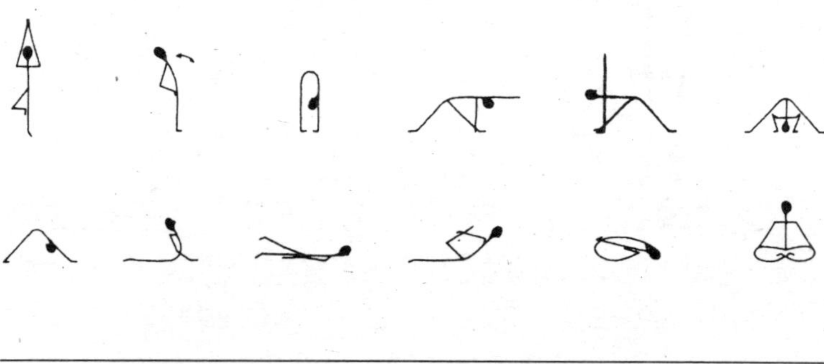

Counterposture	*Stretching in Tadasana*
Contra-indications	*Inguinal hernia* *Displaced vertebrae* *Cervical problems*

Preparatory movements

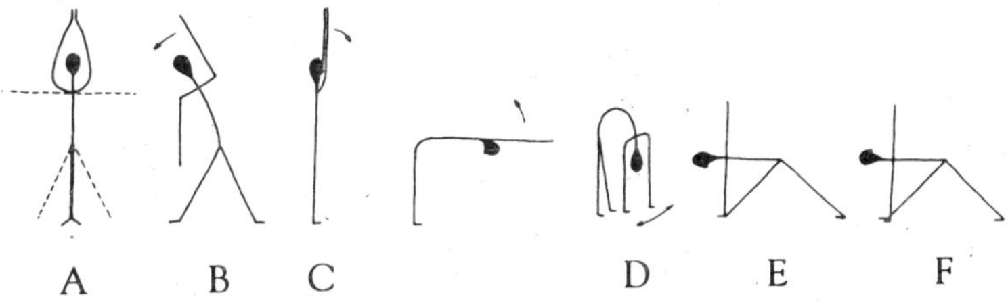

A. Stand with the feet together, arms to the sides. Inhale and jump, spreading legs apart, and raise the arms overhead, palms touching each other. Exhale and jump back to the initial position, bringing the arms down. Repeat ten times.

B. Stand with feet apart. Inhale and bend the trunk to the right, the left arm extending over the head. Exhale and come back to the initial position. Repeat three times on each side.

C. Stand with the feet apart. Inhale and lift up the arms, keeping them close to the ears. Exhale and bend the trunk forward at an angle of 90 degrees, keeping the arms stretched forward and parallel to the ground. Inhale and come back to the initial position. Repeat the movement five times.

D. Stand with the feet apart and the arms to the sides. Inhale and, with full lungs, bend the trunk forward, head and arms totally relaxed. Exhale and swing the trunk and the arms in a slow and relaxed manner like the movement of an elephant's trunk. Inhale and come back to the initial position.

E. Stand with the feet apart. Inhale and lift outstretched arms to shoulder level. Exhale, bend the trunk and touch the right foot with the right hand, while the left arm goes up in a straight line. Inhale while straightening up and continue the same process on the left side. Repeat the entire movement three times.

F. Execute the position as in E above but touch the right foot with the left hand and inversely.

Main benefits of the Asana

Trikonasana gives a lateral exercise to the spine, develops the chest and strengthens the leg and hip muscles.

1. The back muscles are alternately stretched and relaxed and the vertebrae are subjected to a slight lateral compression.
2. The full flexion of the hip increases the blood supply to the lower region of the spine and invigorates the abdominal organs.
3. The leg muscles are toned and the knee joints and the ankles are strengthened.

Trikonasana is a gentle posture with forward bending in which the breathing is slow and intense. The posture combines in a single action rhythmic movements of the different parts of the body, a smooth torsion of the vertebrae and a dynamic tension in the lower limbs.

Trikonasana, like other triangle postures, helps to develop the resistance and flexibility of the lower limbs, which are necessary for general dynamism.

ENERGY PLANE

Trikonasana is a balancing posture, which allows the energy to be evenly distributed to the three sections of the body, the arms, legs and trunk that form the three angles of the asana. Moreover, the lateral flexion, with arms and legs fully extended, stimulates the flow of energy from the spine to the limbs.

In this asana, the intercostal muscles and the rib cage undergo a lateral activity with asymmetrical intense breathing. The energy movement and the respiratory balance are well integrated when the posture is kept for a minimum of two minutes.

During inspiration, the energy moves from the base of the spine to the dorsal area of the spine and during expiration, the energy returns to the root of the spine in the final standing position.

Anahata chakra is the active subtle centre in this posture and it can be stimulated by the following techniques.

As A Preparation For The Asana	*Padahasta Kriya* *Baddhahasta Kriya* *Bhastrika Pranayama* *Kevala Kumbhaka Pranayama*
During The Asana	*Mula Bandha*

DIVINITY PLANE

Trikonasana is a posture of equipoise. It evokes the geometrical pattern of the cosmic bindu, a point expanding into a subtle triad. This asana symbolises the harmonious blending of the three planes of being. The spiritual plane is represented by the upper hand directed towards the sky and the physical plane is evoked by the other hand touching the ground. The psychic plane, which serves as a medium of exchange between the other two planes, is represented by the horizontal line formed by the trunk and the head.

In this posture, the chest is fully expanded and the heart centre is in harmony with the surrounding parts of the body.

In the dynamic meditation, the awareness moves from the base of the spine to the subtle heart centre while four solar mantras are repeated seven times in an ascending order.

Muladhara	*Hram*
Svadhishthana	*Hrim*
Manipura	*Hrum*
Anahata	*Hraim*

After having moved into the posture, the static meditation is performed by concentrating on the subtle heart centre with the appropriate mantra.

Anahata	*Hraim*

ARDHACHANDRASANA
(Half-Moon Pose)

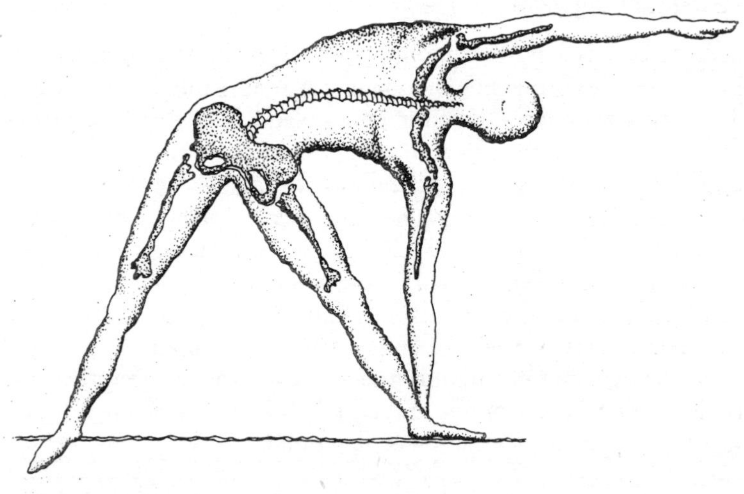

BODY PLANE

Definition and concept

'Ardha' means half and 'chandra' means moon. The sideward bend of the body gives the image of the half-moon and the regular practice of this asana gives the appearance of a soft lunar glow to the practitioner's face

Execution of the Asana

Stand with legs fifty centimetres apart, arms by the sides and feet facing forward and parallel to each other.

Inhale, lift the left arm vertically, arm touching the ear and palm facing inward.

Exhale, bend the trunk to the right until the left arm is parallel to the ground. And, in so doing, the right hand slides down along the right leg to the ankle. The trunk should not be tilted. Stay in the posture with normal breathing.

Inhale, return to the initial position. Repeat the process on the other side.

Counterpostures	*None*
Contra-indications	*Spinal defects in the sacro-lumbar area* *Swelling of the legs*

Preparatory movements

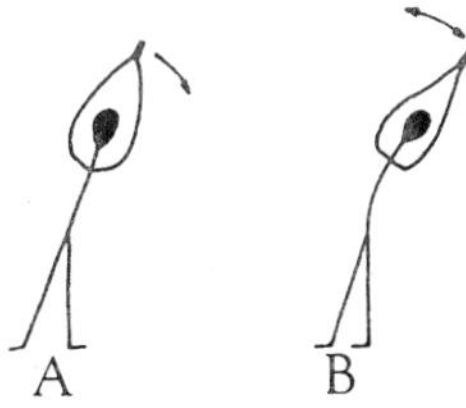

A. Stand with legs half a meter apart. Inhale, lift the arms vertically and cross the fingers of both hands. Exhale and bend the trunk sideward. Inhale and return to the initial position. Repeat on the other side.

B. Standing in the same position, oscillate the trunk at the waist from back to front and vice versa.

Ardhachandrasana in a sequence of Asanas

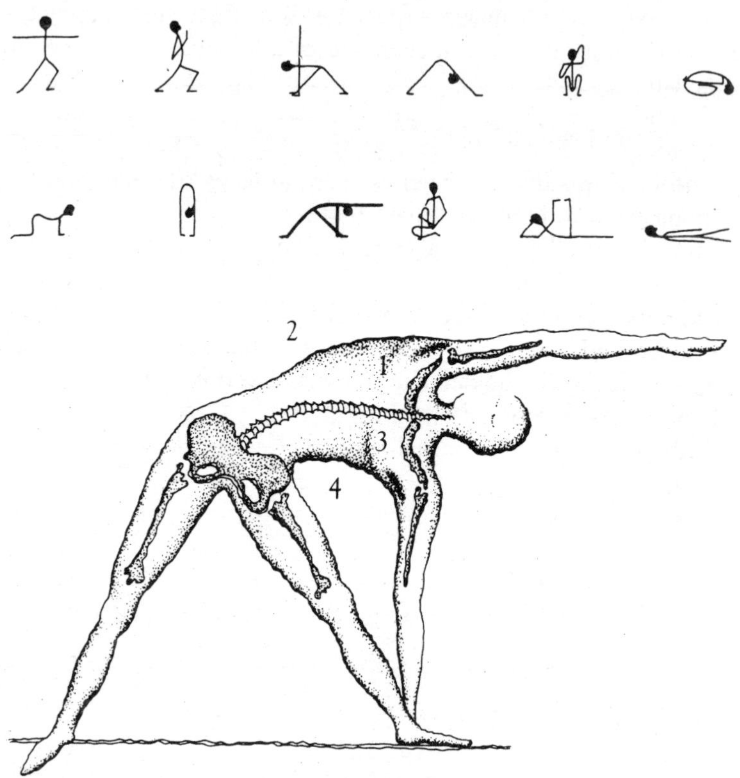

Main benefits of the Asana

1. The stretching and flexing of the spine has a positive, stimulating effect on the spinal nerves.
2. The alternate compression and decompression of the liver area improves the digestive process.
3. The breathing capacity is enhanced.
4. Fatty deposits around the waistline are gradually eliminated.

ENERGY PLANE

In Ardhachandrasana, the whole weight of the body is firmly placed on both feet and the upper part of the body is made to bend from one side to the other.

With the help of the breath, the rib cage expands on the side of the lifted arm and the dorsal section of the spine opens up like a fan. These conditions are favourable to the activity of anahata chakra. The energy flows freely on the side of the lifted arm and there is a good pranic exchange between the navel and heart centres. The following techniques will help to balance the energy flow in the head, trunk, legs and spine.

As A Preparation For The Asana	*Adhama Pranayama*
	Nauli Kriya
	Ashvini Mudra
	Uddiyana Bandha

DIVINITY PLANE

In Ardhachandrasana the energy released at the base of the spine reaches the subtle centre of the heart. In the dynamic meditation, the appropriate mantras are repeated in ascending order seven times.

Muladhara	***Hram***
Svadhishthana	***Hrim***
Manipura	***Hrum***
Anahata	***Hraim***

In the static meditation, the entire awareness is concentrated in the heart centre with the corresponding mantra.

Anahata	***Hraim***

PADAHASTASANA
(Hand-to-Feet Pose)

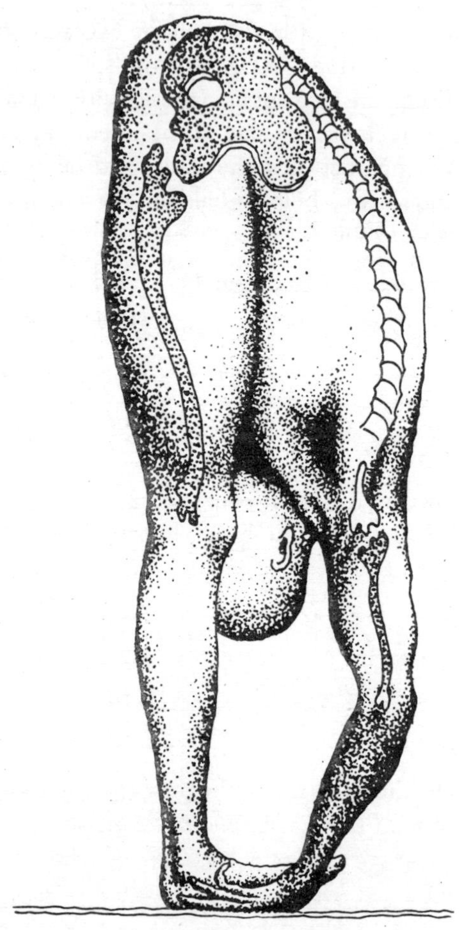

BODY PLANE

Definition and concept

'Pada' means foot and 'hasta' means hand. Since the moving part of the body is usually the second element of the composite Sanskrit word denoting a posture, Padahastasana is to be understood as the hand-to-foot position. What is required in Padahastasana is a great abdominal power to fold the body in two and allow the hands to reach the feet. In this way, the energy flows in a closed circuit created by the posture itself. It is an excellent asana for heating up the body at the beginning of a series of asanas and for the practice of pranayama. It also serves as a preparation for inverted postures or for postures involving intense stretching.

Execution of the Asana

Stand erect, feet together.

Inhale and raise the arms overhead, extending the trunk from the pelvic region.

Exhale slowly and bend the trunk forward until the hands reach the feet and the forehead touches the stretched knees. Remain in the posture with gentle breathing.

Inhale and come back to the initial position.

When the palms are placed under the soles of the feet, the posture is called Padahastasana.

When, in the same posture, the big toes are held by the thumb and forefinger, it is called Padangushthasana.

Counterpostures	*Bhujangasana* *Chakrasana*
Contra-indications	*High blood pressure* *Inguinal hernia* *Renal disorders* *Stomach ulcer* *Sacro-lumbar spinal displacements*

Preparatory movements

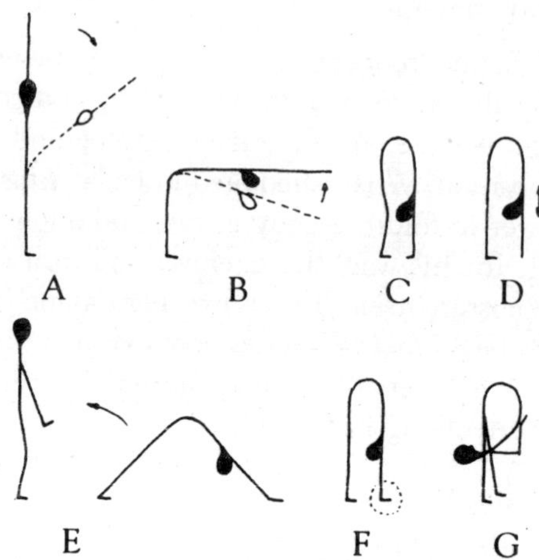

A. Stand with the feet slightly apart. Inhale and stretch the arms up. Exhale, contract the abdomen and bend the trunk forward to an angle of 120 degrees. Inhale and return to the initial position. Repeat five to ten times gradually increasing the amplitude of the forward bending movements.

B. Stand with the feet slightly apart. Inhale, trunk bent forward to an angle of 90 degrees and arms outstretched parallel to the ground. Exhale and bend the trunk lower down. Inhale and come back to an angle of 90 degrees. Repeat five times increasing the amplitude of the forward bending movement.

C. Stand erect, feet slightly apart. Exhale through the mouth and, with bent knees, bend the trunk forward and touch the ground with the hands. Inhale and come back to initial position. Repeat five times.

D. Stand erect. Inhale and stretch the arms up. Exhale, contract the abdomen and bend the trunk forward, knees stretched, head and arms hanging down in a relaxed fashion. In this position, with gentle breathing, move the trunk up and down from the waist, keeping the arms and the head perpendicular to the ground. Repeat five times.

E. Stand erect. Exhale, bend the knees and go into parvatasana. Inhale and return to the initial position.

F. Execute the full posture and try to reach the ground successively with the fingers, the palms, the interlocked hands.

G. Stand with legs apart by half a metre. Inhale and stretch up. Exhale, bend the trunk forward and try to reach as far back as possible with the hands, allowing the head to pass between the legs. Inhale and come back to the initial position.

Main benefits of the Asana

Padahastasana is one of the four folded postures of withdrawal. It has the same characteristics as paschimottanasana but with greater emphasis on the flow of blood to the head. Moreover, it does not present the difficulties of the headstand. In the padangushthasana version, there is also an endocrine stimulation.

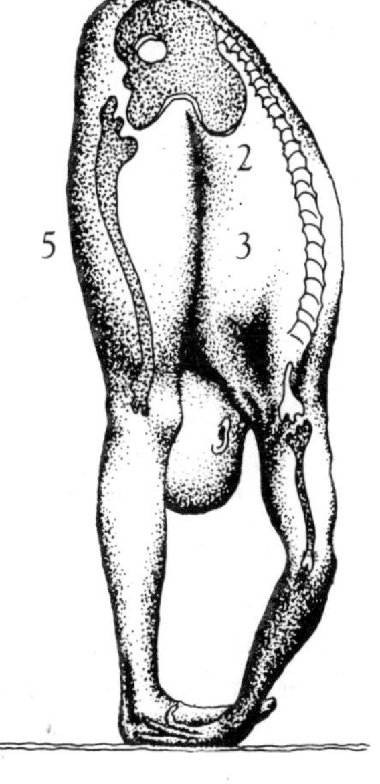

1. The spine is uniformly stretched, especially in the sacro-lumbar area.
2. The compression of the abdomen tones the abdominal organs.
3. The nearness of the cardiac and solar plexuses benefits all the organs situated in the trunk.
4. Cervical tensions are released.
5. Toning and stretching of the leg muscles are achieved.

Padahastasana in a sequence of Asanas

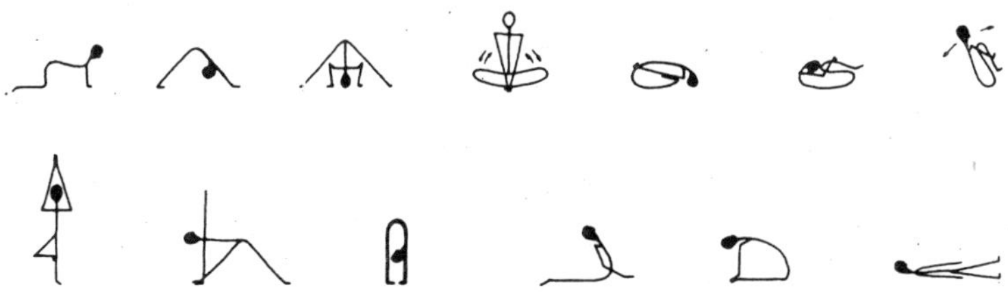

ENERGY PLANE

In Padahastasana, the energy circuit is a closed one. In one direction, the energy flows from the base of the spine to the neck, arms and hands and in the other direction, from the base of the spine to the legs, feet and hands. In this circuit, all the subtle spinal centres are activated as well as the six minor chakras of the legs and the six minor chakras of the arms.

The main chakras involved are muladhara and svadhishthana chakras.

In order to enhance the energy movement, the following practices are suggested:

As A Preparation For The Asana	*Agnisara Kriya*
	Nauli Kriya
	Mula Bandha
	Uddiyana Bandha
	Ashvini Mudra
During The Asana	*Padahasta Kriya*

DIVINITY PLANE

In Padahastasana, the perfect coordination of the six leg chakras and the six arm chakras with the seven important spinal chakras creates a powerful field of energy in which the higher nerve centres of the brain, called the Guru Mandala are extremely active.

The static and the dynamic meditations are performed while remaining in the posture.

The dynamic meditation follows a rhythm punctuated by three stages in which the first solar mantra is repeated seven times, the first six solar mantras are repeated seven times and the last solar mantra is repeated twenty one times, as shown in the following sequence:

Manipura to Muladhara	***Hram***
Muladhara to Ajna	***Hram Hrim Hrum Hraim Hraum Hraha***
Ajna to Sahasrara	***Om***

In the static meditation, the awareness is kept in the ajna chakra with the repetition of a solar mantra seven times. This is followed by the inner visualization of the sun in that chakra.

Ajna	***Hraha***

PARVATASANA
(Mountain Pose)

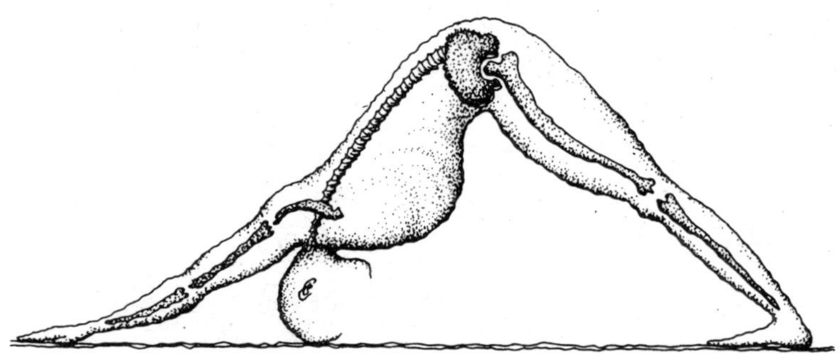

BODY PLANE

Definition and concept

The word 'parvata' means mountain and, by the practice of this asana, the body acquires a stability similar to that of a mountain.

Execution of the Asana

Stand with the feet fifty centimetres apart.

Exhale, bend the trunk forward and place the palms of the hands on the ground so that the body may assume the shape of a triangle.

Remain in this posture with gentle breathing, keeping the arms and legs firmly stretched.

Inhale and come back to the initial posture.

Parvatasana in a sequence of Asanas

Preparatory movements

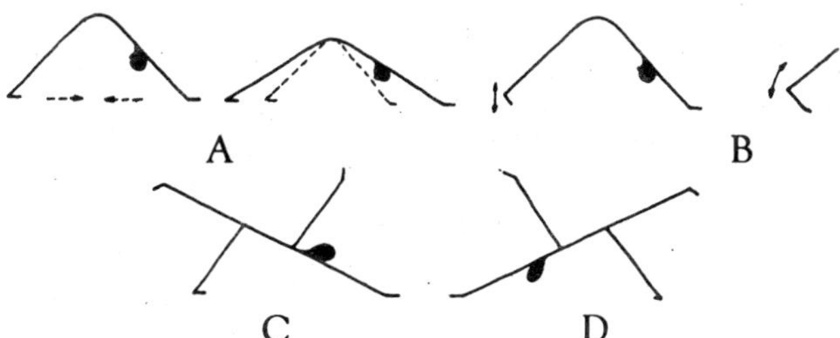

Several dynamic phases of this posture can be practised in order to gain a greater benefit from the static phase of the asana.

A. Gradually bring the arms and legs closer to each other and then move them farther away from each other.

B. Move the heels up and down.
C. Lift the right leg and the left arm simultaneously.
D. Lift the left leg and the right arm simultaneously.

Counterpostures	*Bhujangasana* *Chakrasana* *Suptavajrasana*
Contra-indications	*High blood pressure* *Chronic inflammation of the knees.*

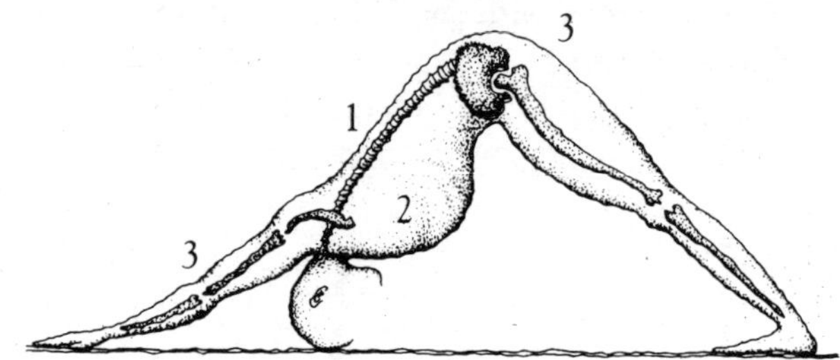

Main benefits of the Asana

This posture is an excellent substitute for the headstand without putting undue strain on the cervical area. It is an important preparatory posture to the 'Salutation to the Sun' series.

1. The spine is completely reinforced in this posture. The pressure created at the junction between the cervical and dorsal vertebrae and at the sacro-lumbar junction (due to the stretching of the arms and legs) is compensated by the flattening and relaxation of the upper cervical and thoracic areas.
2. There is an increased blood flow from the heart to the head.
3. The muscles of the arms and the legs are reinforced and the obstructions at the hip and shoulder joints are released.

ENERGY PLANE

In Parvataṣana, the energy blocks that are usually found at the level of the armpits and the groin are totally removed. The stretching of the legs revitalises the vajra nadi, the subtle counterpart of the sciatic nerve. The relaxed position of the neck allows the energy to

reach the higher subtle brain centres. All these factors contribute to the unimpeded flow of energy from the base of the spine to the head, with a particular intensity in manipura chakra.
The following techniques are suggested:

As A Preparation For The Asana	*Adhama Pranayama* *Savitri Pranayama* *Kapalabhati*

DIVINITY PLANE

Parvatasana is a regenerative rather than a meditative posture. The cycle of solar mantras is thus very simple and helps practitioners to make the effects of their practice subtler.

In the dynamic meditation, the mantras are repeated seven times in an ascending order through the seven chakras:

Muladhara	***Hram***
Svadhishthana	***Hrim***
Manipura	***Hrum***
Anahata	***Hraim***
Vishuddhi	***Hraum***
Ajna	***Hraha***
Sahasrara	***Om***

In the static meditation, the concentration is fixed on the navel centre with the corresponding solar mantra.

Manipura	***Hrum***

VYAGHRASANA
(Tiger Pose)

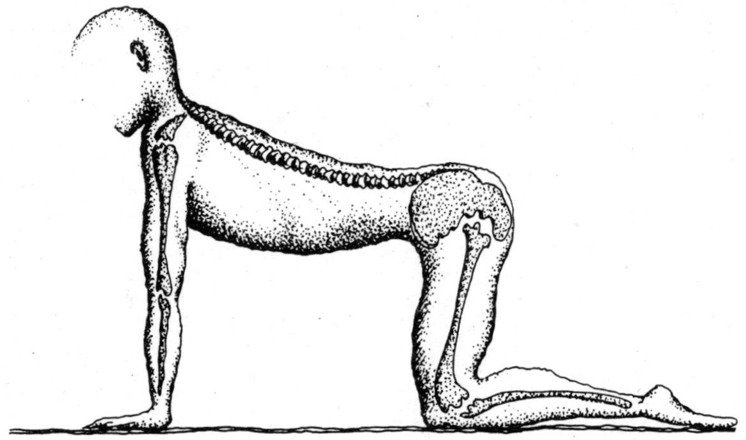

BODY PLANE

Definition and concept

'Vyaghra' means tiger. The movement in this asana evokes the flexibility and the agility of feline animals, hence its name.

Execution of the Asana

Inhale, kneel on the floor with knees about thirty centimetres apart and thighs vertical to the floor. Place the hands on the floor, palms down, about 30 centimetres apart from each other and at the level of the shoulders, fingers pointing forward. The arms and thighs are perpendicular to the ground, the back is straight and horizontal to the floor. The head is in a normal prolongation of the back.

Exhale and slowly raise the back to its furthest extent, hang the head down between the straight arms. Remain without breath for 10 seconds and pull the abdomen in.

Inhale, slowly and deeply, raise the neck and head as high as possible and curve in the lower spine to the maximum, arms and legs remaining fixed. Hold the breath in for about 10 seconds.

As this is a dynamic posture, the movement described above will be repeated in a harmonious and rhythmic manner about ten times without any interruption and without any haste.

Counterpostures	*Maha Mudra*
Contra-indications	*Inguinal hernia* *Migraine* *Spinal disorders*

Using the posture as a basis, certain additional movements of the arms and legs can be performed in order to release the energy, which may be blocked at the joints.

Inhale, stretch out the left arm and the right leg.

Exhale, bring them back to their initial position. Proceed in the same manner with the other arm and leg.

At a more advanced stage of practice, refined breathing techniques can be introduced.

1. Take the posture, exhale and with empty lungs, relax the abdomen and move it in and out about ten times. Inhale, curving in the

lower spine. Exhale and repeat the same process three times.
2. In the posture, inhale through the nose and slowly exhale through the mouth with pouted lips. Repeat ten times
3. In the posture, repeat the movement of the spine rapidly ten to fifteen times, inhaling through the nose and exhaling through the mouth with the sound 'Shu' and simultaneously compressing the abdomen.

Whereas the movements in the posture help in releasing all the joints (neck, shoulders, waist, hips and knees), the breathing techniques, the kriyas and the bandhas stimulate the flow of energy along the spine.

Vyaghrasana in a sequence of Asanas

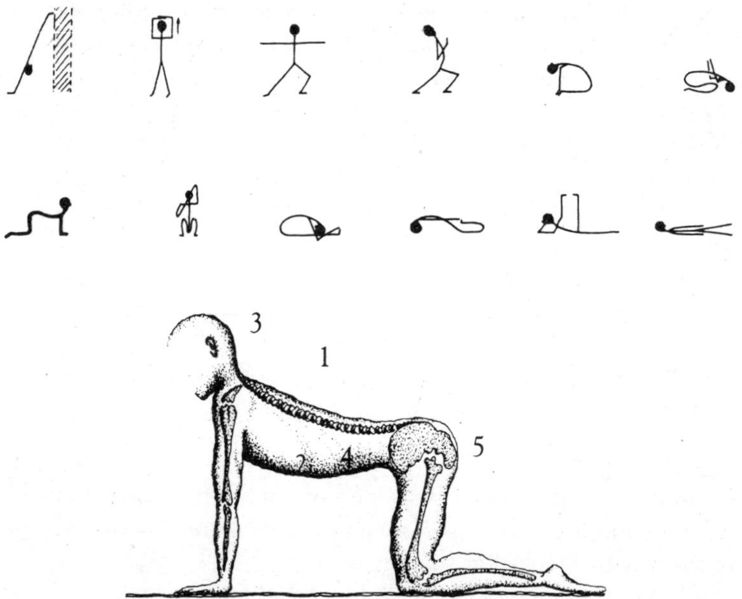

Main benefits of the Asana

This posture is excellent for the spine and the nervous system as it provides a well-coordinated elongation of the anterior and posterior sides of the trunk.

1. Extension of the spine and corresponding expansion of the lungs.

This posture acts on the double curvature of the spine, which constitutes its strength. By stretching and contracting the spine, it inverts the natural curves of the back, strengthens the back muscles and spaces out the vertebrae. This increased space between the vertebrae helps in decongesting the spinal nerve roots with a salutary effect on the entire nervous system.

2. The horizontal position of the lungs and the diaphragm favour the breathing process, which becomes more complete since there is no undue strain on the heart due to the gravity pull and since the diaphragm, being in a natural position, can work more intensely and stimulate the energy movement in the lower back.
3. Tensions are gradually removed in the head and in the neck.
4. The abdominal retraction improves the muscular tone and helps the digestive function.
5. The abdominal retraction increases the pumping of venous blood from the lower limbs.

ENERGY PLANE

In Vyaghrasana, the vertebral column is subjected to a double movement of elongation and contraction, which stimulates the movement of pranic energy in the trunk.

Manipura and anahata chakras are particularly activated in this asana. The energy flows easily along the spine to the head and is evenly distributed throughout the body. The movement of the limbs stimulates the lateral flow of energy whereas the abdominal retraction acts on the energy in the navel area.

The following practices are suggested:

As A Preparation For The Asana	*Agnisara Kriya* *Mahatyoga Pranayama* *Dhouti Pranayama* *Mula Bandha* *Uddiyana Bandha*
During The Asana	*Agnisara Kriya* *Shvana Pranayama*

DIVINITY PLANE

In Vyaghrasana, the subtle centre in the neck region receives the energy activated in the four lower chakras of the trunk. The vital energy liberated from these chakras is purified in the vishuddhi chakra. Since the spinal nerve roots are cleansed in this posture, there will be a purification of the corresponding subtle nadis as well.

In the dynamic meditation, the four solar mantras corresponding to the four lower subtle centres are repeated seven times in an ascending order.

Muladhara	*Hram*
Svadhishthana	*Hrim*
Manipura	*Hrum*
Anahata	*Hraim*

In the static meditation, the awareness is concentrated in the navel centre for a period of two to five minutes, with the corresponding solar mantra.

Manipura	*Hrum*

USHTRASANA
(Camel Pose)

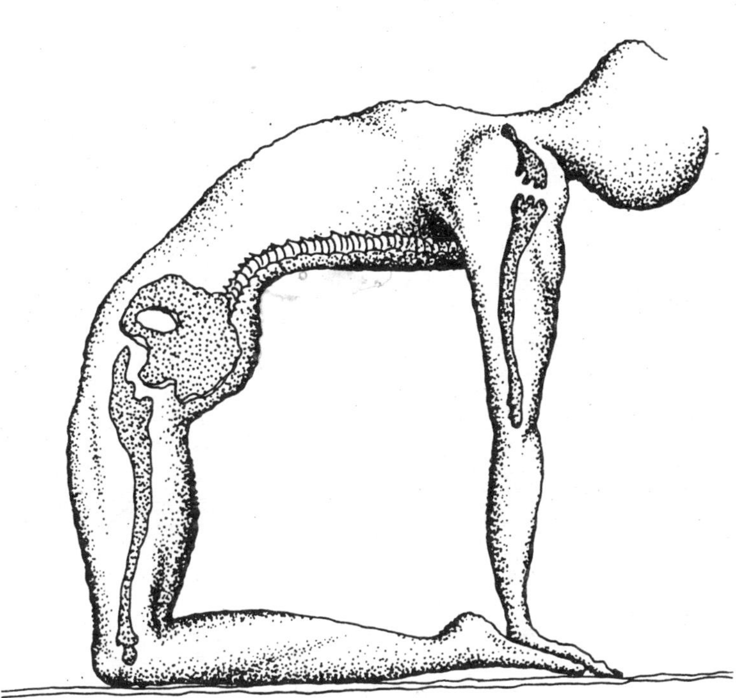

BODY PLANE

Definition and concept

'Ushtra' means camel. It is the resistance of the camel in a barren environment, which is evoked in this posture. Just as the camel survives in the desert by tapping on the reserves of energy in its hump, so human beings pass through life by deriving their energy from an inner spiritual source.

Execution of the Asana

Kneel on the floor, thighs and feet together, toes resting on the floor.

Inhale, rest the palms on the hips and curve the spine backward.

Exhale, place the right palm on the right heel and the left palm on the left heel. Bend the head backward and push the trunk towards the thighs, which are kept perpendicular to the floor. Remain in this posture with gentle breathing and gradually try to stretch the spine still further by contracting the muscles of the glutei.

Inhale and come back to the kneeling position.

Exhale and relax.

Counterpostures	*Vyaghrasana* *Paschimottanasana*
Contra-indications	*Arthritis of the knees* *Severe spinal disorders*

Preparatory movements

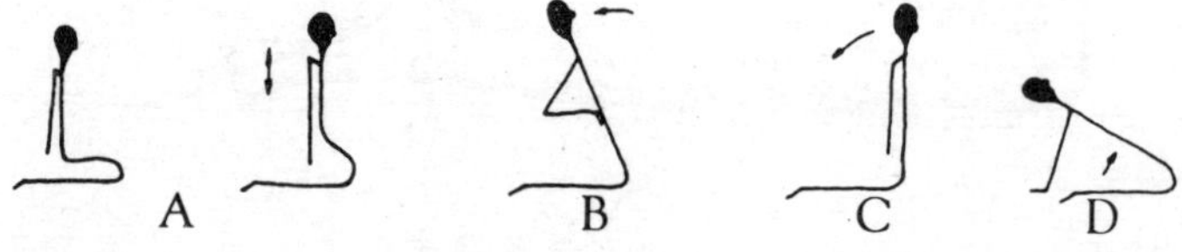

A. Sit in vajrasana, arms alongside the body. Inhale and stretch up on the knees. Exhale and sit again in vajrasana. Repeat five times.

B. Sit in vajrasana. Inhale and support the back with the hands. Exhale, bend the spine backward with the support of the arms. Inhale and return to the initial position. Repeat five times.

C. Repeat the same position as in B above but keep the arms alongside the body.
D. Sit in vajrasana. Inhale and place the palms behind the feet on the floor and raise the buttocks. Exhale and stretch the spine backward, head down. Inhale and return to the initial position.

Ushtrasana in a sequence of Asanas

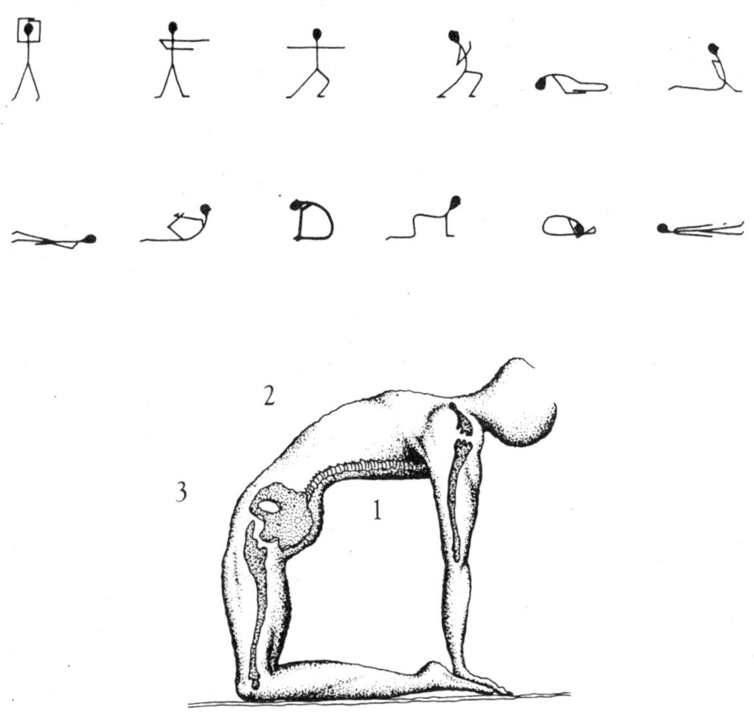

Main benefits of the Asana

Ushtrasana is an ideal posture for improving the health of the spine.

1. The entire spine, and mainly the sacro-lumbar area, is stretched back and invigorated.
2. Breathing in the lower lobes of the lungs is improved.
3. The flow of energy downward from the navel area favours the digestion and elimination processes as well as the ovarian function in women.

ENERGY PLANE

When Ushtrasana is practised with retention of breath, the energy is powerfully emitted from the manipura chakra to the legs, in one direction, and, to the expanded chest in the other direction.

The pranic activity is located mainly in the three lower chakras and the techniques, which will improve the energy circulation, are:

As A Preparation For The Asana	*Adhama Pranayama*
	Agnisara Kriya
	Uddiyana Bandha
During The Asana	*Ushtra Kriya*

DIVINITY PLANE

In Ushtrasana, the cycle of solar mantras practised in the dynamic meditation confines itself to the three lower chakras and it is repeated seven times.

Muladhara	*Hram*
Svadhishthana	*Hrim*
Manipura	*Hrum*

In the static meditation, the awareness is focused on the active energy of the navel centre.

Manipura	*Hrum*

BHUJANGASANA
(Cobra Pose)

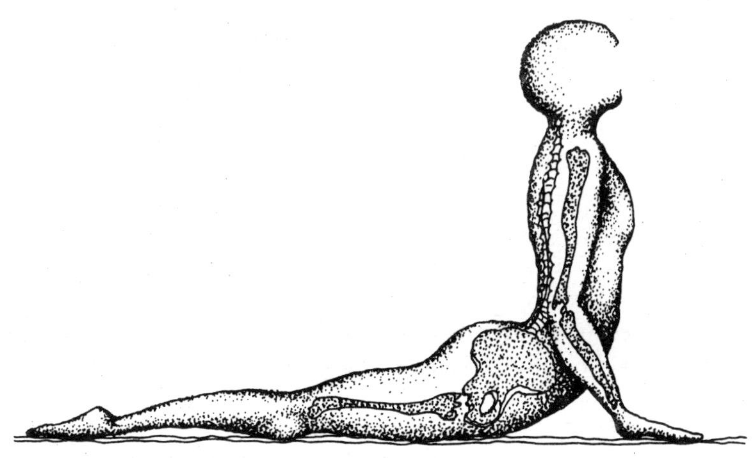

BODY PLANE

Definition and concept

'Bhujanga' means a serpent. When correctly executed, this posture evokes the power and erectness of a snake about to strike. Bhujangasana is a royal posture as it acts mainly on the axis of the body, the vertebral column, and in so doing, it helps to harmonize the three planes of being. Here, the physical level is represented by the fixity of the legs and of the lower back, the psychic level is symbolized by the mobility and flexibility of the trunk and the neck, whereas the spiritual state is evoked by the movement of energy reaching the higher centres in the brain directly from the base of the spine.

Execution of the Asana

Lie on the floor face downwards. Extend the legs, knees tight and feet together with pointed toes. Rest the palms on the floor at shoulder level.

Inhale and slowly pull the trunk up without the help of the arms. First, the head is raised as far as possible, then, by tensing the back muscles, the shoulders and the trunk are lifted farther backward until pubis, legs and hands only remain in contact with the floor. Maintain the posture either for twenty seconds breathing normally or for ten seconds with full lung retention.

Exhale and return gradually to the prone position.

Counterpostures	*Vyaghrasana* *Paschimottanasana* *Pavanamuktasana* *Viparitakaranimudra* *Dharmikasana*
Contra-indications	*Inguinal hernia* *Hypoglicemia* *Acute neuro-vegetative disorders.*

Preparatory movements

A. Execute the position with the support of the arms and place the feet against a wall, thereby increasing the strength of the legs.

B. In case of lumbar weakness, practise the posture with the feet raised on the toes.

C. Execute the position by first lifting the dorsal area of the back, and then lifting the head and finally the lower back. This sequence increases the flexibility of the spine without putting undue strain on the cervical area.

D. Execute the correct posture, first with the support of the arms, then gradually spread the arms away from the body and learn to practise it without the support of the arms.

Bhujangasana in a sequence of Asanas

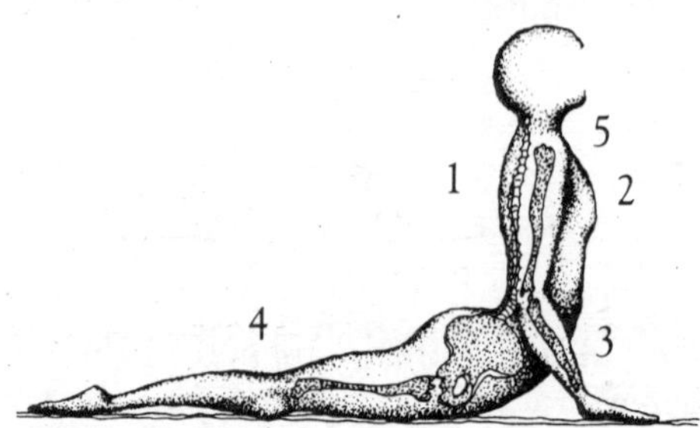

Main benefits of the Asana

Bhujangasana is one of the main postures used for strengthening the back muscles and correcting the vertebral structure. It has a beneficial effect on the entire nervous system since it greatly improves spinal health.

1. The spine is reinforced and rendered more flexible by the gradual sliding of the vertebrae on each other, from the cervical to the lumbar regions. An abundant flow of blood reaches the backbone and the sympathetic nerves.
2. The frontal part of the trunk is stretched, the chest fully expanded. This produces a reflex action on the lumbar area and stimulates the kidney function while improving the breathing capacity.
3. The increase in intra-abdominal pressure effects a calming massage of the viscera with a consequential improvement of the digestion.
4. Through gradual practice, the leg muscles are reinforced and can thus act as a strong support for the arching of the spine.
5. The thyroid gland is stimulated and produces an overall regeneration of the system.

ENERGY PLANE

In Bhujangasana, the energy is concentrated first in manipura chakra and, when this centre is activated, the energy can flow up to vishuddhi chakra if the vertebral column is sufficiently arched during the execution of the posture.

While inhaling, the energy flows upward and awareness is centred on the cervical area. While retaining the posture, awareness is directed along the spine and while exhaling, it reaches the lower part of the spine near the kidneys. Consequently, the energy is

evenly distributed between the three main sections of the spine. In the perfect posture, the energy is concentrated in the coccygeal area with retention of breath and with mulabandha. This should only be performed under the direct guidance of a master and at an advanced stage of practice.
The following practices are recommended:

As A Preparation For The Asana	*Agnisara Kriya* *Ashvini Mudra* *Nagapranayama* *Bhastrika* *Sitali Pranayama*
During The Asana	*Mula Bandha* *Sarpa Kriya* *Bhujangini Kriya* *Ujjayi* *Sitali Pranayama*

DIVINITY PLANE

In Bhujangasana, the spine constitutes the only support for the execution of the dynamic phase of the posture. Spiritually, this posture is symbolic of the practitioners' own inner strength and energy as the only means for attaining self-development.

The dynamic meditation is performed in the posture without the support of the arms. During the inspiration phase, the inner awareness is concentrated at the crown of the head and gradually moves down through the subtle spinal centres until it reaches the base of the spine.
The solar mantras are repeated in the following order:

Sahasrara	***Om***
Manipura	***Hrum***
Ajna	***Hraha***
Svadhishthana	***Hrim***
Vishuddhi	***Hraum***
Muladhara	***Hram***
Anahata	***Hraim***

During the breath retention phase, which can vary from half a minute to one minute, the awareness is brought to one centre with the recitation of one solar mantra.

Sahasrara	*Om*

During the expiration phase, which can vary from half a minute to one minute, the awareness follows the movement of the breath with the mantra ***Om***.

The static meditation, instead, is performed when the posture is held for about five minutes with the support of the arms. In this case, the entire awareness is concentrated with gentle breathing in one subtle centre only with the practice of a single solar mantra.

Manipura	***Hrum***

SHALABHASANA
(Locust Pose)

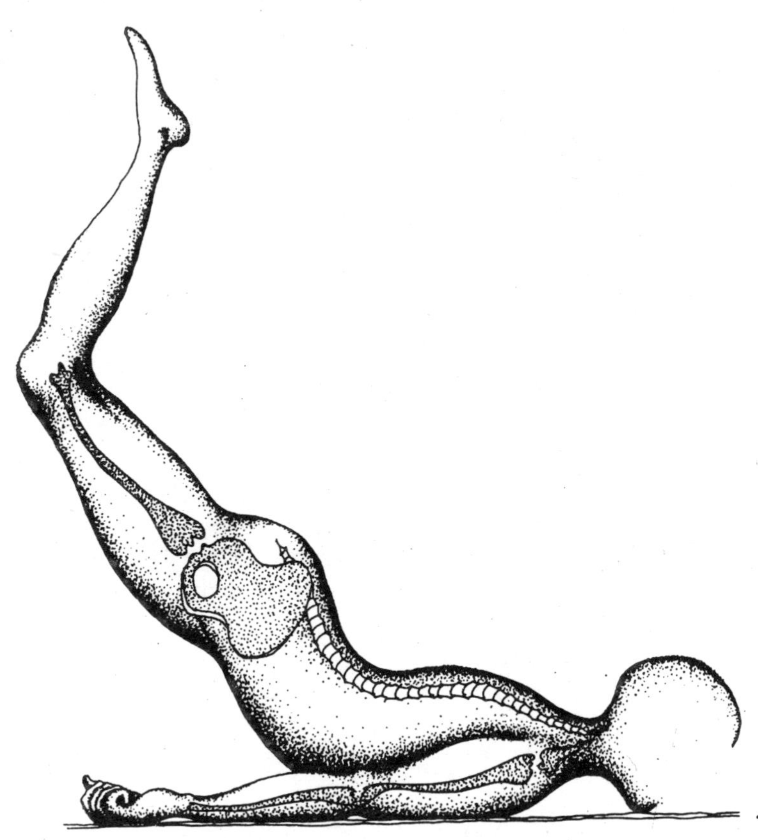

BODY PLANE

Definition and concept

'Shalabha' means a locust. The posture evokes the agility of the insect, hence its name.

Execution of the Asana

Lie full length on the stomach with the legs extended together and the feet flat on the ground. Lay the chin firmly on the ground and place the arms on the floor alongside the body. Clench the fists and place them under the pelvis, keeping the arms fully extended.

Inhale deeply, retain the breath and raise the outstretched legs with a fairly quick motion. Hold the position for fifteen seconds with full lung retention. Still holding the breath, slowly lower the legs to the ground.

Exhale and relax.

At an advanced stage of practice, the abdominal muscles are sufficiently strong and the legs can then be lifted up, with palms on the ground, and the trunk raised up to mid-chest. The posture then becomes somewhat the reverse of sarvangasana.

Counterpostures	*Padahastasana* *Paschimottanasana*
Contra-indications	*Displaced disc* *Inguinal hernia* *Heart and kidney disorders*

Preparatory movement

Shalabhasana should always be preceded by its preparatory posture, 'ardhashalabhasana' or half locust. In the case of most other asanas, preparatory movements have been indicated in order to make the body more flexible. In the case of Shalabhasana, however, the preparation consists in obtaining the correct alignment of the shoulder joints in the half-posture in view of the intense balancing effort required to achieve the final posture. Lie full length on the stomach with legs extended together and feet flat on the ground. Lay the chin on the ground in the body's axis. Push the shoulders firmly to the ground by curving the back and extend the arms alongside the body, fists clenched, back of the hands on the ground.

Inhale, lift one leg up outstretched while pressing symmetrically on both arms.

Exhale and bring the leg down on the ground.

Repeat the same process with the other leg.

Shalabhasana in a sequence of Asanas

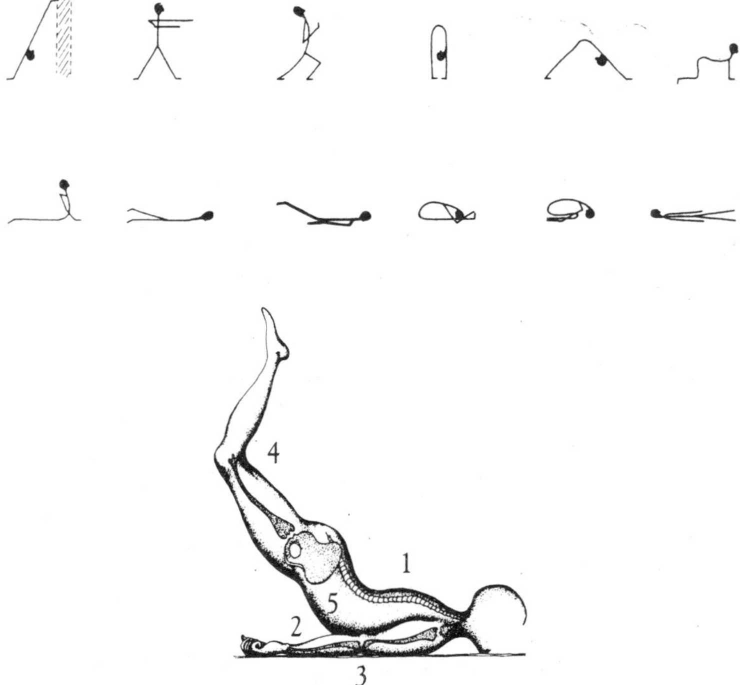

Main benefits of the Asana

This asana, like its complementary bhujangasana, has a powerful effect on the back. Whereas bhujangasana acts on the part of the spine directly above the small of the back, Shalabhasana has a more concentrated effect on the lower part of the back. However, with practice, the technique of Shalabhasana slightly changes and the posture becomes somewhat the reverse of sarvangasana or halasana.

1. The stretching backwards of the spine renders it more elastic. Tensions are eased in the sacral and lumbar areas, the nerves of the small of the back are strengthened, due to the increase of pressure in the abdominal cavity.
2. The concentrated tensing of the abdominal muscles and the elongation of the lower spine improve the digestive function. A highly beneficial effect has been noted for the relief of wind and constipation.
3. With all extensor muscles tensed and flexor muscles relaxed, the chest expands and there is an increased blood flow in the dorsal and cervical areas with a positive effect on the breathing efficiency.
4. The blood circulation in the legs is improved.
5. The increased intra-abdominal pressure, the retained breath and the inclination of the hip joints compress and immobilize the diaphragm while improving its tone.

ENERGY PLANE

Shalabhasana follows bhujangasana in the practice of postures and it precedes dhanurasana. In this postural triad, the energy is moved from the base of the spine to the second subtle spinal centre in order to reach the navel subtle centre. Since Shalabhasana is the middle posture of the three, the centre, which is active, is the svadhishthana chakra.

In this asana, the parasympathetic part of the nervous system is stimulated in two points. First, at the level of the shoulders, the vagus nerve is toned by the pressure of the upper part of the trunk on the ground and, secondly, the pelvic part of the parasympathetic system is stimulated by the contraction of the muscles in the lower back.

The practices, which help in this process, are:

As A Preparation For the Posture	*Adhama Pranayama* *Sarpa Kriya* *Mula Bandha*

DIVINITY PLANE

Since Shalabhasana is essentially a dynamic posture, the only form of meditation is the static one, with concentration on the second subtle spinal centre with the corresponding mantra for a period of up to two minutes.

Svadhishthana	*Hrim*

DHANURASANA
(Bow Pose)

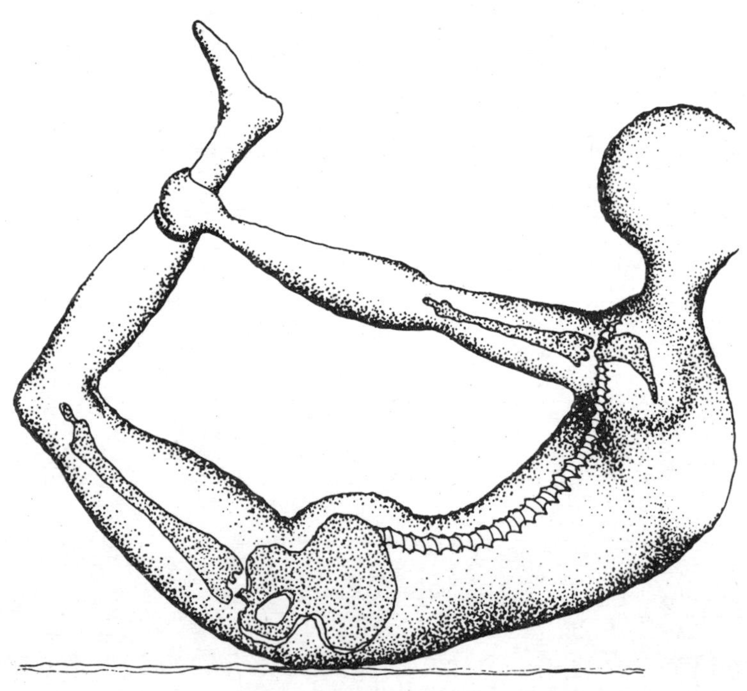

BODY PLANE

Definition and concept

'Dhanu' means bow. In this posture, the body resembles a bow in which the arms and the legs, acting as a tensed bowstring, pull the trunk and head upwards.

Execution of the Asana

Lie on the stomach, face to the floor, arms and legs stretched.

Inhale and bend the knees, stretch the arms backwards and hold the ankles with the hands.

Exhale completely and simultaneously lift the chest and pull the legs from the ground without joining the knees. Stay in the posture with gentle breathing, as long as it is comfortable.

Inhale and come back to the initial position by releasing the ankles and bringing the head and the legs back to the floor.

In the perfect posture, only the abdomen rests on the floor and bears the weight of the body. Moreover, once the full stretch is achieved, the thighs, knees and ankles may be joined together, thus creating a strong intra-abdominal pressure.

When full abdominal strength has been obtained, the posture can be executed in the following manner:

on inhalation, unfold the legs backwards;
with retention, hold the posture, head up;
on exhalation, come back to the initial posture.

Counterpostures	*Paschimottanasana* *Dharmikasana* *Pavanamuktasana*
Contra-indications	*Displaced disc* *High blood pressure* *Stomach ulcer* *Heart disorders*

Preparatory movements

A. Lie on the stomach, palms down at shoulder level. Inhale and raise the head, lifting the trunk up to the waist with the support of the extended arms. Exhale and come back. Repeat five times.
B. Lie on the stomach, arms stretched out in front of the body. Lift one leg up, keeping the other one stretched on the ground.
C. Lie on the stomach, arch the spine backward up to the waistline, bend the knees and tap the buttocks with the heels alternately. Repeat ten to fifteen times.
D. Lie on the stomach. Arch the trunk backwards and stretch the right arm back to grasp the right ankle, the left leg remaining on the floor. Inhale, hold the right leg and lift it as high as possible. This is the half posture. Repeat three times with each leg.

Dhanurasana in a sequence of Asanas

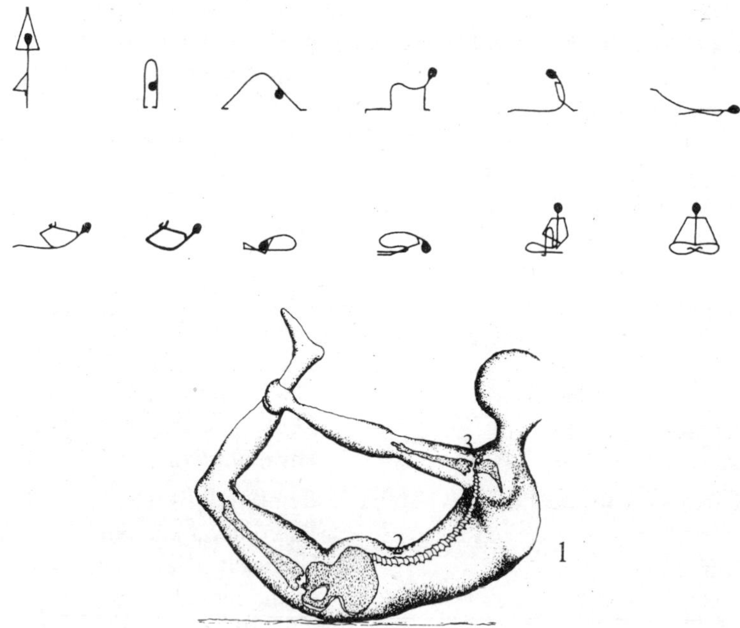

Main benefits of the Asana

This posture produces the combined effects of bhujangasana and halasana. The neutrality of this asana favours the attitude of withdrawal.

1. Extension of the rib-cage area by muscular traction and abdominal pressure. This improves the breathing, tones the diaphragm and the abdominal organs and increases the intercostal mobility.
2. Back-stretching of the spine with a particular extension at the cervical and lumbar areas and a compression at the dorsal area owing to a narrowing of the space between the shoulder blades.
3-4. Increased elasticity of the shoulder and hip joints due to the simultaneous lifting of the trunk and thighs and the full extension of the recti and abdominal muscles.

ENERGY PLANE

Dhanurasana allows practitioners to become aware of two important blocks to the free flow of energy in their systems, namely the shoulder joint and the hip joints. With diligent practice, these obstructions can be overcome and an abundant surge of energy will originate from the manipura chakra and will circulate in the trunk as well as in the arms and the legs.
The helpful techniques are:

As A Preparation For The Asaṇa	*Bhujangini Kriya* *Ushtra Kriya* *Bhastrika Pranayama*
During The Asana	*Dhanur Kriya*

DIVINITY PLANE

Dhanurasana can be mastered once the obstructions to the flow of energy have been removed from the shoulder and hip joints. Furthermore, the total relaxation of the back is the key to success in this asana and the awareness can then be brought to the subtle spinal centres.

During breath retention in the posture, seven cycles of the appropriate solar mantras are repeated in an ascending order.

Muladhara	*Hram*
Svadhishthana	*Hrim*
Manipura	*Hrum*

Anahata	***Hraim***
Vishuddhi	***Hraum***

In the static meditation, the entire concentration is focused on the third subtle centre with the corresponding mantra.

Manipura	***Hrum***

PASCHIMOTTANASANA
(Head-Knee Pose)

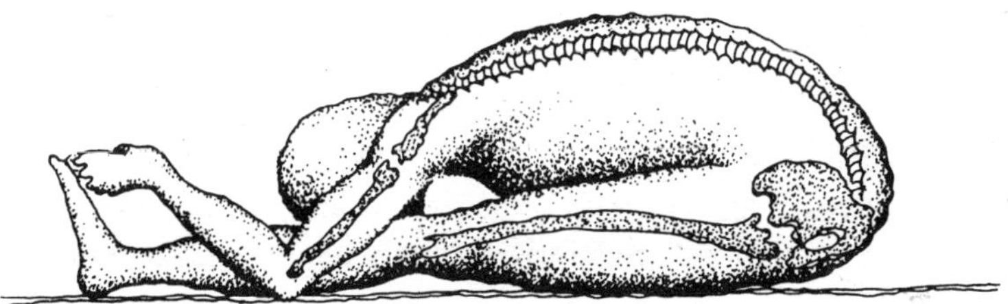

BODY PLANE

Definition and Concept

'Paschima' means West in Sanskrit. 'Ut' indicates an upward movement and 'tan' means vibration. So, in this asana, the energy movement is reversed and flows towards the head. When the posture is perfectly executed, the energy will move through the central core of the spine and produce an upward vibrational pattern.

To be correctly executed, this asana requires a great flexibility of the hip joints and a gradual control over the leg muscles. Hence, a series of preparatory poses will be needed to exercise the different parts of the body and to avoid forced movements that could lead to undesirable muscle pull in the back or in the legs. This series of movements will help in removing back stiffness, opening the hip joints, toning the abdominal muscles and smoothly activating the sciatic nerve.

When these conditions are fulfilled, with diligent practice over a period of time, the knees will stretch naturally and the back will flatten automatically in the final posture. This is made possible by the synergic activity of the back muscles, which stretch the spine to its maximum length.

Execution of the Asana

Sit on the floor, legs stretched out in front and kept together.

Inhale, stretch the arms forward at shoulder level, parallel to the ground.

Exhale, bend the trunk forward right from the pelvic region until the forehead touches the knees and the hands reach the feet, with the big toe of each foot encircled by the thumb and forefinger of the respective hand (left hand to left foot and right hand to right foot). In this position, the back should be flat, the legs should be stretched, knees touching the floor and the elbows, acting as levers, should rest on the ground.

Inhale, come back slowly to the initial position.

Exhale and relax.

Counterpostures	*Suptavajrasana* *Matsyasana*
	Chakrasana *Vyaghrasana*
Contra-indications	*Displaced discs* *Stomach ulcer* *Inflammation of the sciatic nerve* *High blood pressure*

Preparatory Movements

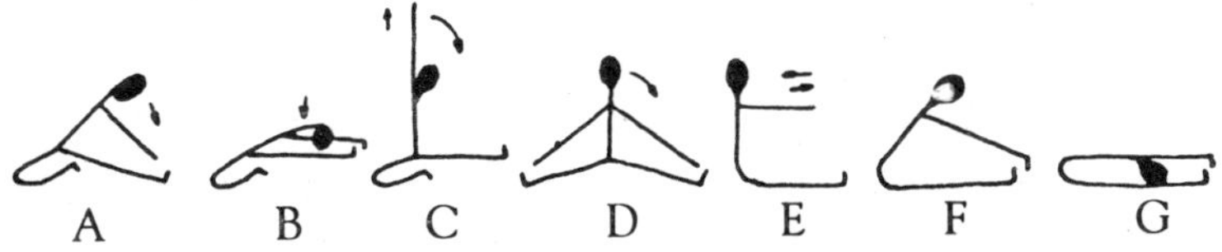

A. Sit with one leg stretched out to the side, the other leg bent at knee, foot near the perineum. Inhale, arms stretched forward and try to reach the foot of the extended leg with the hands and without lifting the knee from the ground. Exhale, come back to the initial position. Change the position of the legs to the other side and repeat the movement at normal speed. In this pose, the effect is concentrated on the hip joints and the legs.

B. Sit in the same position but hold the ankle with both hands. Exhale and bend forward, contracting the abdomen and trying to rest the head on the outstretched knee. Inhale and come back to the sitting position. Change leg position to the other side and repeat. This movement acts against back stiffness.

C. Sit in the same position. Inhale and lift up the arms. Exhale, stretch the trunk from the pelvic region and then bend forward, trying to reach the toes with the hands. Inhale, come back to the initial position. Repeat on the other side. This movement helps to correct the wrong attitude of stretching the back from the shoulder area only while bending forward.

D. Sit, with spine erect and spread the legs as far apart as possible. Inhale, raise the arms up to the shoulder level, keeping them parallel to the legs. Exhale, contract the abdomen and try to touch the feet with the hands. Inhale, return to the initial position. Repeat several times as in a rowing movement, being careful not to curve the back. This pose acts on the entire length of the sciatic nerve and, hence, on the thigh muscles.

E. Sit with legs stretched out together. Inhale, keep the spine erect and stretch the arms forward. Exhale and contract the abdomen. On empty lungs, effect two or three rowing movements backward and forward. Inhale, return to the initial position and relax the arms. Repeat three times. This movement tones the abdominal muscles.

F. Sit in the same position. Inhale, stretch the arms forward, parallel to the ground, palms down. Exhale, bend forward, extending the trunk from the pelvic region and try to stretch the arms beyond the feet until the palms of the hands cover the soles of the feet completely. This position helps to remove contractions and heaviness in the back.

G. Sit in the same position. Inhale, lift up the arms and extend the trunk from the pelvic region. Exhale, bend forward and grasp the big toes with thumb and forefinger. Remain in this position with gentle breathing and gradually develop an awareness of the correct posture. By smooth adjustments, helped by the power of gentle breathing, try to correct the imperfections without any undue strain. Inhale and come back to the initial position.

Paschimottanasana in a sequence of Asanas

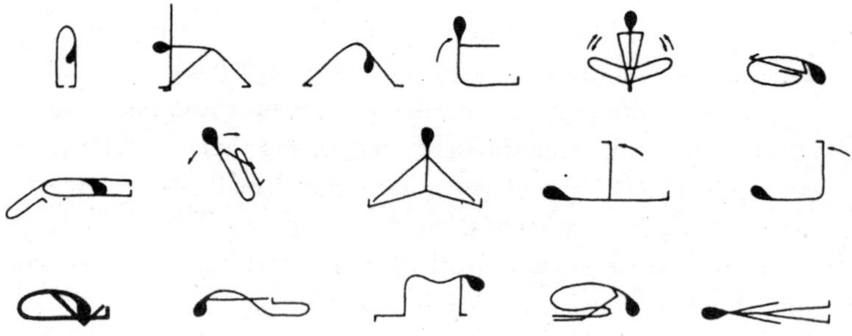

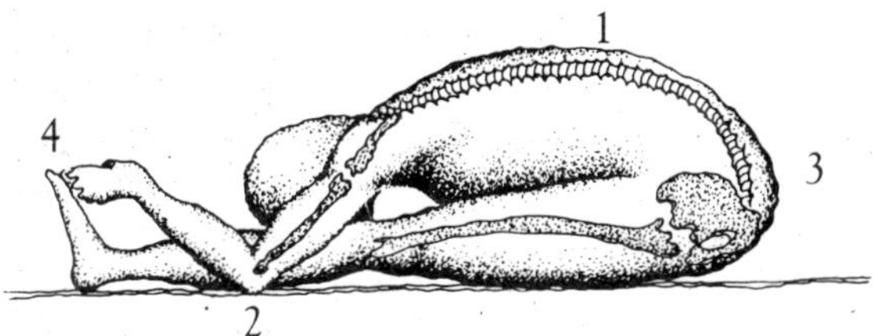

Main benefits of the Asana

The whole body, acting as one unit from neck to toes, is folded in an attitude of inner listening and of withdrawal from the outer world. Paschimottanasana is an excellent posture for the abdominal organs and for the nervous function of the lower back.

1. Since the spine, lungs and heart are in a horizontal plane, they are less subject to the gravity pull. This produces a gentle massage of the heart, an increased blood flow to the head and a relaxed extension of the spinal cord in its full length.
2. When the elbows touch the ground, the associated reflex point has a direct effect on the heart beat.
3. The sacro-lumbar area is fully extended by simultaneously contracting the abdomen and stretching the lumbar spine. This double action has a beneficial effect on the nerve centres and the glands in the sacro-lumbar area with a consequent improvement of the digestive and uro-genital functions.
4. The reflex point located at the base of the big toe, when pressed, acts on the pituitary gland and helps to improve the endocrine activity.

ENERGY PLANE

The energy pattern in Paschimottanasana is determined by three interconnected reflex points located respectively at the elbows, at the base of the spine and at the base of the big toes. When the posture is correctly executed, the energy flows from the two lower chakras, muladhara and svadhishthana, directly to ajna chakra. This energy movement benefits the sacral region of the spine and helps in removing the psychosomatic tensions, which build up in that area. For this reason, Paschimottanasana is said to act mainly on the svadhishthana chakra. This energy movement can be stimulated by the practice of kriyas, bandhas and pranayamas before or during the asana.

As A Preparation For The Asana	*Pavanamukta Kriya* *Agnisara Kriya* *Maha Mudra* *Kapalabhati* *Bhastrika* *Shvana Pranayama* *Sunyaka Pranayama*
During The Asana	*Paschima Kriya* *Ashvini Mudra*

DIVINITY PLANE

In Paschimottanasana, the recitation of the solar mantras follows an ascending order from the lowest chakra to the highest, once all the subtle spinal centres have been properly identified.

Muladhara	*Hram*
Svadhishthana	*Hrim*
Manipura	*Hrum*
Anahata	*Hraim*
Vishuddhi	*Hraum*
Ajna	*Hraha*
Sahasrara	*Om*

Then the solar mantras are repeated seven times for each chakra. This is followed by the solar mantras specific to the three chakras

Anahata	*Hraim*
Vishuddhi	*Hraum*
Ajna	*Hraha*

In the static meditation, the inner awareness is brought to the second lowest chakra with a five-minute repetition of the corresponding solar mantra

Svadhishthana	*Hrim*

GOMUKHASANA
(Cowhead Pose)

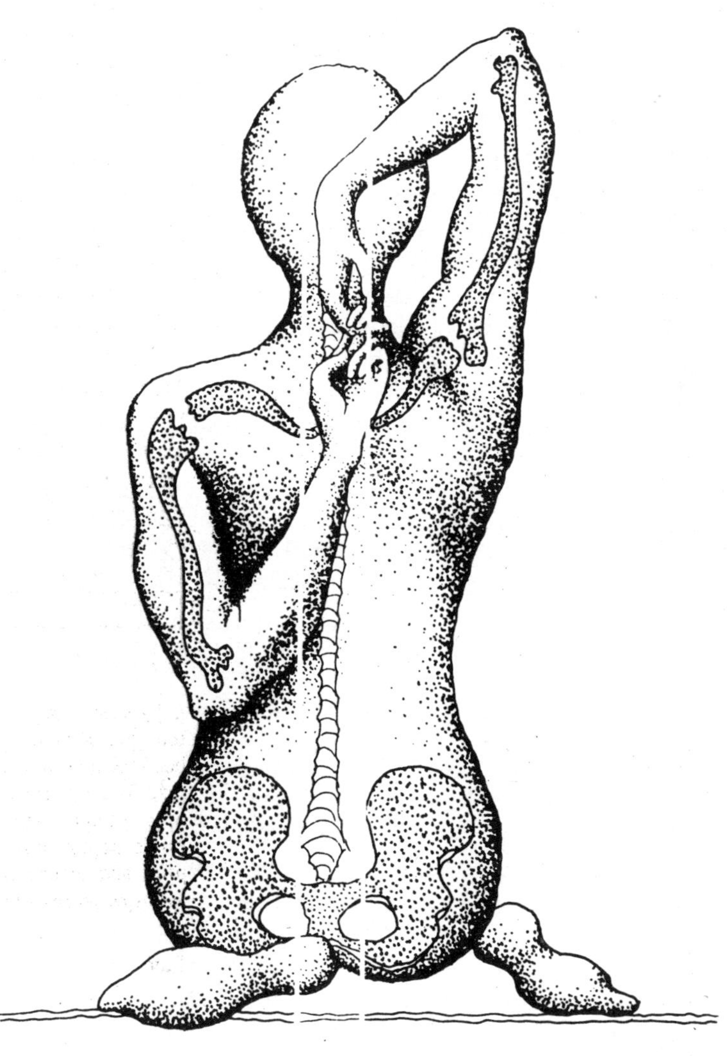

BODY PLANE

Definition and concept

'Go' means a cow and 'mukha' means face. This posture evokes the frontal view of a cow's head.

In Gomukhasana, the work is concentrated in the two main joints of the body, the hips and the shoulders, while the spine is kept static and erect. The arms act as a lever to allow for a greater expansion of the rib cage and the crossed legs provide a firm base for the practice of the asana.

Execution of the Asana

Sit on the ground with the legs stretched out, palms of the hands on the floor. Bend the left knee back and sit on the left heel. Lift the right leg and place the right thigh over the left one.

Inhale and place the arms: raise the left arm over the head, bend it at the elbow and place the left palm between the shoulders. Lower the right arm, bend it at the elbow and raise the right forearm up behind the back at the level of the shoulder blades.

With retention of breath, clasp the hands in this position and firmly pull the raised elbow up, keeping the neck and head erect and looking straight ahead.

Exhale, unclasp the hands, loosen the legs and the arms.

Counterposture	*Dharmikasana* *Namaskarasana*
Contra-indications	*Arthritis of the shoulder joints* *Weakness of the knees*

Preparatory movements

A. Practise the opening of the shoulder joints.

B. Practise the crossed leg posture: sit on the floor, legs stretched out together, hands behind the back on the floor. Bend the right knee and keep the right foot next to the right buttock. The left leg remains stretched out and the knees are touching each other. Breathe normally. This preparatory position requires patience since the tensions and the contractions in the hip joints will have to be overcome before one can sit symmetrically on the buttocks. Do not force the movement if pain is felt in the knee.

C. Sit in vajrasana and practise the placing of the hands as described in the full posture above. Do not force the shoulder joints. If, at the beginning, the hands do not join, use a handkerchief to bridge the distance between the hands.

Gomukhasana in a sequence of Asanas

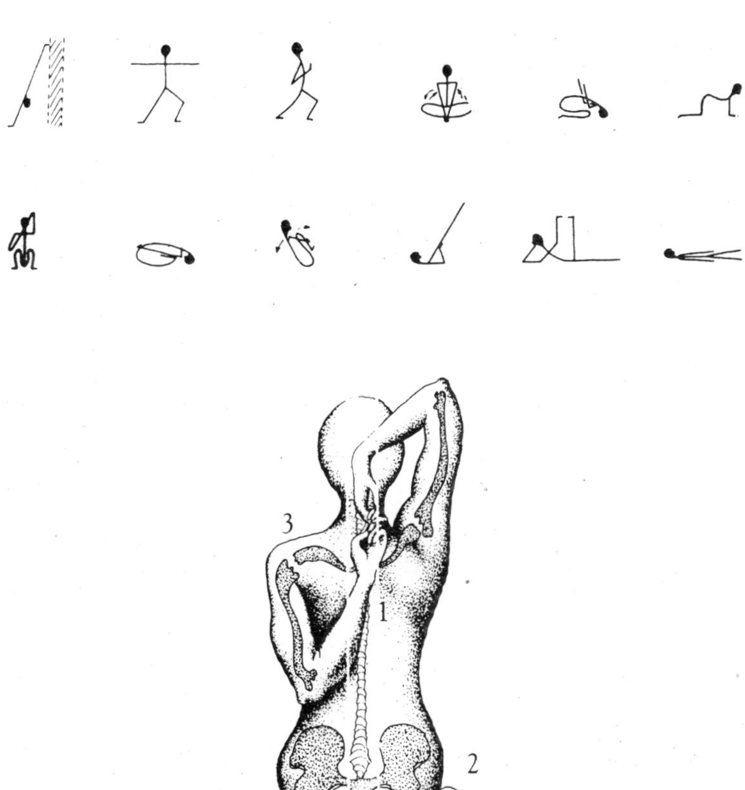

Main benefits of the Asana

1. This posture allows the chest to expand fully in a two-stage movement; it stretches the spine and improves the elasticity of

the shoulder joints by balancing the tension in the muscles of the arms and the shoulders.

2. The crossed-leg position, while rendering the leg muscles more elastic and the hip joints more flexible, stimulates the blood flow from the trunk to the head. This extra blood supply benefits the pituitary and the pineal glands.
3. Tensions and contractions in the neck and the shoulders are alleviated.

ENERGY PLANE

In Gomukhasana, the upper and middle lobes of the lungs are fully expanded and there is a lateral increase of energy flow to the side of the brain corresponding to the folded lower arm.

Anahata chakra is activated by the practice of this asana.

The energy movement can be stimulated by the following pranayamas and kriyas:

As A Preparation For The Asana	*MahatYoga Pranayama* *Baddhahasta Kriya* *Adhyam Pranayama*
During The Asana	*Gopucha Kriya*

DIVINITY PLANE

Gomukhasana acts on the heart centre and is thus well suited as a preparatory posture for meditation. The energy is allowed to radiate from that centre to the higher subtle centres of the brain.

In the dynamic meditation, the concentration moves from the heart centre to the subtle centre between the eyebrows with the repetition of seven cycles of solar mantras:

Anahata	***Hraim***
Vishuddhi	***Hraum***
Ajna	***Hraha***

In the static meditation, the awareness is kept for a period of two minutes in the heart centre with the appropriate mantra:

Anahata	***Hraim***

ARDHAMATSYENDRASANA

(Half Spinal Twist Pose)

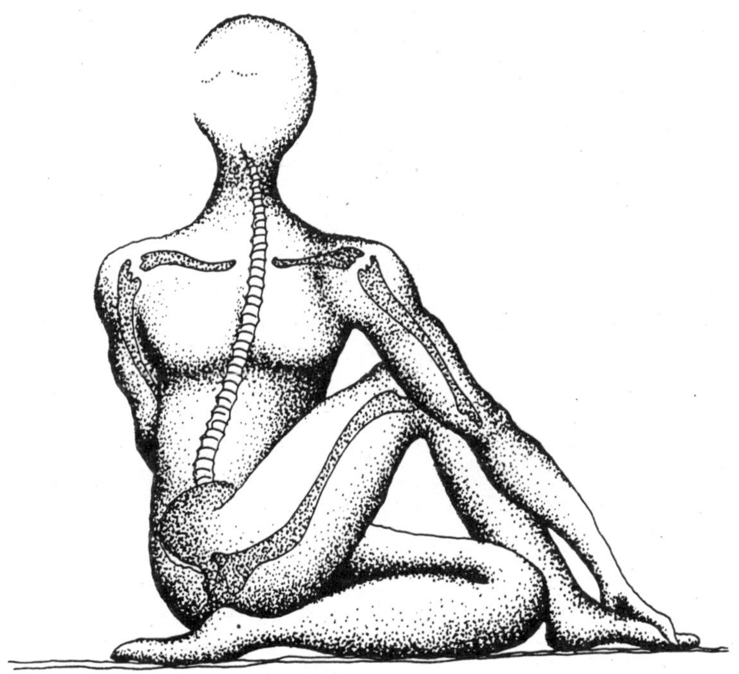

BODY PLANE

Definition and concept

'Ardha' means half, an expression used to depict a milder version of the asana by the same name. And 'Matsyendra' signifies the 'Lord of Fishes', the name given to one of the founders of the yogic science. This posture is otherwise known as the 'Half Spinal Twist'.

Execution of the Asana

Sit on the floor with legs outstretched. Bend the right knee and place the right foot under the right buttock. Then, cross the right thigh with the left leg so that the outer side of the left ankle touches the outer side of the right thigh. Find the proper balance in this position.

Turn the trunk to the left, bring the right armpit over the left knee and grasp the left leg with the right hand. The left arm is swung back and the left hand catches the right thigh.

Inhale, keep the spine erect and secure the proper balance in this posture.

Exhale and slowly twist the trunk to the left, from the sacro-lumbar area to the cervical one, allowing the neck to turn towards the left shoulder. Remain in this posture for fifteen seconds and, then, inhale again.

Exhale and slowly return to the initial position. Release the hands and legs.

Repeat the posture on the other side by changing the position of the limbs.

Counterpostures	*Parvatasana* *Vyaghrasana*
Contra-indications	*Displaced disc* *Inguinal hernia* *Hypertension* *Sciatica*

Preparatory movements

In this asana, the positioning is very important. The waist should be stretched and the back should not be curved despite the lateral twist. The rotation is caused by the neck, the trunk and the abdominal muscles whereas the impulse is given by the forward shoulder and the arm.

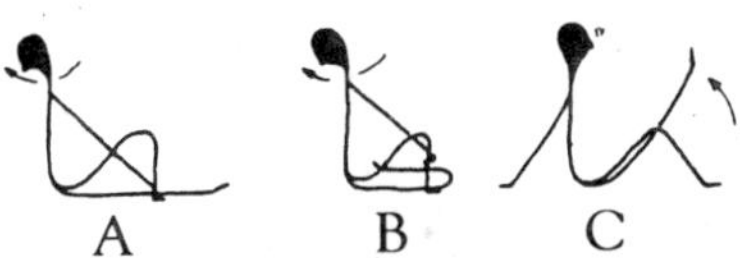

The following stages are given for a better execution of the movements involved in this complex posture:

A. Sit with legs outstretched and arms alongside the body. Bend the right knee and place the right foot on the floor along the outer side of the left thigh. Inhale and grasp the right ankle with the left hand. With full lung retention, turn the trunk to the right allowing the right arm to swing back around the waist. Exhale and come back. Change the position of the limbs and repeat on the other side.

B. Sit in vajrasana. Lift the left leg and place the left foot on the outer side of the right knee. Lock the bent left knee tightly against the chest with the help of the left arm, keeping the spine erect. Inhale and twist the trunk to the right, allowing the right arm to swing back around the waist. Exhale and come back. Change the position of the limbs and repeat on the other side.

C. Sit with both legs bent at the knees, feet close to the perineum. Place the palms behind the back on the ground, inhale and slightly lean back. Exhale, contract the abdomen and swing the left leg across the right one, twisting the lower spine. Inhale and come back. Repeat three times with each leg.

Ardhamatsyendrasana in a sequence of Asanas

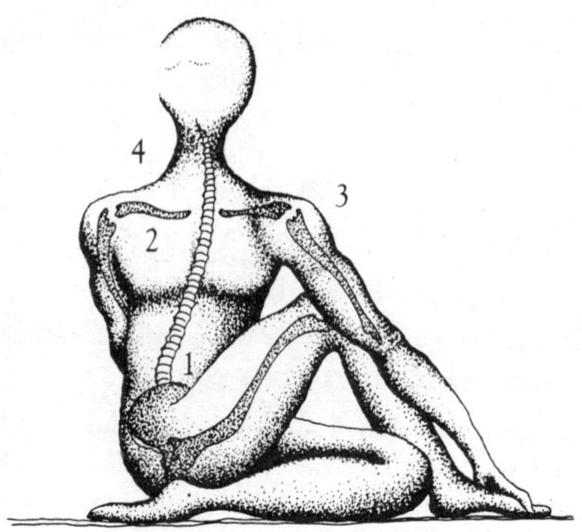

Main benefits of the Asana

Ardhamatsyendrasana produces a quasi-perfect rotation of the trunk on a fixed base formed by the lower limbs. It is excellent for detoxifying the system and is therefore usually practised at the end of a series of asanas.

1. Between the fixed hip joints and the symmetrically moving shoulder joint, the spine is subjected to an axial rotation with a salutary spacing of the vertebrae from the lumbar to the cervical region. The blood supply to the nerves branching out from the backbone is thus increased to its maximum.
2. Due to the chest expansion and the abdominal compression, the breathing process improves and the digestive organs are toned up.
3. The shoulder joints are strengthened and the shoulder movements become freer.
4. The neck muscles are made more powerful without any strain or pressure.

ENERGY PLANE

In ardhamatsyendrasana, an abundant flow of energy moves along the elongated spine because of the abdominal compression and the expansion of the chest produced by the lateral twist. Moreover, both sides of the trunk are exercised and the energy flows evenly on the right and on the left sides of the body.

Anahata chakra receives the energy, which springs from the base of the spine.

The following kriyas and pranayamas help the movement of energy:

As A Preparation For The Asana	*Bhastrika in Vyaghrasana* *Agnisara Kriya* *Madhyama Pranayama*

DIVINITY PLANE

Ardhamatsyendrasana increases the vitality and the well being of practitioners and helps in the arousal of the latent spiritual energy in the innermost core of the spine. Through a regular practice of this asana, the choroid plexus as well as the cerebrospinal fluid are stabilized.

This equilibrium is further enhanced by the practice of the dynamic form of solar meditation in which seven cycles of four solar mantras are repeated in the four lower centres.

Muladhara	*Hram*
Svadhishthana	*Hrim*
Manipura	*Hrum*
Anahata	*Hraim*

In the static meditation, the awareness is kept in the subtle heart centre for a period of about two minutes with the appropriate mantra.

Anahata	*Hraim*

NAVASANA
(Boat Pose)

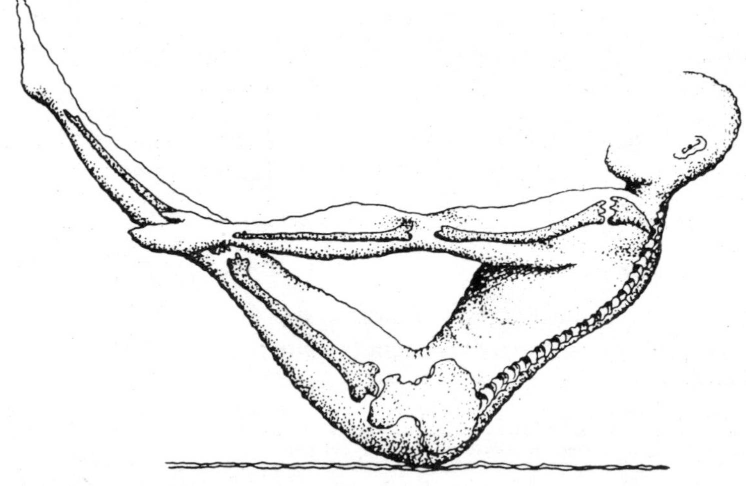

BODY PLANE

Definition and concept

'Nava' or 'nowka' means boat. This posture evokes the shape of a boat with oars, hence the name 'Navasana' which means 'the posture of the boat' in Sanskrit.

In Navasana, the body obtains an excellent balance as in the case of a boat, which has to find its proper equilibrium to sail on the waters.

Navasana is a very energizing posture and its effects are directly manifested in the abdominal belt. A regular practice of this asana will produce a buoyant feeling in the whole system.

Execution

Sit on the floor with the legs stretched together in front. Place the palms on the floor by the hips, fingers pointing forward.

Inhale, keep the back erect and the arms straight.

Exhale, recline the trunk slightly back and simultaneously raise the legs from the floor, knees tight and toes pointing forward. At the same time, stretch the arms forward, keeping them parallel to the floor and on the outer side of the thighs, palms facing each other. Keep the posture with normal breathing for half a minute. Then, gradually increase to one minute. In this asana, the body is balanced on the buttocks only and the legs are kept at an angle of 60 degrees from the ground with the feet being held higher than the head.

Exhale, lower the arms, rest the legs on the floor and relax lying on the back.

Counterpostures	*Bhujangasana*
Contra-indications	*Displaced disc* *Nervous disorders* *Sciatica* *Advanced stages of pregnancy*

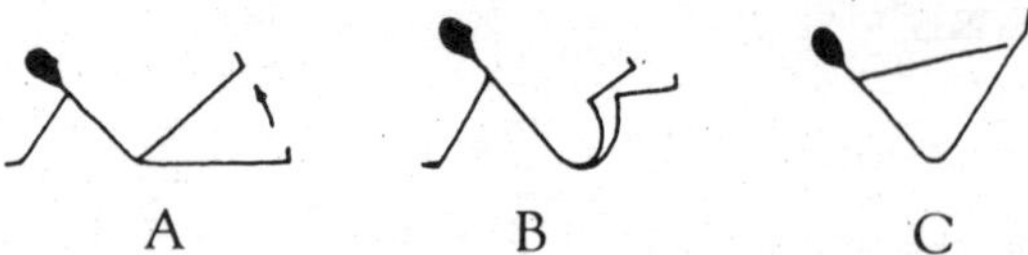

Preparatory movements

These preparatory movements are particularly useful in the case of Navasana because the back is usually too weak to bear the strain of the posture in the initial stages of the practice.

A. Sit on the floor, legs stretched out together. Place the hands behind the body on the ground and recline the trunk slightly back. Inhale and lift one leg as high as comfortable. Exhale and bring it down to the ground. Repeat with the other leg. Execute this movement five times with each leg.

B. Sit on the floor as in A above and perform different movements, such as cycling, rowing, scissors, rotations, with each leg separately and then with both legs together.

C. Sit on the floor, legs stretched out together. Bend the knees, move the arms between the legs and grasp the big toes with the fingers. Try to stretch the legs upwards while balancing the body on the buttocks.

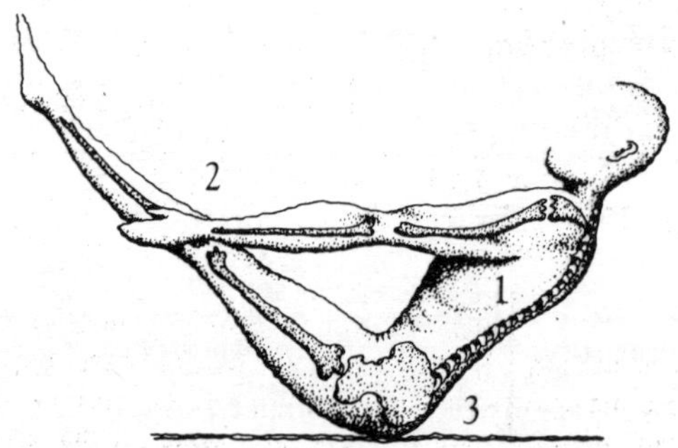

Main benefits of the Asana

This asana, when coupled with a lateral twisting movement of the spine, is a great regenerator of the back.

1. The posture has a beneficial effect on the digestive system particularly on the intestines, and it tones the kidneys.

2. It strengthens the arms and the legs.
3. It reinforces the lower back and tones the spinal nerves.

Navasana in a sequence of Asanas

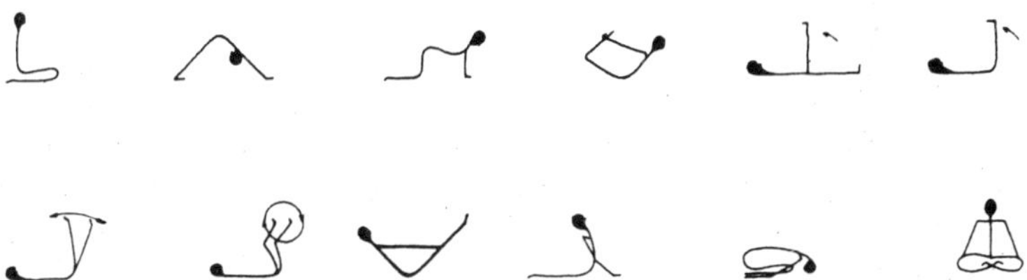

ENERGY PLANE

Navasana produces a powerful reaction at the base of the spine and the energy recoiled in the subtle root centre known as muladhara chakra can be channelled in an upward direction through the different spinal centres up to the neck centre. Owing to the powerful energy movement it produces in the sacro-lumbar area of the spine and the concomitant energy vibrations this movement creates in the abdominal region, Navasana has proved itself to be a rejuvenating and revitalizing posture.

Since Navasana is in itself an energy-producing asana, the only techniques recommended are the ones, which are practised:

As A Preparation To The Asana	*Nauli Kriya* *Uddiyana Bandha* *Mula Bandha* *Ashvini Mudra* *Agnisara Kriya*

DIVINITY PLANE

In Navasana, the energy released from the root of the spine should be utilized as a support for the repetition of the five solar mantras, which correspond to the five lower subtle centres.

The cycle of mantras is repeated seven times in a clockwise fashion from the root centre to the neck centre.

Muladhara	*Hram*
Svadhishthana	*Hrim*
Manipura	*Hrum*
Anahata	*Hraim*
Vishuddhi	*Hraum*

In the static meditation, the vital power is transformed into a pacifying spiritual energy by repeating the appropriate mantras sixty times in the root centre of the spine in the state of kevala kumbhaka.

Muladhara	*Hram*

PAVANAMUKTASANA
(Foetus Pose)

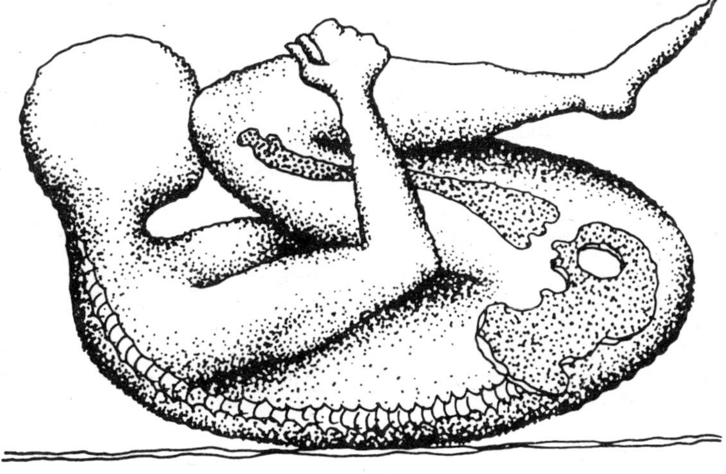

BODY PLANE

Definition and concept

'Pavana' is one of the Sanskrit names for the wind and 'mukta' gives the idea of liberation or release. In its final phase, this posture evokes the foetus stage in which the flow of life is free from the necessity of air intake.

Execution of the Asana

The full posture is generally preceded by the half-posture.

Half Posture

Lie on the back, legs stretched together on the floor.

Inhale and fold the right leg at the knee, bringing it towards the chest. With full lung retention, press the folded leg on the chest, with the help of both hands, the left leg remaining straight on the ground.

Exhale and bring the leg back to the initial position. Repeat this movement three times with each leg. Then, execute the full posture.

Full Posture

Inhale and bring both legs towards the chest. With full lung retention, press the folded legs on the chest and lift the head towards the knees.

Exhale and return to the initial position.

Counterposture	*Bhujangasana* *Shalabhasana* *Setubandhasana* *Suptavajrasana*
Contra-indications	*Inguinal hernia* *Stomach or duodenal ulcer*

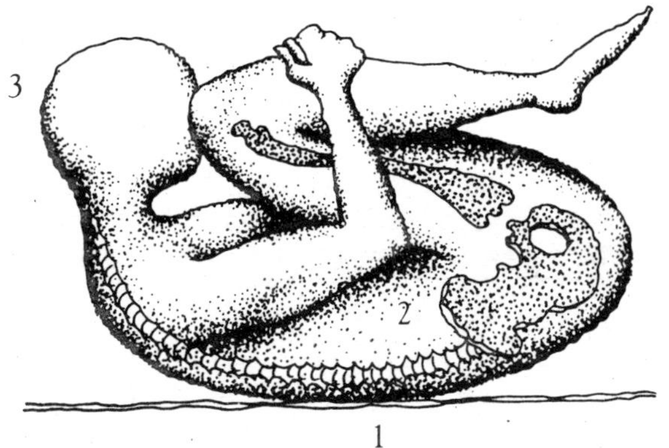

Main benefits of the Asana

This posture creates an intrathoracic compression, immediately followed by a release action, which tends to eliminate the build up of wind in the digestive tract.

1. Full stretching of the spine, especially in the lumbar area.
2. Compression of the abdominal viscera owing to the intrathoracic pressure build-up created by the action of the folded knees.
3. Relaxation of the nervous system in the final pose.

Pavanamuktasana in a sequence of Asanas

ENERGY PLANE

In Pavanamuktasana, the movement of apana is stimulated in the appropriate direction by blocking its upward tendency and allowing it to flow naturally from the navel downwards.

Muladhara chakra is activated in this posture.

The techniques recommended are:

As A Preparation For The Asana	*Ushtra Kriya* *Adham Pranayama* *Agnisara Kriya* *Viparitakarani Mudra* *Prishta Tadana Kriya*
During The Asana	*Pavanamukta Kriya*

DIVINITY PLANE

In Pavanamuktasana, the dynamic meditation consists in reciting seven cycles of solar mantras on a held-in breath.

Muladhara	*Hram*
Svadhishthana	*Hrim*
Manipura	*Hrum*

The static meditation consists in repeating fifty times the solar mantra corresponding to the subtle navel centre.

Manipura	*Hrum*

SETUBANDHASANA
(Bridge Pose)

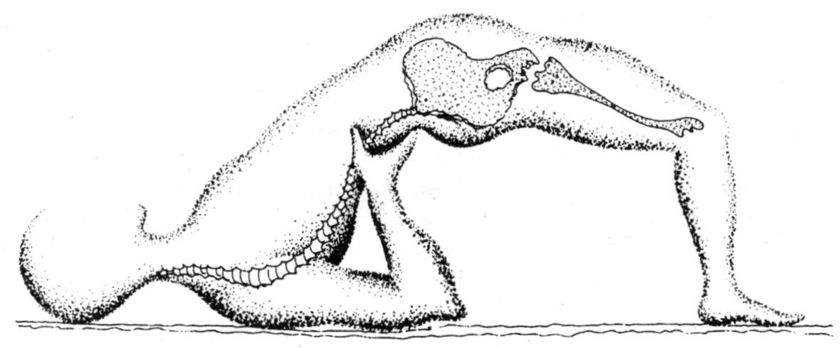

BODY PLANE

Definition and concept

'Setu' means bridge and 'bandha' gives the idea of binding. In this posture, the trunk is elevated as a bridge and the entire body rests only on the feet, on the upper part of the back and on the head. The vulnerable sacro-lumbar junction of the spine, which constitutes a bridge in the evolution of the animate species, is protected by the regular practice of this asana. Millennia ago, the passage from the condition of primate to that of man implied a bending back of the vertebral column in the hip region in order to assume the standing position. Although the lumbar vertebrae are the largest and heaviest of the spine, their position in a vertical plane is thus relatively recent and has to be constantly reinforced. This is the main purpose of Setubandhasana.

Execution of the Asana

Lie on the back, legs folded at the knees and feet resting on the ground. The arms are stretched on the ground alongside the body, the tip of the fingers touching the heels.

Inhale, slowly lift up the trunk to form an arch between the feet and the shoulders, and support the back with the folded arms on the ground. Remain in this posture with gentle breathing.

Exhale and, with the muscles of the glutei contracted, slowly bring the trunk to the ground, unfolding the vertebral column from the dorsal to the lumbar area. Relax.

Preparatory movement

Lie on the back as in the posture described above but execute the movement several times at a normal speed, gradually increasing the amplitude of the arching. Keep inhalation steady but gradually lengthen the exhalation time in order to slow down the descending movement of the trunk and to obtain more benefits for the spine.

Counterpostures	*Vyaghrasana* *Paschimottanasana*
Contra-indications	*Displaced lumbar disc* *Kidney disorders* *Inflammation of the Sciatic nerve* *Arthrosis of the neck.*

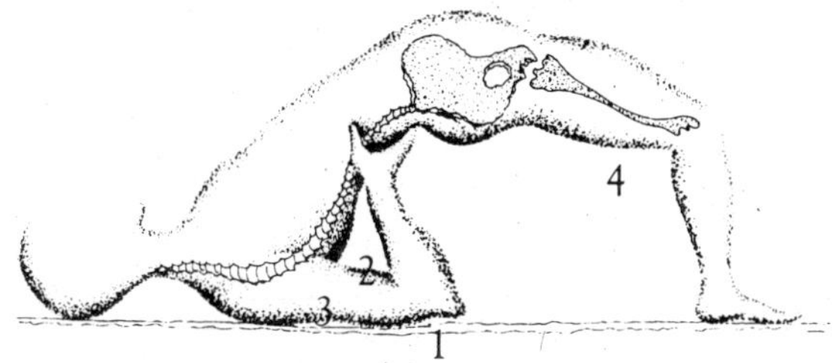

Main benefits of the Asana

Setubandhasana is an excellent preparatory posture for the practice of bandhas and pranayamas.

1. The lumbar curvature is inverted to the maximum with abdominal retraction, causing a reversal of the pressures accumulated in the sacrolumbar area.
2. There is an increased blood flow to the abdominal organs and to the kidneys.
3. The natural diaphragmatic control improves the breathing process.
4. There is an easing of the thigh muscles due to the hyperextension of the hip and a reflux of venous blood from the legs.

Setubandhasana in a sequence of Asanas

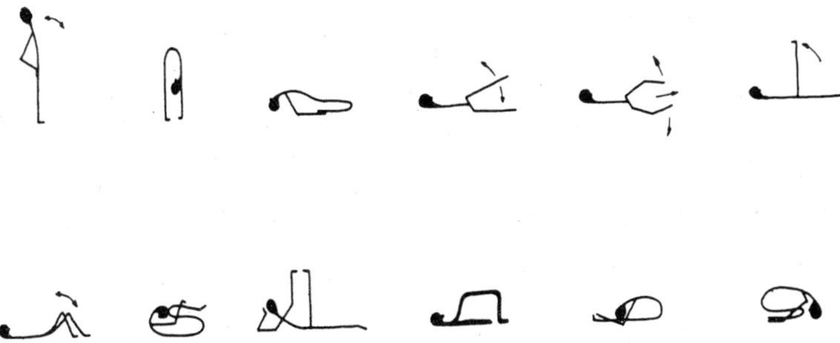

ENERGY PLANE

In Setubandhasana, the tensions created in the sacro-lumbar area by the imbalance between prana and apana are released because the energy is concentrated in manipura chakra. This allows the energy to flow freely in two directions: from manipura to vishuddhi chakra in the upper semi-arching of the spine and from manipura to muladhara chakra in the lower semi-arching of the spine.

The techniques, which stimulate the flow of energy, are:

As A Preparation For The Asana	*Agnisara Kriya* *Bhastrika Pranayama* *Adhama Pranayama* *Sunyaka Pranayama*
During The Asana	*Uddiyana Bandha* *Mula Bandha* *Vibrations Ha, A*

DIVINITY PLANE

Setubandhasana should be kept for at least five minutes to allow an effective flow of energy from manipura to vishuddhi chakra to occur. This balances the cellular mechanisms, which regulate the respiratory, digestive and circulatory systems. The physiological harmony produced by the removal of energy blocks will, in turn, create a feeling of mental peace and tranquillity.

This condition of inner peace is conducive to the static meditation on the navel centre with the corresponding mantra.

Manipura	***Hrum***

The dynamic meditation consists instead in repeating fifty times, focusing on the same chakra, the cycle of solar mantras in an anti-clockwise fashion.

Manipura	***Hram Hrim Hrum Hraim*** ***Hraum Hraha Om***

VIPARITAKARANIMUDRA

(Inverted Pose)

BODY PLANE

Definition and concept

In this posture, the body, the flow of energy and the effect of time are inverted, as the three elements of the Sanskrit name rightly indicate. 'Viparita' means inverted, 'karani' means effect and 'mudra' means gesture.

This mudra is the generic posture of all the inverted asanas and it is practised as a dynamic postural technique to modify the flow of energy.

Apart from being an excellent purification and anti-stress posture, Viparitakaranimudra acts mainly on the lumbar vertebrae of the spine allowing an intense blood flow to reach that area and to relax it.

Execution of the Asana

Lie on the back.

Inhale and raise the legs to a vertical position.

Exhale and gradually raise the trunk until it rests on the shoulder blades. While doing so, support the hips, and not the trunk, with the hands. The legs are inclined behind the head, without reaching the ground. Hold the posture without exertion and practise gentle abdominal breathing.

Exhale and slowly return to the first position. Relax.

An advanced variation of this posture consists in keeping the legs at an angle of 45 degrees.

Counterpostures	*Matsyasana*
Contra-indications	*High blood pressure* *Cervical Problems* *Renal failure* *Heart disorders* *Displaced discs*

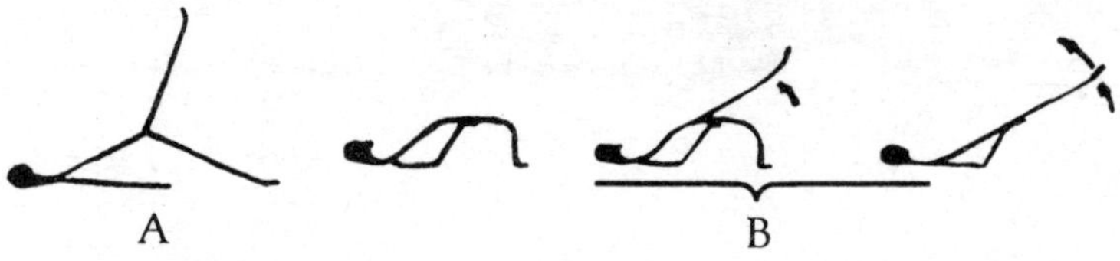

Preparatory movements

A. Lie on the back, arms alongside the body. Bend the knees and keep the feet near the buttocks. Inhale and lift up the back, and, from that position, lift one leg up. Exhale and bring the leg down and, finally, bring the back to the ground. Repeat five times with each leg.

B. Execute setubandhasana, supporting the hips with the hands, elbows on the ground. Inhale and raise one leg up. Exhale and with a swift movement raise the other leg, while keeping the first leg up. The body is inclined at an angle of 45 degrees and the legs are perpendicular to the ground.

Viparitakaranimudra in a sequence of Asanas

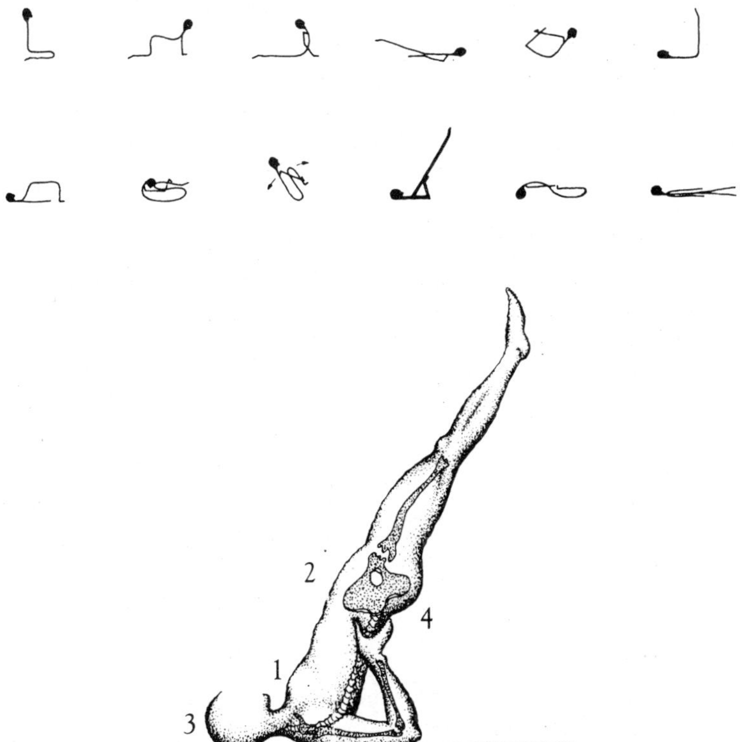

Main benefits of the Asana

1. The absence of a chin lock in this inverted posture allows the free flow of blood and energy from the trunk to the head.
2. The practice of abdominal breathing or 'bhastrika' breathing in the posture activates the energy in the solar plexus and thus tones up the major organs in the trunk, such as kidneys, liver, intestines, lungs, stomach and heart.
3. The unimpeded flow of energy from the navel to the head greatly benefits the nervous and endocrine systems.
4. The spine is reinforced at the sacral and lumbar areas.

ENERGY PLANE

In Viparitakaranimudra, the flow of telluric currents passing through the body is inverted. This balances the nervous system and produces a positive effect on the mind. In this posture, a powerful exchange of energy takes place between the manipura and vishuddhi chakras.

The energy is withdrawn from the legs and stimulates the entire sacro-lumbar area. This movement creates a strong vibratory effect in the umbilical region and the energy is then allowed to flow freely to the neck area, owing to the pull of gravity. Since there is no chin lock in this posture, the head will also receive an abundant supply of energy.

The following techniques are recommended to activate the solar plexus:

As A Preparation For The Asana	*Kapalabhati* *Bhastrika* *Nauli Kriya* *Agnisara Kriya*
During The Asana	*Bhastrika with contraction of the abdomen* *Mula Bandha in Kumbhaka.*

DIVINITY PLANE

Viparitakaranimudra, like the other asanas, which have received the title of mudra, is a great symbol of Yoga. The main aim of Hatha Yoga can be experienced while practising this posture. In the word 'Hatha', the sound 'Ha' which symbolises the moon whose pranic influence is felt mainly in the throat and neck region, is in resonance with the sound 'Tha' which represents the sun whose pranic energy is concentrated predominantly in the navel area. In this semi-inverted posture, the constant exchange of energy between these two subtle centres harmonises the life force and the spiritual power and brings both strength and peace to the practitioners.

The dynamic meditation consists in linking the navel and the throat areas with the appropriate solar mantras and, then, focusing the awareness on the subtle centre between the eyebrows. This cycle is to be repeated twenty-one times.

Manipura	*Hram*
Anahata	*Hrim*
Vishuddhi	*Hraha*
Ajna	*Om*

In the static meditation, the awareness can be oriented towards the subtle centre in the navel area or towards the subtle centre in the throat region according to the desired purpose of the practice.

Manipura		*Hrum*
	or	
Vishuddhi		*Hraum*

SARVANGASANA
(Shoulderstand)

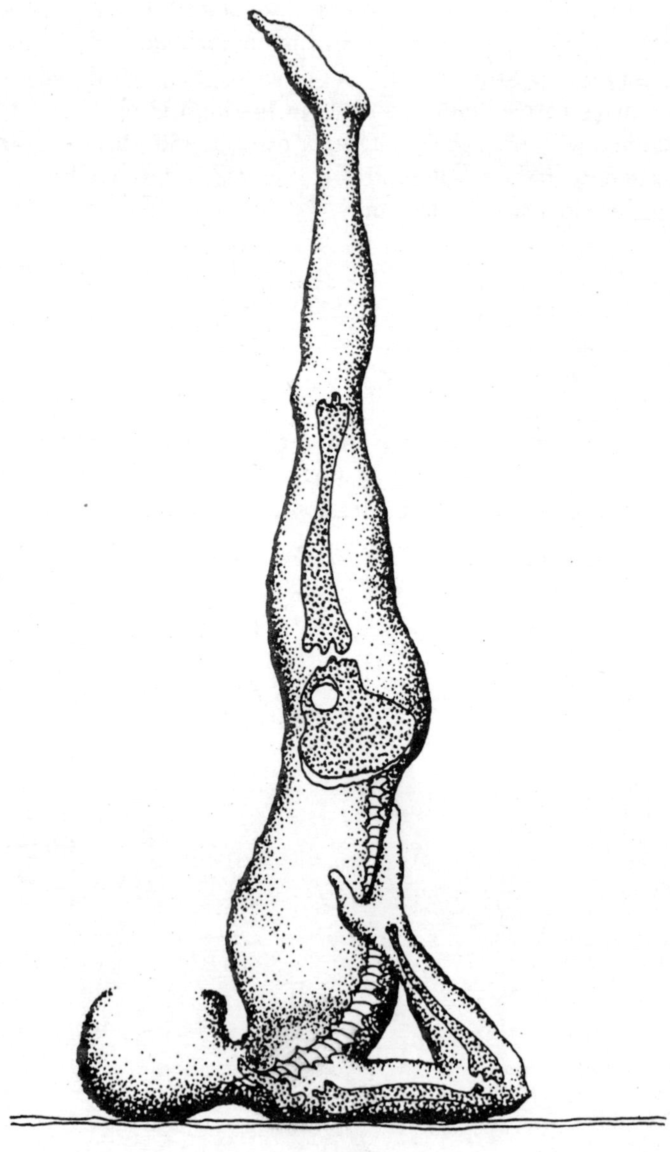

BODY PLANE

Definition and concept

'Sarvangasana' is composed of the word 'sarva' meaning whole, complete and 'anga' meaning limb. In this posture, commonly known as the candle, the entire body is benefited as the Sanskrit word itself indicates.

Execution of the Asana

Lie on the back, legs stretched out, with the arms alongside the body, palms down.

Exhale, bend the knees and bring the legs towards the stomach. Breathe normally.

Exhale again and raise the hips from the floor, resting the hands on them. Breathe normally.

Exhale, raise the trunk perpendicularly to the ground until the chest touches the chin while supporting the middle of the spine with the hands. Stay in this posture with abdominal breathing.

Exhale, gradually lower the trunk, release the arms, slide down the legs and feet. Rest on the ground and relax. Beginners should keep the posture for a very brief moment and then, gradually increase the time.

Counterpostures	*Matsyasana* *Suptvajrasana*
Contra-indications	*Cervical problems* *Hypertension* *Eye defects* *Heart and kidney disorders* *Displaced disc* *Vertigo*

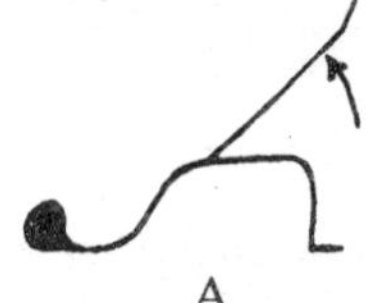
A

B

C

Preparatory movements

The practice of Sarvangasana warrants a note of caution. The posture should be introduced in one's regular practice once the muscles of the lumbar region have been sufficiently strengthened by the practice of other asanas and once the vertebrae are well aligned. The posture should be practised without expending excessive energy, without loss of balance and without straining the vertebrae.

It is advisable to practise Sarvangasana at regular intervals in a plan of work so as to monitor its effects on the body. The posture should be followed by some rocking movement and by setubandhasana.

A. Lie on the back and go into setubandhasana supporting the back with the hands. From there, kick up the right leg, then the left leg and finally both legs. Repeat five times.
B. Go into viparitakaranimudra, supporting the back with the help of the hands. Exhale and raise the back and legs perpendicularly to the ground.
C. Practise Sarvangasana with the support of a wall.

Sarvangasana in a sequence of Asanas

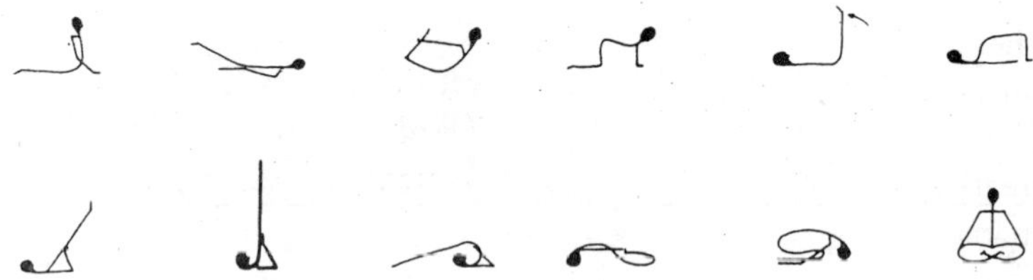

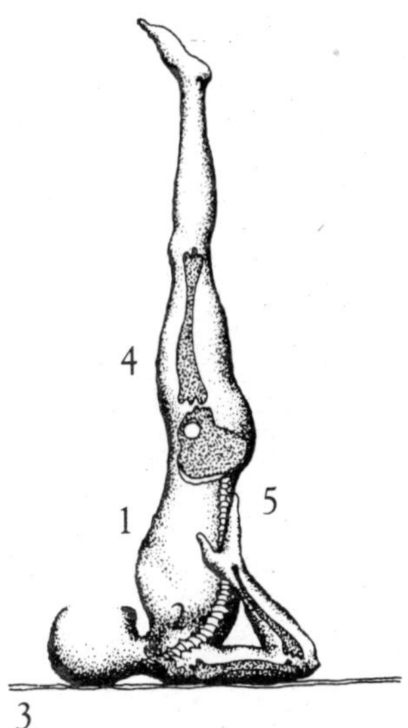

Main benefits of the Asana

Sarvangasana is among the most beneficial postures. It increases the flow of energy, helps to eliminate the toxins from the organism and produces overall harmony in the system.

1. The effect of the force of gravity is reversed, which increases the blood flow to the organs of the upper trunk without exerting the heart unduly.
2. The chin lock increases the blood supply to the neck and helps in regulating the thyroid and parathyroid functions.
3. The blood flow to the head is regulated by the practice of the chin lock with a consequent calming of the cranial nerves.
4. The practice of abdominal breathing in this inverted posture greatly reduces the venous congestion in the legs and in the abdominal organs.
5. The spine is strengthened with a relaxation of the lower back and a stretching of the neck.

ENERGY PLANE

Sarvangasana is an inverted posture in which the telluric current is minimized and the cosmic current strongly concentrated in the head and in the brain. In the posture, the energy is withdrawn from the leg chakras into the base of the spine and is then allowed to flow easily to the chest and to the neck. Due to the chin lock, there is a strong concentration of energy at the base of the neck.

Vishuddhi chakra, as the nexus of cosmic and individual energies, is activated in this asana.

The following practices will help the flow of energy:

As A Preparation For The Asana	*Viparitakaranimudra* *Hala Kriya* *Savitri Pranayama* *Jalandhara Bandha*

DIVINITY PLANE

Sarvangasana produces an inversion of the electric current in the body, which is highly beneficial to the mind and the Spirit. The divine energy and the lower energies meet at the vishuddhi chakra, which is the subtle centre of purification. In this inverted posture, the lower energies are more easily sublimated into a higher and subtler form of energy suited for meditation.

In the dynamic meditation, the awareness is brought with the appropriate solar mantras to the five lower subtle centres during breath retention. This is repeated seven times.

Muladhara	*Hram*
Svadhishthana	*Hrim*
Manipura	*Hrum*
Anahata	*Hraim*
Vishuddhi	*Hraum*

In the static meditation, the inner awareness is concentrated on the subtle centre at the neck, with gentle breathing, for a period that should not exceed seven minutes.

Vishuddhi	*Hraum*

HALASANA
(Plough Pose)

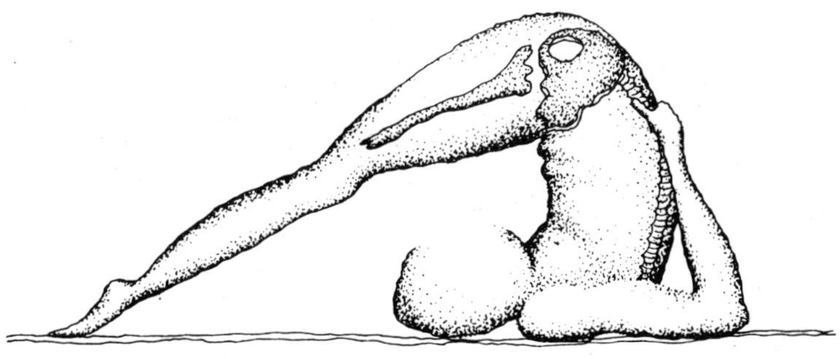

BODY PLANE

Definition and concept

'Hala' means a plough, the shape of which is evoked by this asana.

Execution of the Asana

Lie on the back with arms outstretched alongside the body, palms down.

Exhale slowly, raise the legs outstretched and bring the feet over and beyond the head until the toes touch the floor. While doing so, support the back with the hands, elbows on the ground. In this posture, the back is perpendicular to the ground, the chin is pressed against the chest, the legs are stretched out and the feet are at right angles to the legs.

Remain in this posture for fifteen seconds without breathing.

Inhale, bring the feet somewhat closer to the head so that the back comes slightly down, hold the breath and slowly unroll the body until the feet return to the initial position.

Exhale and relax.

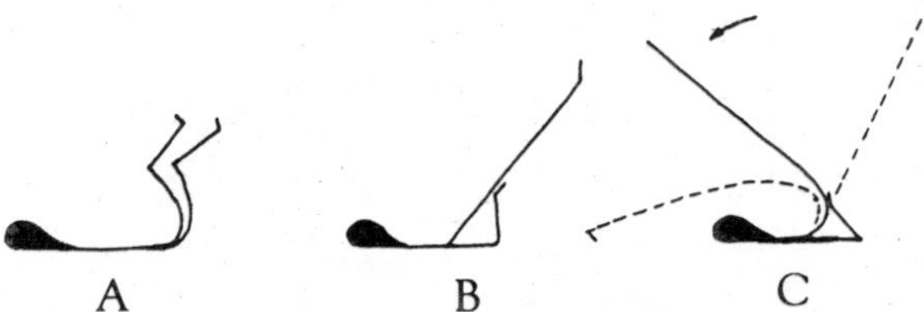

Preparatory movements

A. Lie on the back. Inhale, raise both legs until they are perpendicular to the ground. Practise cycling movements for half a minute.
B. Go into the viparitakaranimudra position.
C. Exhale and bring the feet over the head towards the ground. Inhale and return to viparitakaranimudra. Repeat five times.

Counterpostures	*Matsyasana* *Suptavajrasana*
Contra-indications	*Cervical Problems* *High blood pressure* *Heart disorders* *Spinal disorders*

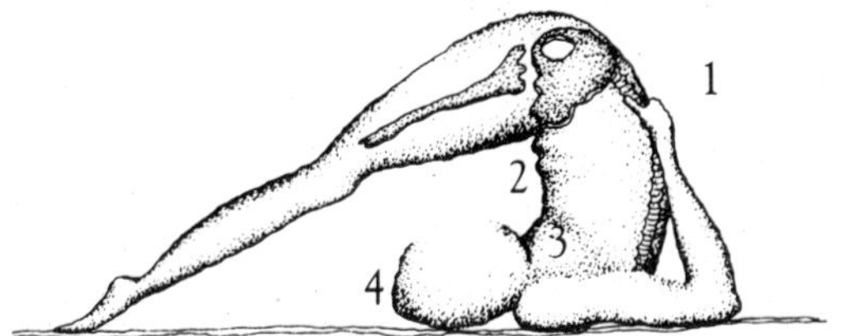

Main benefits of the Asana

1. Every part of the spinal column is subjected to compression or tension with a beneficial effect on the vertebrae and the spinal nerves. Tensing and flexing of the back muscles creates perfect body symmetry and strengthens the entire back.
2. The abdominal contraction increases the blood supply to the organs of the abdominal cavity, strengthening them, reducing fatty deposits and alleviating digestive disorders.
3. The thyroid and parathyroid glands are stimulated. The pressure on the carotid sinus lowers the blood pressure and slows down the heart rate.
4. The forward bend brings an extra supply of blood to the spine thereby relieving tensions in the head and allowing the brain activity to be stimulated.

Halasana in a sequence of Asanas

ENERGY PLANE

In Halasana, the energy is ploughed back from the sacro-lumbar area to the heart and to the neck. Due to the constriction at the neck, breathing becomes rather shallow in this posture and concentration should be directed to the vishuddhi chakra.

The techniques, which will enhance the revitalizing effect of this asana, are:

As A Preparation For The Asana	*Kapalabhati* *Agnisara Kriya* *Adhyama Pranayama* *Pavanamukta Kriya* *Hala Kriya*
During The Asana	*Padachalana Kriya*

DIVINITY PLANE

The dynamic meditation is performed with mild breathing once the posture is obtained.

Seven cycles of solar mantras are recited in the appropriate subtle centres.

Muladhara	***Hram***
Svadhishthana	***Hrim***
Manipura	***Hrum***
Anahata	***Hraim***
Vishuddhi	***Hraum***

The static meditation consists in keeping the awareness in the throat centre and repeating the corresponding solar mantra 108 times.

Vishuddhi	***Hraum***

MATSYASANA
(Fish Pose)

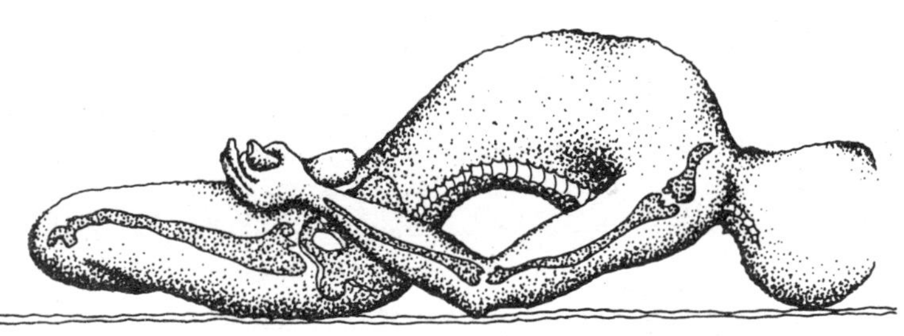

BODY PLANE

Definition and concept

'Matsya' means fish. This posture is dedicated to the incarnation of the mythological Hindu god Vishnu as a fish. It evokes the continuity and maintenance of life even when the physical universe is threatened with dissolution.

Execution of the Asana

Inhale and sit in padmasana.

Exhale and, with the help of the elbows, lower the trunk backward, arch the chest and rest the top of the head on the floor. Hold the toes with the hands. Remain in this posture, breathing in the thoracic region (15 to 30 seconds) and try to arch the back further by increasing the curvature of the neck.

Exhale while coming out of the posture, rest the back of the head on the floor and lie flat on the back.

Inhale and come back to the initial position. Release the legs and relax. Cross the legs the other way and repeat the posture.

If the posture is difficult to execute in padmasana, it can be practised with the legs outstretched and the arms alongside the body. In the intermediary stage, it can be practised in padmasana with the arms stretched overhead on the floor.

Counterpostures	*Paschimottanasana* *Paripurna Shashasana*
Contra-indications	*Depressive states* *Cervical problems* *Neuro-vegetative troubles* *Vertigo* *Arthrosis of the hip and/or shoulder joints*

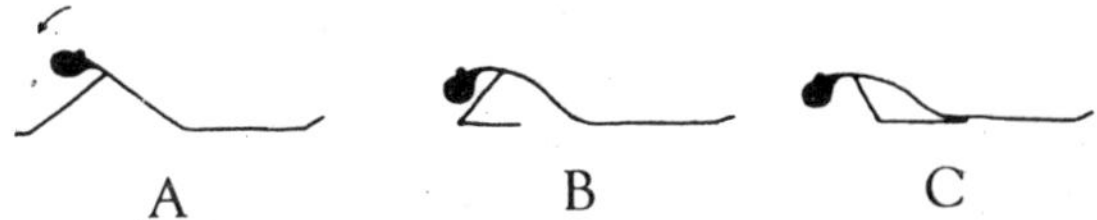

Preparatory movements

A. Sit with legs outstretched and close together. Lean back on the elbows, palms down. Arch up the spine gradually and rest the crown of the head on the ground. Breathe in the thoracic region of the lungs for twenty seconds. Repeat three times.

B. Lie on the back, arms alongside the body. Inhale and arch the chest up, rest the crown of the head on the floor and look behind. Exhale and return to the initial position. Repeat three times.

C. Sit with legs outstretched. Lean back supporting the body on the elbows and the forearms. Exhale, arch the back and look behind. Remain in the posture for fifteen seconds. Repeat three times.

Matsyasana in a sequence of Asanas

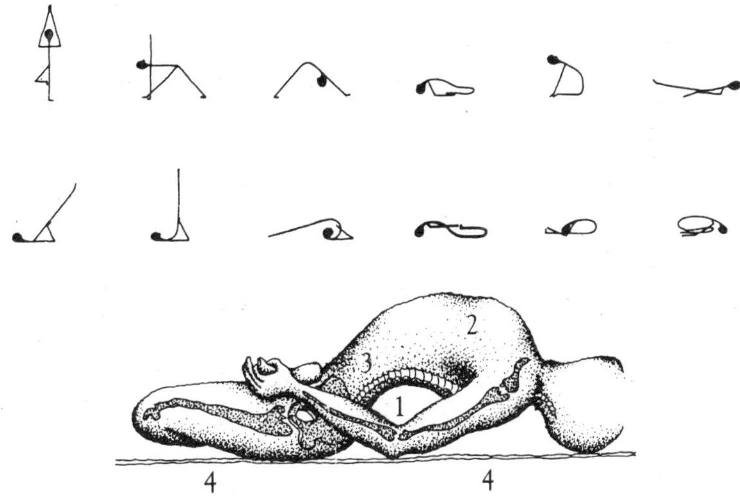

Main benefits of the Asana

Matsyasana, stimulates the blood flow to the neck and has a powerful effect on the thyroid function.

1. The spine undergoes a flattening in the lumbar area and a stretching in the dorsal and cervical sections.
2. The chest is fully expanded.
3. The pelvic joint is made elastic with a maximum extension of the waist.
4. The muscles of the thighs and arms are stretched.

ENERGY PLANE

Matsyasana increases the feeling of floating by bringing the centre of gravity closer to the centre of the body. In this posture, the energy flow is restricted in the legs and is concentrated in the chest, the upper back and the neck. This, in turn, produces a decongestion of the solar plexus and releases the key point of anxiety. The vishuddhi chakra is activated in this asana, as the backward pressure of the head on the ground increases the flow of energy in the neck. When the arms are crossed and each hand is holding the opposite foot, the electric and magnetic currents in the body are well balanced. The following pranayamas and kriyas can be practised:

As A Preparation For The Asana	*Mahatyoga Pranayama* *Ujjayi* *Shvana Pranayama* *Hastabaddha Kriya*

DIVINITY PLANE

Matsyasana is a posture of complete rest with a great calming effect on the mind and a regulating effect on the breathing rhythm. In the dynamic meditation, three subtle centres are activated by the repetition of seven cycles of the appropriate solar mantras.

Anahata	***Hraim***
Vishuddhi	***Hraum***
Ajna	***Hraha***

In the static meditation, the awareness is kept in the subtle centre of the neck for a period of two to five minutes with the appropriate mantra.

Vishuddhi	***Hraum***

SHIRSHASANA
(Headstand)

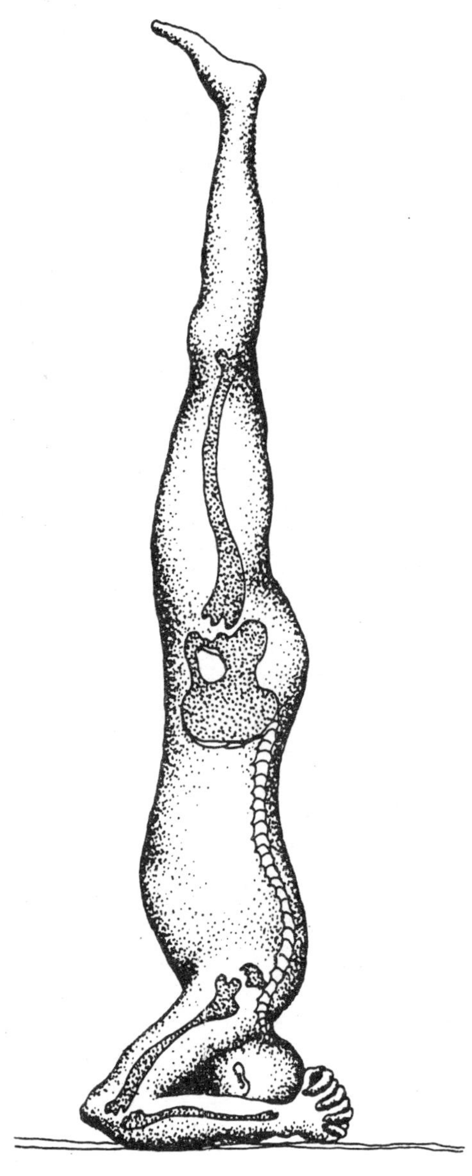

BODY PLANE

Definition and concept

'Shirsha' means head. This is the headstand, one of the most important classical postures.

Execution of the Asana

Kneel on the floor and rest the forearms on the ground in front of the body. The distance between the elbows should be equal to that of the shoulders. Interlace the fingers tightly so that the palms form a cup in which to rest the head. Leaning forward, place the crown of the head only on the floor so that the back of the head can be firmly secured in the cupped palms.

Exhale and with the support of the stretched legs, raise the hips and then, with a gentle swing, lift the legs off the ground and bend the knees. Secure this phase of the posture and find the proper balance of the body, which is resting only on the head. Breathe gently.

Exhale and gradually bring the legs to a perpendicular position. The whole body is then in a vertical line. With gentle breathing, remain in this posture from one to five minutes.

To come down, bend the trunk at the hips and bend the knees until the kneeling position is reached. Rest in this position, placing the fists on top of each other and the head on top of the upper fist. In this way, the head and heart are at the same level and the legs are compressed. This gives a rest to the heart and produces a decongestion of the legs.

There are a number of variations, which can be practised in shirshasana.

1. Practise the posture, resting the head just beyond the folded forearms.
2. Practise the posture, arms stretched in front of the chest towards the feet, palms up.
3. Practise movements of the legs, such as scissors, rotations, in shirshasana.
4. Practise shirshasana with the legs in the lotus position.

Counterpostures	*Paripurna Shashasana* *Dharmikasana with arms outstretched*
Contra-indications	*Hypertension* *Weak eye capillaries* *Chronic constipation* *Weak heart* *Inner ear disorders* *Arthrosis of the neck and shoulders* *Vertigo*

General indications about Shirshasana

All the movements of Shirshasana should be practised on an exhalation.

Use a folded blanket to rest the head. Practise all the adjustments necessary to find the proper balance: avoid swaying, swinging or tilting the body.

In the case of loss of balance, loosen the fingers, bend the knees and roll over in a relaxed fashion. The body should be in a vertical line: back of the head, trunk, heels and back of the thighs.

The weight of the body should rest on the head and not on the arms. The elbows and the shoulders should form a straight line and the shoulders should be as high above the floor as possible. The legs should be fully stretched and move together, toes pointing up.

Preparatory movements

A. Kneel down. Place the head on the ground between the cupped hands. Stretch the legs on the toes and raise the buttocks. Move the feet alternately backwards and forwards without bending the knees. Then lift the legs up alternately.

B. Practise Shirshasana in a corner of a room where two walls form a right angle. Place the head ten to fifteen centimetres away from the wall.

Exhale, swing the legs up, support the hips against the side of the wall and raise the feet up.

To come down, exhale, rest hips and feet against the wall, slide down and rest the knees on the floor. With practise, stretch the back up vertically and gradually do without the support of the wall.

Shirshasana in a sequence of Asanas

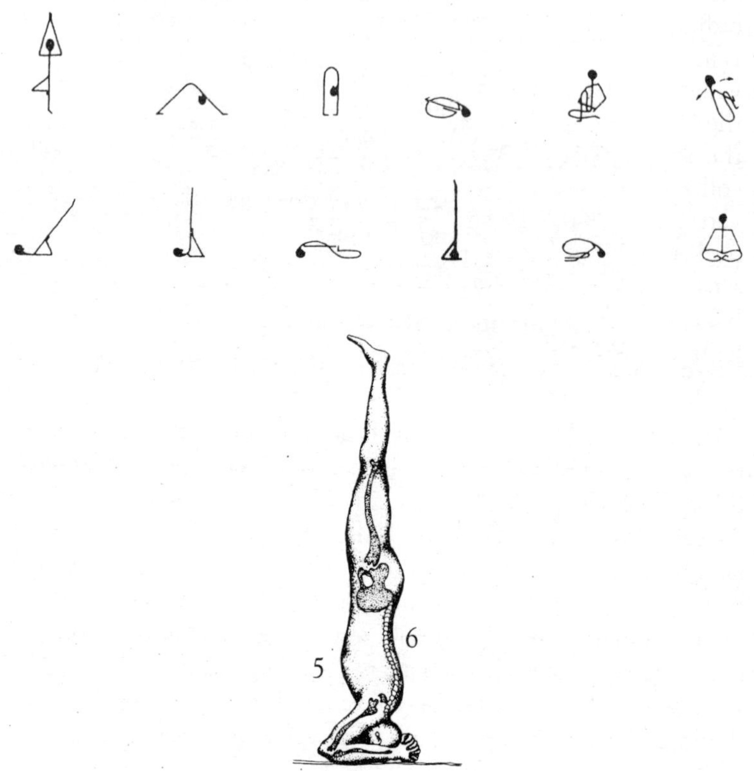

Main benefits of the Asana

1. The rich blood supply to the nervous centres in the brain has a positive effect on the nervous system. This helps in awakening the latent brain faculties.
2. The pituitary and pineal glands are benefited, bringing overall health and vitality to the system.
3. The posture tones up the endocrine, nervous and digestive systems.
4. Reversal of the blood flow acts against the effects of ageing.
5. Mid-lung breathing is favoured.
6. The headstand helps to attenuate the excessive curvature of the spine.

ENERGY PLANE

Shirshasana is the crown of the Hatha Yoga practice. When the ordinary standing posture is completely inverted and the entire body is made to rest on the crown of the head, the flow of pranic energy will be greatly influenced. The energy is gradually withdrawn from the leg chakras. This release of energy from the lower limbs favours the venous circulation and relaxes the leg muscles. The energy collected at the base of the spine starts flowing naturally along the vertebral column towards the higher subtle centres located in the neck and head. This energizes the major cranial nerves and the five senses. This posture helps to develop the sixth sense. This asana has a purifying and cleansing effect on the spinal nerves and on the brain and it allows most of the pranic obstructions to be removed.

This asana acts directly on the sahasrara chakra.

DIVINITY PLANE

Shirshasana gives the practitioners a sense of the balance of the psycho-physical human system and promotes the expansion of the mind. When the asana can be kept without any undue tension and when the breath has been regulated, the inner concentration can be brought to the base of the spine.

The dynamic meditation starts from this root centre and consists of the entire cycle of solar mantras repeated at the appropriate subtle spinal centres, for the entire duration of the posture.

Muladhara	*Hram*
Svadhishthana	*Hrim*
Manipura	*Hrum*
Anahata	*Hraim*
Vishuddhi	*Hraum*
Ajna	*Hraha*
Sahasrara	*Om*

The static meditation combines the visualization of the inner sun with the repetition of the cosmic solar mantra, at the appropriate centre, for a period of two to five minutes.

Sahasrara	*Om*

YOGAMUDRA
(Lotus Seal Pose)

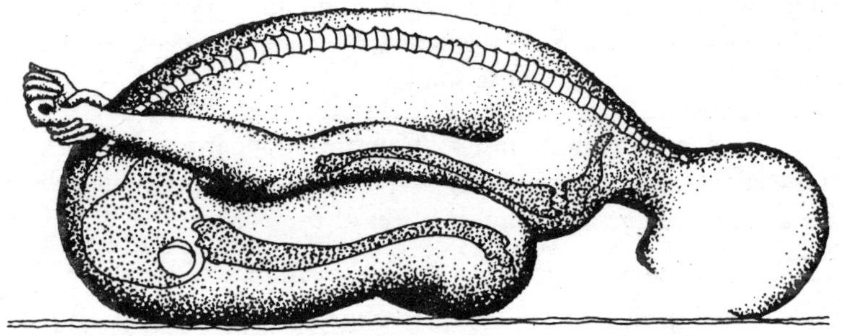

BODY PLANE

Definition and concept

'Mudra' means gesture, symbol. This asana is the perfect symbol of Yoga as it is especially useful in awakening the spiritual energy. This posture is called a mudra because it seals a particular aspect of the yogic practice and produces a deep effect on the three planes of being with a great economy of physical movement and energy. This is an asana of rest in which passivity becomes the leading force.

Execution of the Asana

Sit in padmasana.

Inhale and bring the arms behind the back, clasping the right wrist with the left hand, spine erect.

Exhale and bend the trunk slowly forward until the head touches the ground. During the forward movement, the spine is straight and the chin slightly raised. Remain in this position without breathing for as long as is comfortable. When the trunk has reached its maximum forward bend, the head is lowered to the ground while the neck is completely relaxed.

Inhale and gradually straighten up the trunk to the initial position and relax.

Preparatory movements

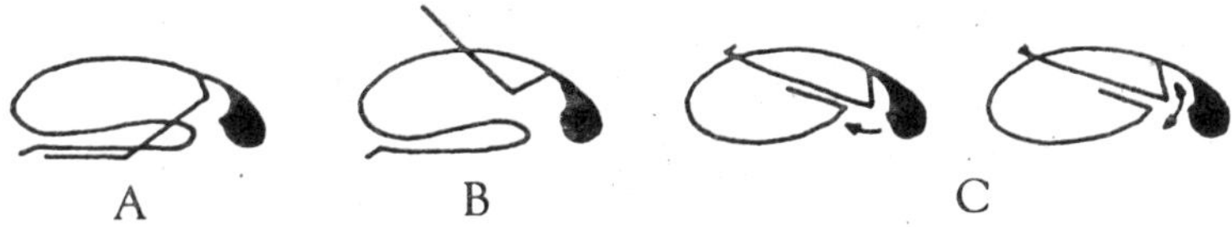

A. Sit in vajrasana. Exhale and bend forward in dharmikasana. Inhale and return to the initial position. Exhale again and bend forward in mahamudra. Inhale and return to the initial position.

B. Sit in padmasana, ardhapadmasana or sukhasana, hands clasped behind the back. Exhale and bend the trunk slowly towards the right knee. With full lung retention, keep the pose for twenty seconds. Inhale and straighten up. Repeat on the left side and in the centre.

C. Sit in padmasana. Exhale and bend the trunk forward. With full lung retention, move the trunk to the right, to the left and complete a full circle. Inhale and slowly come back to the initial position and relax.

Counterpostures	*Ushtrasana* *Suptavajrasana*
Contra-indications	*Displaced disc* *Cervical problems*

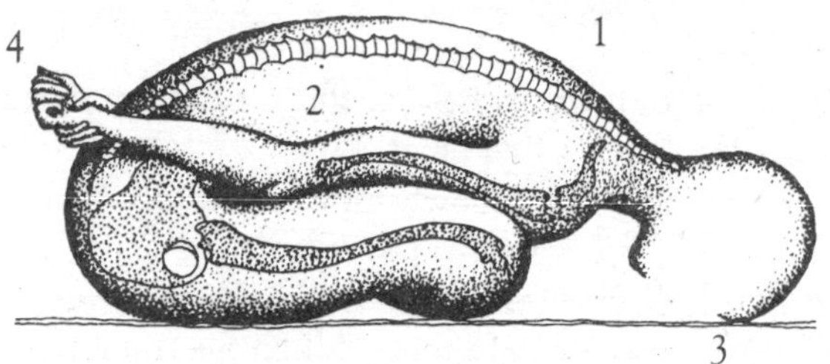

Main benefits of the Asana

This major classical asana is particularly useful as a calming and balancing posture. Therefore, it is usually practised before pranayama or as a relaxing pose before meditation.

1. Due to the weight of the head, the spine is stretched with a release of tensions, particularly in the dorsal and cervical areas, with a consequent toning up of the spinal nerves.
2. The intra-abdominal pressure creates an internal muscular massage, which helps in regenerating the organs of the abdominal cavity and in intensifying the peristaltic activity.
3. The abundant flow of energy to the brain has a great calming effect on the mind. Moreover, when properly executed, the centre point between the eyebrows is pressed against the floor producing a calming of the mental vibrations.
4. The position of clasped hands behind the back expands the chest and improves the breathing capacity.

Yogamudra in a Sequence of Asanas

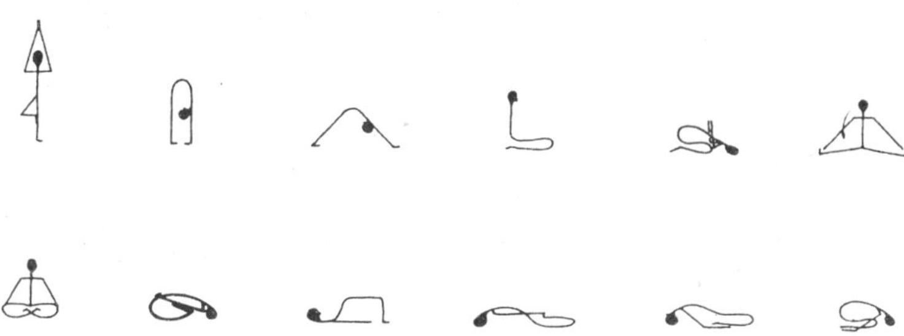

ENERGY PLANE

In Yogamudra, the leg-lock prevents the energy from moving downwards and the extreme stretching of the spine allows it to reach the head easily. When the arms are clasped behind the back, the rib cage expands, the energy blocks at the armpits are removed and this further intensifies the upward movement of the energy.

In this asana, the active subtle centre is the vishuddhi chakra and the abundant flow of energy from that centre to the higher centres of the brain has a great calming effect on the mind. Moreover, when the forehead touches the ground and the ajna chakra is stimulated, the thought process can be effectively controlled. This mental calm induces meditation and, for this reason, the posture has been called yogamudra, the synthesis of Yoga.

The following practices will stimulate the energy movement:

As A Preparation For The Asana	*Nadi Shodhana* *Nadi Shuddhi* *Kapalabhati* *Uddiyana in Vyaghrasana* *Agnisara Kriya*
During The Asana	*Mula Bandha*

DIVINITY PLANE

In Yogamudra, the Vishuddhi chakra is activated and allows the energy to flow to the higher subtle centres of the brain, which form the 'Guru Mandala'. These centres, in turn, respond to the practitioners' own superior vibrations.

In the dynamic meditation, the entire cycle of solar mantras is repeated from the lowest chakra to the highest. A beautiful movement of energy follows this from the base of the neck to the crown of the head and back to the base of the throat with the repetition of the appropriate solar mantras. This shorter cycle is repeated seven times and involves the four higher chakras.

From Muladhara To Sahasrara	*Hram Hrim Hrum Hraim Hraum Hraha Om*
Vishuddhi	*Hraum*
Sahasrara	*Om*
Ajna	*Om*
Vishuddhi	*Hraha*
From Vishuddhi To Sahasrara	*Hraum*
Through Ajna To Vishuddhi	*Om*

The static meditation consists in staying in the subtle centre of the neck for about two to five minutes with gentle breath while repeating the appropriate mantra.

Vishuddhi	*Om Hraha*

SHAVASANA
(Corpse Pose)

Definition and concept

'Shava' means a corpse. In this relaxing posture, the immobility of the physical frame evokes the image of a corpse. The asana is also called 'mritasana' or 'shanti asana'.

Execution of the Asana

Lie on the back, head towards the North, arms alongside the body, palms up. The legs are stretched out, heels together and toes apart. The posture may seem unnatural at the beginning owing to psychosomatic tensions, which can be felt in different parts of the body. These are the areas, which will require more attention during the practice of the asanas. If a slight pain is felt in some parts of the body, this may indicate that the energy is circulating again in areas which were previously damaged or diseased. But if the pain is sudden and violent, it should be reported immediately to the Guide or the Master.

Nevertheless, some minor adjustments can be effected in the first stages of the practice in order to give the body and the mind the maximum ease.

1. Cover the body with a blanket since the relaxed condition will lower the body temperature.
2. If there is tension in the lumbar area, fold the knees during the relaxation time.
3. If the tension is felt in the neck, roll the head from right to left and find the correct position before starting the relaxation process.
4. Adjust the distance between the trunk and the arms in order to discover the most comfortable posture.

When the body is motionless and the mind is still, bring the awareness to the breathing process: practise abdominal breathing ten times, thoracic breathing ten times and clavicular breathing ten times. Then, perform a full breathing ten times. Allow the exhalation to be deep and slow and concentrate more on the exhalation than the inhalation. Relax all the muscles of the body, starting from the feet and ending with the head.

By a mental process of concentration, withdraw all the energies from the legs to the lower back and from the arms to the base of the neck. Then, bring the unified energies to the centre between the eyebrows and allow the body and the mind to be completely still.

Remain a detached but alert witness, within a motionless body and a pacified mind.

Shavasana can be used as a relaxation posture, as a research technique on breathing or as a rest period between asanas.

Breathing and energy

In the initial stage of practice, the energy moves to all the cells of the body. When the relaxation becomes deeper, the energy is withdrawn from the periphery and is confined to the spine and the brain cells. At a later stage, the energy is concentrated in the centre between the eyebrows and awareness of the breathing process stops. Withdrawal from the mind and the senses is complete.

Effects of the Asana

In this asana, the blood circulation is balanced, the nervous system is rested, the blood pressure is equalized and the heart is relaxed. This produces a regeneration of the main vital functions of the body and a relaxation of the mind.

There are neither counter postures nor contra-indications to the practice of Shavasana.

PADMASANA
(Lotus Pose)

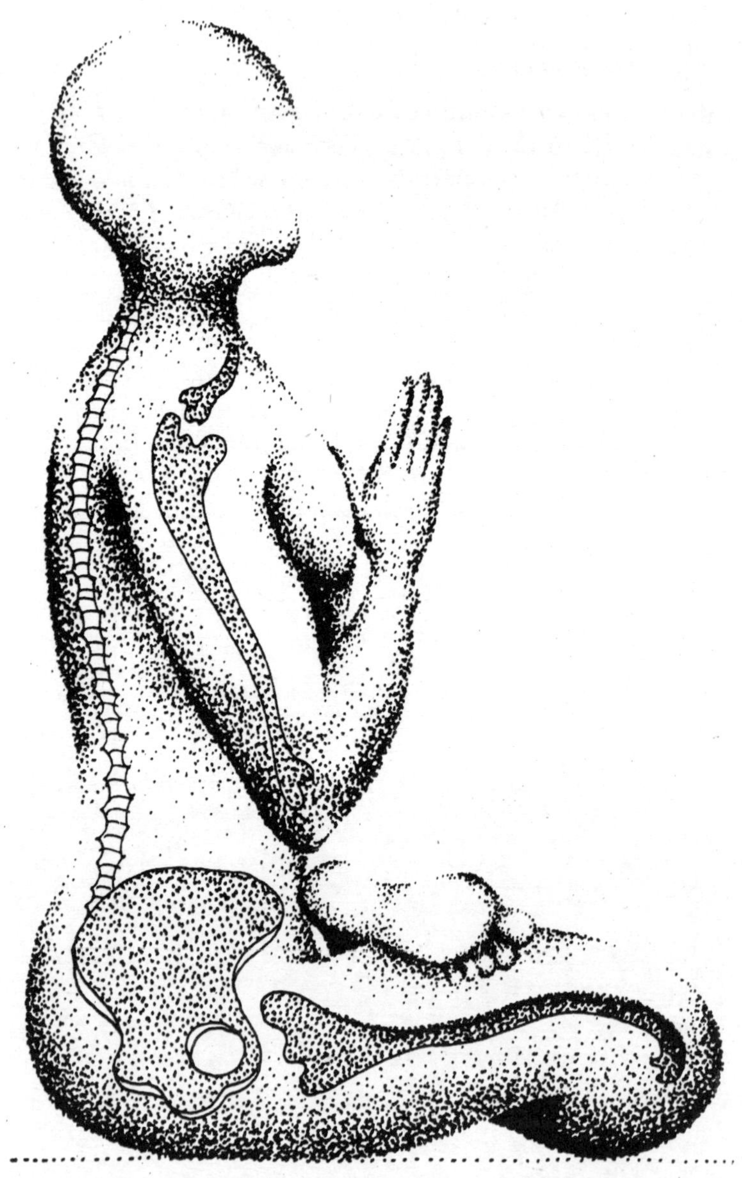

BODY PLANE

Definition and concept

'Padma' means lotus and 'asana' is the seat. This posture is commonly referred to as the Lotus Seat. It evokes the state of expanded consciousness floating above the relative existence in the image of the lotus flower, which points its petals towards the sun when its stem is caught in the muddy waters of the pond.

Execution of the Asana

Sit on the ground with the legs stretched out and with the spine erect. Bend the right leg at the knee and place the right foot at the root of the left thigh. Try to keep the right heel as close as possible to the navel.

Bend the left leg at the knee and place the left foot at the root of the right thigh, trying to keep the left heel as close as possible to the navel.

Ideally, the soles of the feet should be turned up, the spine should remain erect and the chin should be slightly tilted downward. The arms can be stretched out with the hands resting on the knees. The hands can also be crossed, palms upon each other, at the point where the feet are crossed. Repeat the posture, which is kept with gentle breathing, by changing the position of the legs.

Preparatory movements

A. All the exercises for the joints of the ankles, knees, legs and hips.
B. Trikonasana
C. Ushtrasana
D. Vyaghrasana
E. Butterfly posture
F. Ardhapadmasana.

Sit on the buttocks. Bend the right knee and place the right foot under the left thigh. Bend the left knee and place the left foot on the right thigh, the heel of the foot being near the groin. Stay in this position with gentle breathing. Practise the same movement with the other leg.

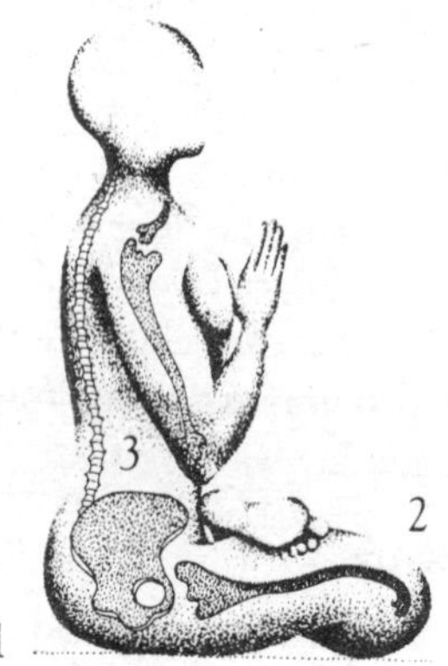

Main benefits of the Asana

1. The stability of the base and the erectness of the spine have a calming effect on the nervous system and a beneficial effect on the endocrine system.
2. Any stiffness in the knees and the ankles is reduced.
3. The blood flow is increased in the lumbar area of the spine and in the abdominal region with a consequent toning of the abdominal organs.

Padmasana in a sequence of Asanas

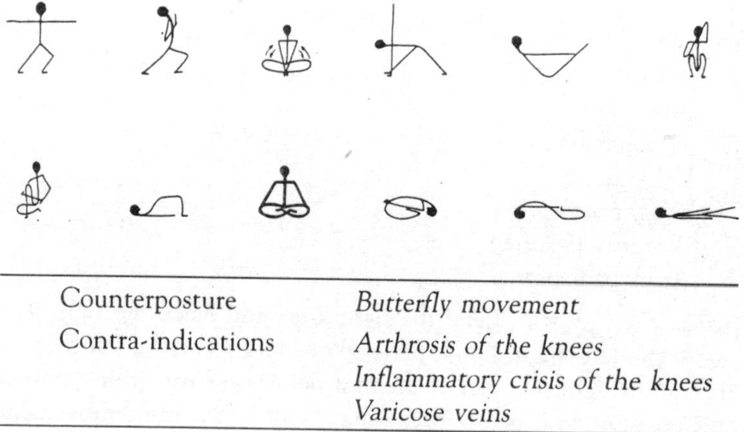

Counterposture	*Butterfly movement*
Contra-indications	*Arthrosis of the knees* *Inflammatory crisis of the knees* *Varicose veins*

ENERGY PLANE

Padmasana is one of the main postures adopted for the practice of pranayamas and for meditation. This is due to the fact that, in this posture, the spine is kept erect and the energy can move freely from the muladhara chakra, which is the subtle centre activated in this posture, to the base of the head and to the brain. The complete symmetry of the body provides a harmonious distribution of the energy and a perfect balance between the positive and negative currents influencing the gross and subtle bodies. The flow of energy into the lower limbs is constricted owing to the leg lock. With the practice of mudras and bandhas, all the effects of pranayama are enhanced in this posture, as can be seen in the Part Two of the book, in the chapter dedicated to pranayama.

In order to gain mastery over this difficult asana, the following energy practices are recommended:

As A Preparation For The Asana	*Ushtra Kriya* *Agnisara Kriya* *Ashta Sandhi Vimochana Kriya* *Savitri Pranayama*
During The Asana	*Yoga Mudra* *Nadi Shodhana* *Nadi Shuddhi*

DIVINITY PLANE

In Padmasana, the energies liberated at the muladhara chakra are made to flow upwards to the ajna chakra where they are purified by the practise of the solar mantras and fused into a creative divine energy, which follows an ascending path to the sahasrara chakra.

In the dynamic meditation, the practice of the solar mantras is done with the retention of the breath and the inner awareness is brought through the seven spinal centres, starting at the base of the spine and ending at the crown of the head, by repeating seven cycles of the appropriate mantras.

Muladhara	***Hram***
Svadhishthana	***Hrim***

Manipura	*Hrum*
Anahata	*Hraim*
Vishuddhi	*Hraum*
Ajna	*Hraha*
Sahasrara	*Om*

This is followed by the repetition of seven cycles of solar mantras in each of the subtle spinal centres, with the retention of the breath.

Muladhara	*Hram Hrim Hrum Hraim Hraum Hraha Om*
Svadhishthana	*Hram Hrim Hrum Hraim Hraum Hraha Om*
Manipura	*Hram Hrim Hrum Hraim Hraum Hraha Om*
Anahata	*Hram Hrim Hrum Hraim Hraum Hraha Om*
Vishuddhi	*Hram Hrim Hrum Hraim Hraum Hraha Om*
Ajna	*Hram Hrim Hrum Hraim Hraum Hraha Om*
Sahasrara	*Hram Hrim Hrum Hraim Hraum Hraha Om*

The dynamic meditation ends with a shorter cycle of solar mantras repeated fifty times as a cycle, with gentle breathing, in the three superior subtle centres

Vishuddhi	*Hraum*
Sahasrara	*Om*
Ajna	*Hraha*

The static meditation in Padmasana can be performed for a period of up to twenty-four minutes, if the posture can be kept with ease. It consists in keeping the awareness at the crown of the head in the highest subtle centre with the constant repetition of the solar mantra.

Sahasrara	*Om*

YOGASANAS (Meditation Postures)

In all the classical Yóga texts, certain asanas have been specifically designated as postures suitable for the practice of pranayama and meditation.

They are all sitting postures, which allow the body to be relaxed and steady and the spine to remain straight. These asanas, when kept over a period of time, will produce mental calm and emotional balance and will help to reduce the physical tensions and prevent energy dissipation. These postures create perfect body architecture. The legs are generally crossed or folded: this gives a firm and solid base to the buttocks, the pelvis and the spine and prevents the energy from being dissipated in the lower limbs. The hip and shoulder joints are parallel to the ground and to each other: this keeps the trunk in a correct position, especially for the practice of pranayama, and it gives ample space in the torso for the movement of the diaphragm and the expansion of the lungs. This enables the energy to be distributed evenly in the trunk. The spine is kept erect through the action of the muscles of the back and the torso and this allows the energy to move easily to the brain.

When the asanas are used for meditation, the head is held erect, in direct prolongation of the spine and the eyes are closed, facial muscles and tongue relaxed. The five senses are withdrawn from their objects and the mind is concentrated on the inner Light or Sound. When the same asanas are adopted for pranayama, the head is kept slightly forward with a chin lock in the case of breath retentions.

The facial muscles are relaxed, the eyes are closed or slightly opened with the glance directed to the tip of the nose. The mind is relaxed and the five senses are tranquil with the exception of the nose and the ears, which remain alert to the movement of the breath. Since these asanas require a fair degree of body flexibility and a great power of concentration on the subtle movements of energy inside the body, it is advisable to practise the joint opening movements and the classical asanas before attempting to sit in these asanas for a prolonged period of time. The following are the asanas in order of ascending difficulty: sukhasana or easy posture, vajrasana or the adamantine posture, ardha padmasana or half lotus posture, virasana or the hero posture, padmasana or lotus posture, siddhasana or the accomplished posture and bhadrasana or the self-restraint posture.

Ardha Padmasana

This posture has been described in the section on asanas.

Bhadrasana

Sit on the ground. Bring the feet close to the perineum and allow the soles of the feet to touch each other. Gradually move the trunk towards the clasped feet and sit, with spine erect, on the joined edges of the feet. Find the proper balance and keep the arms stretched with the hands, in adhi mudra, resting on the knees.

Padmasana

This posture has been described in the section on asanas.

Siddhasana

Sit on the ground. Bring the left heel to the perineum and press the base of the heel tightly against it. Then, place the right foot above the pubis. Keep the spine erect, with the upper part of the vertebral column more stretched and the chin slightly brought down on the sternum. The arms are stretched and the hands, in adhi mudra, are resting on the knees.

Sukhasana

Sit on the ground. Bring the left foot near the perineum without straining the knee. Then, slide the right foot towards the left one without forcing the knee. Keep the spine straight and remain comfortably in this posture with legs easily crossed. The arms are stretched and the hands, in adhi mudra, are resting on the knees.

Vajrasana

This posture has been described in the section on asanas.

Virasana

Sit in sukhasana. Place the right heel under the perineum. Bend the left leg in such a way that the left foot slides towards the outer edge of the left buttock. Keep the spine erect, the arms stretched and the hands, in adhi mudra, resting on the knees.

Photo. 4: Caroline Rosso Cicogna in Sukhasana (hands in Brahma Mudra).

Photo. 5: Yogacharya Janakiraman in Bhadrasana.

Photo. 6: Yogacharya Janakiraman in Padmasana (left hand in Chin Mudra).

Photo. 7: Caroline Rosso Cicogna in Ardhapadmasana
(right hand in Vishnu Mudra).

Photo. 8: Yogacharya Janakiraman in Siddhasana (hands in Chin Mudra).

A TWELVE -WEEK ASANA PROGRAMME

This programme is given as an illustration for beginners. It is recommended to learn in-depth two asanas a week following the indications given in Part Two of the book. If practitioners wish to add a pranayama programme to their practice of asanas, they should consult the 'Twelve-week pranayama programme' given in the section on pranayama practices and integrate the two sets of exercises into one full Solar Yoga programme. The following instructions should be respected:

1. Clearly imagine the plane on which you mainly want to obtain results: physical, psychic, spiritual or on the three planes simultaneously.
2. Choose a quiet, clean, tidy and well-aerated place for the yoga session. Practise in loose clothes and barefooted, on a mat covered with a clean towel.
3. Choose a proper time for the practice: the stomach should be empty and the body outwardly and inwardly cleansed. The ideal time of practice is around sunrise and sunset. The asana session should always precede the pranayama and meditation sessions.
4. Refrain from practising when tired, exhausted or ill: Yoga is not a substitute for the necessary medical treatment.
5. Keep a diary of the practice and perform weekly breathing capacity checks.
6. Moderate living habits and give up any noxious habit.
7. Start the practice with one minute of silence and repeat the mantra *Om* three times.
8. During the practice, try to keep a constant awareness of the breathing pattern during the performance of asanas. Move slowly and harmoniously into and out of the asanas. Keep the eyes open during the practice of dynamic postures. Learn to stay comfortably in the static asanas.
9. Close the Yoga session with a full relaxation in shavasana.

Remember that the practice of asanas is not simply body culture; it needs the cooperation of a calm mind and a regulated breath as well as enthusiastic and constant training associated with the right spiritual attitude.

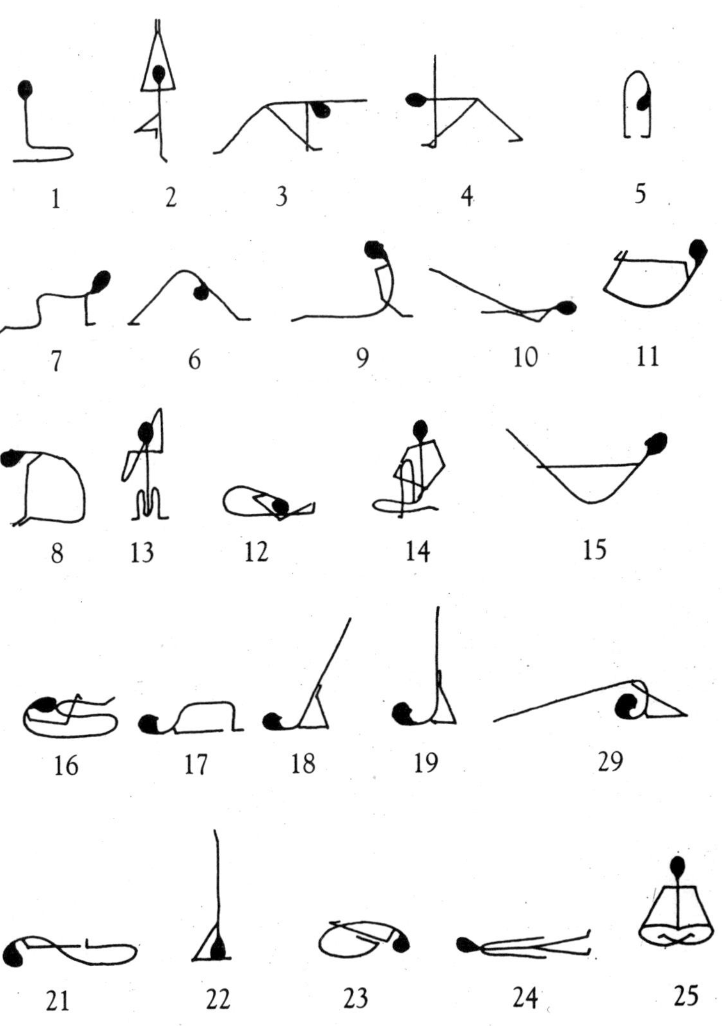

Illus. 3: Complete Solar Sequence

List of sanskrit names (and their English translations) of the asanas

Prescribed in the order of execution of a twelve-week programme.

	Names of Asanas	Starting Week	
1.	Vajrasana	Kneeling Pose	1
2.	Vrikshasana	Tree Pose	2
3.	Trikonasana	Triangle Pose	3
4.	Ardhachandrasana	Half Moon Pose	4
5.	Padahastasana	Hand-to-feet Pose	3
6.	Parvatasana	Mountain Pose	2
7.	Vyaghrasana	Tiger Pose	1
8.	Ushtrasana	Camel Pose	4
9.	Bhujangasana	Cobra Pose	6
10.	Shalabhasana	Locust Pose	6
11.	Dhanurasana	Bow Pose	7
12.	Paschimottanasana	Head-to-knee Pose	10
13.	Gomukhasana	Cowhead Pose	5
14.	Ardhamatsyendrasana	Half Spinal Twist Pose	9
15.	Navasana	Boat Pose	7
16.	Pavanamuktasana	Foetus Pose	8
17.	Setubandhasana	Bridge Pose	8
18.	Viparitakaranimudra	Inverted Pose	9
19.	Sarvangasana	Shoulderstand	11
20.	Halasana	Plough Pose	11
21.	Matsyasana	Fish Pose	5
22.	Shirshasana	Headstand	12
23.	Yogamudra	Lotus Seal Pose	12
24.	Shavasana	Corpse Pose	1
25.	Padmasana	Lotus Pose	10

Illus. 4: Surya Namaskar

"SURYA NAMASKAR MANTRAS"

Pranamasana – Prayer posture
"Om Hram Mitraya Namah"

Hasta Uttanasana – Stretching posture
"Om Hrim Ravaye Namah"

Padahastasana – Hand to feet posture
"Om Hrum Suryaya Namah"

Ashvasanchalanasana – Equestrian posture
"Om Hraim Bhanave Namah"

Parvatasana – Mountain posture
Om Hraum Khagaya Namah"

Ashtanga Namaskara – Eight point salutation
"Om Hraha Pushne Namah"

Bhujangasana – Cobra posture
"Om Hram Hiranayagarbhaya Namah"

Parvatasana – Mountain posture
"Om Hrim Marichaye Namaha"

Ashvasanchalanasana – Equestrian posture
"Om Hrum Adityaya Namah"

Padahastasana – Hand to feet posture
"Om Hraim Savitre Namah"

Hasta Uttanasana – Stretching posture
"Om Hraum Arkaya Namah"

Pranamasana – Prayer posture
"Om Hraha Bhaskaraya Namah"

SURYA NAMASKAR – THE SALUTATION TO THE SUN

A brief outline of Surya Namaskar or the Salutation to the Sun series has been included for sake of completeness although it does not form part of the traditional asanas.

This dynamic succession of movements is based on the same principle as the practices of Solar Yoga. It comprises a sequence of twelve asanas executed in a rhythmic fashion, with controlled breathing and the utterance of the solar mantras followed by the twelve names of the Sun. Practised at sunrise, it is a prostration of the entire being, body, mind and spirit, to the sun, the source of all life.

Surya Namaskar has a powerful effect on the glandular, circulatory and digestive systems and it harmonizes them. It exercises all the main muscles of the body and it is excellent for the suppleness of the joints. It has a balancing effect on the nervous system and it tones up the energy. It acts as a strong antidote to stress.

It should be practised at the beginning of a Yoga session as a warming up exercise and should be followed by a short relaxation in shavasana. It can also be practised on its own.

The rhythmic and loud repetition of the pranava, the bij solar mantras and the names of the sun creates vibrations that allow the mind to concentrate properly. The mantras also help to revitalize the energy centres, the chakras, by tuning them into one of the most important sources of cosmic energy, the sun.

For a thorough description of this practice the reader is referred to any classical book on Hatha Yoga.

The purpose here is simply to point out the mantric similarity between Surya Namaskar and the practices of Solar Yoga.

CHAPTER 2

PRANAYAMAS

The Sanskrit word Pranayama has been defined as the method of control and expansion of energy. In fact, the entire field of pranayama can be considered as a melody which starts from simple notes — simple breathing techniques — passes through several degrees of musical complexity — the classical pranayama techniques — and ends in a beautiful symphony — the state of kevala kumbhaka — a state of perfect concentration in which physical and mental limitations vanish.

But, as a musical composition requires a structure, a code and a gradual unfoldment, the practice of pranayama likewise should follow certain basic principles and should not be undertaken indiscriminately.

Therefore, the techniques given in this section have been grouped according to their main characteristics into six categories.

Moreover, the main classical pranayama practices have been presented in a separate list in an ascending order of complexity.

This is followed by the detailed description, in alphabetical order, of all the pranayama techniques discussed in the book.

Finally, some pranayama series are given as a general indication for daily practice over a period of twelve weeks.

TYPES OF PRANAYAMA PRACTICES

Purifying Pranayamas	Dhouti	Cleansing Breath
	Anunasika	Nasal Cleaner
	Nadi Shodhana	Nerve Purifier
	Nadi Shuddhi	Nerve Purifier
	Shvana	Dog Breathing
Stimulating	Kapalabhati	Brain Brightener

	Ujjayi	Victorious Breathing
	Antara Kumbhaka	Restrained Breathing
	Bhastrika	Bellows Breathing
Cooling	Sitali	Cooling Breathing
	Shvana	Dog Breathing
	Kevala Kumbhaka	Breathless State
Harmonizing	Savitri	Rhythmic Breathing
	Vibhaga	Sectional Breathing
	Sukha	Easy Breathing
	Mahat Yoga	Complete Breathing
Regenerating	Sahita	Compound Breathing
	Pranava	Cosmic Breathing
	Surya	Solar Breathing
	Ujjayi	Victorious Breathing
	Naga	Serpent Breathing
Binding	Any Pranayama Practised with one or more Bandhas.	

Main Classical Pranayamas

Sukha Pranayama	Easy Breathing
Savitri Pranayama	Rhythmic Breathing
Vibhaga Pranayama	Sectional Breathing
Nadi Shuddhi Pranayama	Nerve Purifier
Ujjayi Pranayama	Victorious Breathing
Bhastrika Pranayama	Bellows Breathing
Kapalabhati Pranayama	Brain Brightener
Mahat Yoga Pranayama with Kumbhaka	Complete Breathing

ADHAM PRANAYAMA – ABDOMINAL BREATHING

This breathing is part of the vibhaga pranayama described later. It is the abdominal breathing.

Lie on the ground and place the hands on the area of the diaphragm. Breathe in and feel the hands move outwards as the lower lung area expands. Breathe out and feel that area contracting as the hands move inwards.

This breathing technique can also be practised sitting in vajrasana and the hands can be placed on the sides of the body to feel the movement of the lower rib cage with inhalation and exhalation.

The hands can also be placed in the back with the fingers pointing towards the spine. This enables the breath movement to be felt in the lower lobes of the lungs.

ADHYAM PRANAYAMA – UPPER-CHEST BREATHING

This breathing technique is part of the vibhaga pranayama described later. It is the upper chest breathing. It can be practised lying down or sitting in any pranayama posture. In the early stages, the practice can be helped by placing the hands on the chest, just below the clavicles, in order to feel the movement of the breath.

ANUNASIKA PRANAYAMA–ATOMISING BREATHING

This is a cleansing breath known also as the atomising breath.

Technique

Sit in any pranayama posture.

1. Close the left nostril. Breathe in fully through the right nostril. Then, force the air out of the same nostril in six short spurts.
2. Close the right nostril. Breathe in fully through the left nostril. Then, force the air out of the same nostril in six short spurts.
3. Breathe in fully. Then, force the air out of the nostrils in six short spurts.

This cleansing breath should be repeated daily. With time, the number of short exhalations can be increased and the rhythm of exhalation can become more powerful. This pranayama helps to clear the upper respiratory passages and the sinuses. The forcing out of the air through a small aperture from a larger cavity creates a vacuum at the sides of the nasal cavity. This allows the excess mucous to be drained out properly. This breathing technique is also an excellent preparation for higher forms of pranayama.

BHASTRIKA PRANAYAMA- BELLOWS BREATHING

This is one of the eight major pranayamas described in the Hatha Yoga Pradipika. It is a technique of forced rhythmic breathing in which the exhalation sets the pace and both exhalation and inhalation are vigorous. Its foundation is the three-staged yogic breath with control of the abdominal belt.

Mastery of this pranayama is gradually obtained by gaining a complete control of the abdominal belt, by enhancing the exhalation and by accelerating its rhythm while contracting the abdominal belt. After some practice, the exhalations will become more vigorous than the inhalations. But, in the perfected and advanced practice, at higher speeds of breathing, inhalation and exhalation become perfectly harmonious and the abdominal and intercostal muscles coordinate properly with a smooth movement of the diaphragm.

The varieties encountered in the practice of bhastrika pranayama are related to the use of both nostrils or one nostril, presence or absence of partial closure of the glottis and use or absence of bandhas.

Technique

Bhastrika - Variation I

Sit in padmasana or vajrasana. Keep the spine erect and the ribcage slightly raised. Keep the palms of the hands on the sides of the lower ribs and the fingers turned downwards.

Inhale deeply and then exhale, allowing the lungs to contract naturally. Repeat this breathing ten times.

Inhale deeply again and, then, contract the abdominal muscles, causing a forced expulsion of air.

Repeat this breathing ten times.

When both forceful inhalation and exhalation have been learned, combine the two movements.

Inhale and concentrate on the downward movement of the diaphragm.

Exhale and concentrate on the contraction of the abdominal and intercostal muscles. Perform one cycle of twenty breaths.

At the end of this cycle, inhale very deeply and without haste and allow the chest to expand fully. Do not force the air in rapidly and do not increase the friction by closing the glottis.

When this inhalation is completed, retain the air in the lungs with the practice of aprakasha mudra, mayura mudra, jalandhara bandha and keep the nostrils closed with the fingers in vishnu mudra.

The retention period lasts about thirty seconds in the early stages of the practice and it can go up to two minutes at an advanced stage.

Slowly exhale after releasing the nostrils, opening the glottis and releasing the jalandhara bandha. The exhalation is thorough and deep and the chest and abdomen contract.

This completes one bhastrika pranayama, which is followed by a few normal breaths before starting the next round.

The number of air expulsions, which can go up to one hundred and eight, and the time of retention will depend on the practitioners' lung capacity and on the regularity and intensity of their practice. In any case, there should be a gradual development of the technique over a period of eight weeks.

Bhastrika Pranayama - Variation II

This is the same as for Variation I but with a partial closure of the glottis.

After a round of air expulsions, inhale slowly and deeply through the right nostril. Retain the air for as long as comfortable and slowly exhale through the left nostril.

Repeat three rounds of breathing in this fashion.

Bhastrika Pranayama - Variation III

Sit in padmasana or in vajrasana. Close the right nostril with the right hand in vishnu mudra and inhale through the left nostril.

Close the left nostril and make a series of air expulsions through the right nostril.

Keep the left nostril closed and inhale through the right nostril deeply. Retain the breath for a comfortable period and, then, slowly exhale through the left nostril whilst closing the right one.

Repeat the same process with the other nostril and perform three cycles of bhastrika for each nostril with the alternate nostril breathing technique. After this, do gentle breathing and relax.

This variation of bhastrika is more powerful than the first one and should be practised only when the first variation has been completely mastered.

At the beginning, the hand movements, the alternate nostril breathing and the bhastrika rhythm will have to be harmonized. This requires skill, time and patience whereas great caution will have to be applied in the practice, which has to be progressive and should not exceed fifty breaths per minute.

Effects of Bhastrika Pranayama

Since it is a hyperventilation technique, it accelerates cellular breathing and has profound regenerating effects on the organism. Moreover, it helps to cleanse the nadis and harmonizes prana, apana and samana. When the practice is performed with full concentration on the muladhara chakra, it favours the practitioners'inner awakening.

DHOUTI PRANAYAMA- CLEANSING BREATHING

This is a cleansing breath, which helps to alleviate uncomfortable chest conditions, to overcome acidity in the stomach and to remove tiredness and tension.

Technique

Sit in vajrasana or in any other pranayama posture. Place the hands on the thighs and take a full inhalation. Pucker the lips into the shape of a small tube: this is called kaki mudra. Blow out the air through the mouth in short and regular exhalations whilst bending the trunk forward. With these short exhalations, produce the sound 'TSH, TSH, TSH' by forcing the tongue against the back of the teeth. When the forehead touches the ground at the end of the exhalation, remain in this position and force out the remaining air from the lungs. Then, sit up in the initial position on an inhalation.

This pranayama is practised at the beginning of a sitting of asanas or of pranayama and it is usually executed three times. It can also be practised, in the case of tiredness, during the sitting itself.

KAPALABHATI – BRAIN BRIGHTENER

This practice is sometimes called a pranayama and, at other times, as in the Hatha Yoga Pradipika, it is called a kriya. In any case, it is usually performed after asanas and before ujjayi and bhastrika pranayamas.

In kapalabhati, both inhalation and exhalation are performed through both nostrils but the latter is forceful whereas the former is passive.

This practice consists of a series of rapid and brief spurts during exhalation, followed by a very short retention at the end of which a passive inhalation is triggered. In this pranayama, the abdominal belt plays a fundamental role and the power of the exhalation will determine the quality of the practice. Since kapalabhati is a very powerful pranayama, it is advisable to train the lungs progressively. The concentration of the mind is on the navel area and on the corresponding subtle centre along the spine.

For beginners, the practice of bandhas is to be avoided. After a few weeks of practice, mulabandha can be introduced. In the advanced stage of practice, mulabandha occurs naturally.

Technique

Sit in padmasana, spine erect, trunk tilted slightly forward. The arms are stretched and the hands are resting on the knees. The chest muscles are kept slightly contracted in order to keep the chest as immobile as possible.

Inhale quickly but deeply and follow this by a rapid exhalation. Repeat this process five to ten times. This prepares the ground for the execution of fast expulsions of air during the exhalation phase.

Inhale while relaxing the abdominal muscles. Exhale by a quick and forceful contraction of the abdominal muscles. This sudden and vigorous contraction on exhalation raises the diaphragm and causes the lungs to contract. The facial muscles should be relaxed, the chest immobile, the shoulders should not lift and the abdomen should not retract.

The practice of kapalabhati should be divided into progressive units of number and speed.

Beginners may start with thirty to forty breaths a minute and gradually increase the number to sixty in two weeks in order to reach a number of one hundred and twenty in eight weeks. After each round, practise normal breathing for thirty to sixty seconds. Three to six rounds of kapalabhati may be performed in one sitting and repeated twice a day.

Effects of Kapalabhati

This pranayama produces a complete cleansing of the lungs with a massive expulsion of carbon dioxide, which, in turn, has a beneficial effect on the cellular activity.

Blood is fully oxygenated thus stimulating cellular breathing. A good return circulation of venous blood takes place owing to the strong diaphragmatic activity. There is good toning of all the abdominal muscles and a deep massage of the abdominal organs.

All these factors favourably influence the neuro-vegetative system but the main effect is recorded in the brain and in the flow of cerebro-spinal fluid.

Contra-indications

Persons suffering from pulmonary and cardiac disabilities or high blood pressure should refrain from this practice.

KEVALA KUMBHAKA PRANAYAMA–BREATHLESS STATE

The four breathing phases involved in pranayama are inhalation, exhalation and two retentions, one with breath and one without breath. When the retention of breath is performed with the help of willpower, it is known as sahita kumbhaka. In the case of kevala kumbhaka pranayama, the breathing process is completely suspended and the practitioner remains in an easy and natural breathless state

This state can be achieved by the practice of breathing, mental concentration, vibrations or mantras. The respiratory process becomes so perfect, through practice that the retention is made absolute and pure. The Hatha Yoga Pradipika describes kevala kumbhaka as a state of total absorption, an intuitive state of joy and peace.

A subtle vibration, known as 'So Ham', accompanies the normal breathing process. 'So' being emitted during inhalation and 'Ham' during exhalation. Since this vibration takes place unconsciously but continuously, it is known as 'ajapa japa'. When this vibration is consciously concentrated on the muladhara, anahata and ajna chakras, it is known as 'hamsa kriya'.

In normal breathing, the number of respirations will reach an average of fifteen per minute. In the case of yogic breathing performed in order to achieve the state of kevala kumbhaka, the number of respirations is increased to thirty per minute with the mind fixed on the mantra 'So Ham'. By this practice, fixity of the mind can be achieved.

Technique

Sit in padmasana. Practise three rounds of bhastrika and kapalabhati pranayamas. Then, with the eyes closed and mind relaxed, follow the breath with the mantra 'So Ham'. Then, take in a long and slow breath and hold the air within the lungs, with the practice of three bandhas and for a period of one minute. After some time the breath will become very subtle and when the mind is fully concentrated in the ajna chakra, the breath will automatically stop. The power of inhalation and of exhalation cancel each other and cause a complete breath suspension.

The same process can be performed by fully expelling the air from the lungs and then remaining in an empty lung condition.

The practice of kevala kumbhaka leads to the higher stages of Raja Yoga.

MADHYAMA PRANAYAMA – THORACIC BREATHING

This breathing technique is part of the vibhaga pranayama described later. This is the middle-chest or thoracic breathing.

Technique

Lie on the ground and place the palms of the hands on the chest. Breathe in and feel the hands move out and the ribcage expand. Breathe out and feel the hands move in and the rib-cage contract.

This breathing technique can be practised in vajrasana and the hands can then be placed to the sides of the chest in order to feel the movement of the breath in this area of the chest. Then, the hands can be placed as far as possible onto the back. Concentrate the mind in the mid-back area and breathe in that area.

MAHAT YOGA PRANAYAMA – COMPLETE BREATHING

This is the full yogic breath. It should be practised regularly every day as it produces an excellent flow of prana in the entire organism. This method of breathing combines all the effects described in the general part on pranayama.

Technique

Sit in vajrasana. Breathe abdominally, then in the mid-chest area and finally in the upper chest, without any interruption between the three forms of breathing. Then, retain the breath. Release the breath in the same order.

Initially the hands can be used to check the movement of the air in the lungs. This helps in fully filling the three sections of the lungs.

Use a count of three seconds to fill each section of the lungs. When they are filled, swallow the breath and hold the air in the lungs for a count of three seconds. Use a count of three seconds to empty each section of the lungs in the order prescribed. Then, remain without breath for a count of three seconds. Repeat this cycle three times.

With practice, count and rhythm can be increased gradually up to a ratio of thirty-two seconds for inhalation and exhalation each and sixteen seconds for each retention.

NADI SHODHANA PRANAYAMA – NERVE PURIFIER

This technique, otherwise known as surya bhedana pranayama, acts directly on the subtle energy channels called nadis, which carry the prana throughout the pranic or energy body. These subtle channels should be kept free and pure for the pranic energy to flow along them.

The purpose of this pranayama is to purify the subtle energy channels and it is thus recommended that it should be practised daily as a regular preparation for the meditation sittings.

Nadi shodhana is a grosser form of purification that acts mainly on the pingala nadi. About eighty percent of the body energy flows on the right side along the pingala nadi, the current of solar, positive energy. By breathing repeatedly through the right nostril and exhaling through the left one, there is an increase of this positive energy, which removes the tensions or the obstructions that might have accumulated in the area governed by the pingala nadi.

Technique

Sit in any pranayama posture. Place the palms of the hands on the thighs and find the correct, comfortable posture for the practice. Lift the right hand to the level of the nose, practise vishnu mudra with the right hand and close the left nostril.

Inhale through the right nostril in a slow and deep manner. When the inhalation is completed, swing the fingers of the hand in vishnu mudra to the other side, thereby closing the right nostril.

Exhale slowly through the left nostril. When the exhalation is completed, swing the fingers of the hand in vishnu mudra to the original position and close the left nostril again.

Inhale through the right nostril again, keeping the left one closed.

Exhale slowly through the left nostril.

IN	RIGHT NOSTRIL	
OUT	LEFT NOSTRIL	ONE CYCLE
IN	RIGHT NOSTRIL	
OUT	LEFT NOSTRIL	

Effects of Nadi Shodhana

This pranayama increases the body heat, improves the digestive power, cleanses the sinuses and calms the nerves.

NADI SHUDDHI PRANAYAMA – ALTERNATE NOSTRIL BREATHING

The second purification method is more refined and it affects the subtle channels as a whole. It balances the pranic energy along the subtle channels and thereby brings a great mental peace and rest. As breathing through the right nostril activates the positive energy, and breathing through the left nostril activates the negative one, the fact of alternating the breaths produces a continuous reversal of the electrical charge of the bio-magnetic body. This removes the impedance of the magnetic field created by the pranic flow along the subtle channels. This alternate breathing technique revitalizes the two hemispheres of the brain in a harmonious manner: it allows the energy to reach the remotest parts of the brain and the nervous system through the network of the nadis.

Nadi shuddhi pranayama is a difficult technique, which requires great sensitivity and an excellent coordination of all the senses. It is a pranayama of concentration and withdrawal. In the advanced stages of the practice, kumbhakas and bandhas are introduced. The practice of these bandhas during the retention periods produces a deeper cleansing of the nadis and allows the prana to penetrate deeply into the organism, thereby calming the nerves and the mind. This is one of the main reasons why this pranayama is always recommended before the practice of meditation.

Technique

Sit in any pranayama posture with the hands resting on the thighs. The head should be slightly lowered and the spine fully erect. Lift the right hand to the level of the nose and place the fingers in vishnu mudra. Close the left nostril with the fingers.

Inhale deeply and slowly through the right nostril. At the end of the inhalation, swing the fingers of the hand in vishnu mudra onto the right nostril and close it.

Exhale slowly and deeply through the left nostril. At the end of the exhalation, leave the fingers in the same position and keep the left nostril open.

Inhale slowly and deeply through the left nostril. When the inhalation is completed, swing the fingers of the hand in vishnu mudra onto the left nostril and close it.

Exhale through the right nostril.

This constitutes one cycle of nadi shuddhi pranayama. Repeat this cycle at least ten times.

IN	RIGHT NOSTRIL	
OUT	LEFT NOSTRIL	ONE CYCLE
IN	LEFT NOSTRIL	
OUT	RIGHT NOSTRIL	

NAGA PRANAYAMA – SERPENT BREATHING

'Naga' means serpent in Sanskrit. This breathing simulates the special skin breathing of the serpent. The human skin has an elimination function like the kidneys or the lungs. It contains a great number of pores which allow toxins to be properly released. It is thus advisable to practise this purification technique before any cycle of pranayamas for regeneration. It also improves the breathing capacity.

Technique

Sit in vajrasana. Inhale deeply through the nose. Hold the breath for a period of ten seconds. Then, take another inhalation and hold the breath again for ten seconds. Exhale slowly through the mouth.

With this practice, the skin becomes warm and perspiration may even begin to form on the arms. Repeat this process three times and, then, lie on the back and relax totally.

This is a very powerful kumbhaka and persons with weak lungs, bronchial problems or a weak heart, should not practise it.

PRANAVA PRANAYAMA – COSMIC BREATHING

This pranayama combines the techniques of vibhaga pranayama, mahat yoga pranayama and the pranava vibration ***Aum***. It produces a complete regeneration of the organism and it is recommended to practise it every day.

Technique

Sit in any pranayama posture.

1. Place the fingers in chin mudra into the groin area or on the thighs. Breathe in deeply in the abdomen and produce mentally the sound 'AAA'. Exhale through the mouth in a slow, regular manner while producing the sound 'AAA' loudly. Concentrate on the navel area to feel the place of origin of the sound. Repeat six to ten times.
2. Place the fingers in chinmaya mudra in the same position as for (1). Breathe in deeply into the thoracic area and produce mentally the sound 'OOO'. Exhale through the mouth in a slow, regular manner while producing the sound 'OOO' loudly. Concentrate on the heart region and experience the vibrations produced by the sound. Repeat six to ten times.
3. Place the fingers in adhi mudra in the same position as in 1. Breathe in fully in the clavicular area of the lungs and mentally produce the sound 'MMM'. Breathe out slowly through the mouth while producing the sound 'MMM' loudly. Concentrate on the nape of the neck and feel the vibration produced by the sound reverberate in the entire head. Repeat six to ten times.
4. Place the fingers in adhi mudra and bring the fists together, fingers upwards on the abdomen, just above the navel. Practise the full yogic breath, producing the three sounds mentally, one for each section of the lungs. Breathe out in the manner prescribed for the full yogic breath but through the mouth and producing the

three sounds 'AA, OO, MM' in succession. Experience the vibration produced by the sound along the entire spine. Repeat six to ten times.

SAVITRI PRANAYAMA – RHYTHMIC BREATHING

This is a balancing, harmonic and rhythmic breathing technique. It consists in giving a constant ratio to the different parts of the breathing process, in which the retention periods are usually half of each exhalation and inhalation respectively. This breathing calms the nerves and improves mental concentration. The ratio between the four parts of the breathing process can be increased with practice.

Technique

Sit in any pranayama posture.

Inhale for a count of six seconds. Hold the air in the lungs for a count of three seconds.

Exhale for a count of six seconds. Remain without breathing for a count of three seconds.

RATIOS			
In	Hold with breath	Out	Hold without breath
6	3	6	3
8	4	8	4
10	5	0	5
12	6	12	6

SAHITA PRANAYAMA – COMPOUND BREATHING

This is a pranayama programme that regenerates the five important vital organs: lungs, liver, stomach, kidneys and heart. It is practised over a period of forty-five days for a complete rejuvenation of the organism.

In this technique, the ratios of the four parts of the breathing process are constantly modified in order to help the prana to reach effectively the organs concerned. The timing of the breathing is the crucial element of this pranayama.

It is recommended to practise the full sahita pranayama programme under expert guidance.

The ratios of the four parts of the breathing process are as follows:

Organ	inhalation	retention (full lungs)	exhalation (empty lungs)	retention
Lungs	4	16	8	4
Liver	4	4	16	8
Stomach	8	4	4	16
Kidneys	16	8	4	4
Heart	4	16	8	0

The sequence of forty-five days of practice should be divided as follows:

Days	Practice	Ratio
Days 1 to 9	9 cycles of lung pranayama	4/16/8/4
Days 10 to 18	9 cycles of lung pranayama	
	9 cycles of liver pranayama	4/4/16/8
Days 19 to 27	9 cycles of lung pranayama	
	9 cycles of liver pranayama	
	9 cycles of stomach pranayama	8/4/4/16
Days 28 to 36	9 cycles of lung pranayama	
	9 cycles of liver pranayama	
	9 cycles of stomach pranayama	
	9 cycles of kidney pranayama	16/8/4/4/
Days 37 to 45	9 cycles of lung pranayama	
	9 cycles of liver pranayama	
	9 cycles of stomach pranayama	
	9 cycles of kidney pranayama	
	9 cycles of heart pranayama	4/16/8/0

SHVANA PRANAYAMA – DOG BREATHING

The Sanskrit word 'shvana' means dog. This breathing simulates the breathing of a dog. It is performed through the mouth. Dogs are not equipped with sweat glands and to cool down they are obliged to breathe through the mouth. Human beings also adopt this technique in case of strong physical exertion because it allows the carbon dioxide to be expelled more forcefully from the lungs.

This cooling breath acts in the same way and helps to eliminate the toxins from the organism. By forcefully blowing out the carbon dioxide, tension and fatigue can be overcome more easily and a new burst of energy is given to the system. Moreover, the panting movement executed in this pranayama stimulates the renal region and when the sound 'Ha' is emitted during the breathing, it acts directly on the kidneys. This pranayama produces a vibratory movement along the spine down to the coccyx, which is beneficial to the entire spine.

This purification technique is practised before advanced pranayamas in order to improve the lung capacity.

Technique

Sit in vajrasana. Inhale deeply through the nose. Then, roll the tongue right out, expelling the breath through the mouth on an exhalation. Pant like a dog, as fully as possible, about ten times. Rest and repeat again three times.

SITALI PRANAYAMA – COOLING BREATHING

This is a cooling breath, which soothes the eyes and the ears. It activates the liver function, improves digestion, relieves excessive thirst and creates a feeling of freshness.

Technique

Sit in virasana. Curl the tongue lengthwise and stretch it out. This moistens the breath. Breathe in through the mouth over the rolled tongue and fill the lungs completely.

With full breath retention, withdraw the tongue and close the mouth. Then, breathe out through the nose. During the exhalation, feel a cool sensation along the spine. Practise this breathing ten times and, then, breathe normally through both nostrils and relax in shavasana.

SUKHA PRANAYAMA – EASY BREATHING

Before attempting any pranayama technique, practitioners should spend the first week of their practice on this preliminary breathing exercise that will help them to open up the three sections of the lungs fully.

This is the simplest form of breathing. It consists in regulating the length of the inhalation and the exhalation according to a given ratio. The ratio can go up to 16/16. This breathing technique can be learned in a sitting or a lying position. Start with three breaths, then five, then seven breaths. Afterwards, learn to hold the breath for ten seconds between the inhalation and the exhalation. The movement of the arms, in a vertical or in a horizontal direction, will help to develop a good sense of rhythm in the breathing process. This is an important feature because this breathing technique is used to accompany the dynamic asanas where rhythm is the most important element as, for instance, in bhujangasana, trikonasana, vyaghrasana or padahastasana.

SURYA PRANAYAMA – SOLAR BREATHING

This is a rejuvenating and energizing pranayama, which is best performed early in the morning, preferably facing the rising sun. Try to adopt a very relaxed, loving attitude of drawing the energy from the sun into the heart.

Technique

A. Stand with the hands on the chest in the namaskara mudra.
   Inhale, cross the fingers and push palms and arms straight out at shoulder height and stretch. Hold the breath.
   Exhale, bring the hands back onto the chest in namaskara mudra. Repeat five times with the savitri rhythm of breathing.

B. In the same position, practise the same breathing but place the hands at a forty-five degree angle and practise the same movement of arms and the same breathing rhythm.

C. In the same position, practise the same breathing but place the hands directly above the head. Repeat five times with the same savitri rhythm.

D. In the same position, practise the same breathing but stretch the arms as far back above the head as possible, keeping the head in the vertical position. Repeat five times with the same savitri rhythm.

E. After this pranayama, there will be a certain amount of tension in the arms, hands and fingers. Remove this tension by shaking the hands in all directions and by bending the fingers backwards and forwards.

This pranayama produces a natural sectional breathing by lifting the arms in different positions. In the first position, with the arms at shoulder level, the lower lobes of the lungs are ventilated and the mudra in this position opens the duodenal sphincter. In the second position, with the arms at a forty-five degree angle, the middle lobes of the lungs are ventilated. In the third position, with the hands above the head, the area under the armpits is opened and the pranic energy can flow freely along the ida and pingala channels. This helps also to unblock the nostrils. In the fourth position, with the arms stretched back as far as possible, the back muscles are fully extended, the area under the armpits is fully opened and the prana can flow along the entire spine. The upper lobes of the lungs are fully ventilated in this position.

UJJAYI – VICTORIOUS BREATHING

This is one of the eight classical kumbhaka pranayamas mentioned in the Hatha Yoga Pradipika. It is practised on its own as a pranayama and it is used also as a technique during the practice of asanas.

As a pranayama, it has been transmitted by the great exponents of Hatha Yoga in two main forms: Gheranda recommends its practice with bahya kumbhaka (empty lung retention) and Kuvalayananda recommends it with abhyantara kumbhaka (full lung retention). Nevertheless, in the early stages, it is recommended to practise ujjayi without any kumbhaka.

The technique consists in keeping the glottis partially closed thereby allowing the movement of air to produce a gentle and continuous sound. This partial-resistance breathing revitalizes the respiratory tract by increasing the intra-thoracic depression during inhalation and by increasing the intra-pulmonary pressure during exhalation. This has a positive effect on the venous circulation and on the lung elasticity. Moreover, through this deep respiratory activity, the blood is fully oxygenated, the nerves are soothed and the mind is calmed.

Ujjayi without Kumbhaka

Sit in padmasana, siddhasana or vajrasana. The trunk is leaning slightly forward, the spine is erect and the arms are stretched out allowing the hands to rest on the knees with fingers in chin mudra.

Inhalation is performed slowly and deeply through both nostrils. The abdominal belt is controlled, the glottis is partially closed and the breathing is mainly thoracic. The air produces a regular sound.

At the end of the inhalation, close the glottis completely for a short retention of two seconds.

During exhalation, keep the abdominal belt under tighter control, open the glottis slightly so as to allow the air to flow out with the same continuous sound. Then, contract the thoracic muscles and lower the clavicles in order to force all the air out of the lungs. Keep the spine fully erect. Exhalation should be twice as long as inhalation.

Practise one round of three breaths, relax and repeat another two rounds. With practise, it is possible to achieve seven rounds.

Ujjayi with Abhyantara Kumbhaka (full lung retention)

Sit in padmasana or siddhasana. Start with a complete exhalation, keeping the spine fully erect. During the inhalation, which follows, the breath is slowly and deeply drawn in through the nostrils. The glottis is partially closed, the facial and nasal muscles are kept relaxed. When the chest is fully expanded and the lungs are full, practise jalandhara bandha and close the nostrils with the fingers of the right hand.

This full lung retention is accompanied by mula bandha and is kept for a ratio of 4 to 1 compared with the inhalation phase. The upper limit of this ratio is reached when a slight vibration is felt in the navel area.

Exhalation is practised through the left nostril only, with the glottis partially closed and it should last twice as long as the inhalation. The abdominal muscles contract, the chest deflates while the spine is kept fully erect and the lungs are completely emptied.

Remain with a short empty-lung retention of two seconds and inhale again. The third inhalation should not be hasty otherwise it is a sign that the retention period was exaggerated and should be reduced.

The full cycle of ujjayi has a ratio of 1-4-2 and should last approximately thirty-two seconds. Three rounds of nine breaths each can be practised and followed by shavasana.

Ujjayi with Bahya Kumbhaka (empty lung retention)

Sit in padmasana or siddhasana. Inhale through both nostrils. Then, pull up the internal air from the lungs and throat into the mouth. Retain the air in the mouth with lips tightly closed.

Exhale this air very slowly through the mouth. At the end of the exhalation, perform jalandhara bandha and mula bandha and perform kumbhaka for as long as is comfortable.

Practise one cycle of nine breaths. Rest and repeat two more rounds.

During ujjayi pranayama, the concentration of the mind is on the passage of air through the nostrils and on the sound produced by the air at the level of the glottis. This pranayama strengthens the throat, tones the nervous system, improves digestion and develops a better harmony between the breath and the respiratory organs and between the mind and the nervous system.

Antara kumbhaka is advised in the case of low blood pressure and a tendency to laziness and depression. Bahya kumbhaka is advised in case of high blood pressure, nervous tension. In a sequence, ujjayi follows kapalabhati and precedes bhastrika.

VIBHAGA PRANAYAMA – SECTIONAL BREATHING

This is the sectional breathing in which the three parts of the breathing process are first performed separately and, then, successively: abdominal, thoracic and clavicular breathing. This breathing technique is an introduction to the full yogic breath.

Technique

Lie in a relaxed posture or sit in any pranayama posture. Start with abdominal breathing and place the hands above the navel. Breathe ten times in this area.

Continue with mid-chest breathing and place the hands on the chest. Breathe ten times in this area.

Follow with upper-chest breathing and place the hands below the clavicles. Breathe ten times in this area.

End the sectional breathing by a full and complete movement. Inhale by breathing in the abdomen for a count of three seconds, in the chest for a count of three seconds and in the upper chest for another count of three seconds. Retain the breath for a count of six seconds. Exhale by breathing out from the abdomen for a count of three seconds, from the chest for a count of three seconds and from the upper chest for a count of three seconds. Relax and repeat the entire cycle.

It is easier to learn this breathing by placing the hands on the appropriate parts of the body to check if the correct movement is occurring. For the complete breathing, place one hand on the abdomen and the other on the chest and then on the upper chest. Release the hands in the same order with the appropriate rhythm. Later, when proficiency has been attained, the hands can be removed.

The aim of sectional breathing is to ventilate fully the three main areas of the lungs. The breathing in the three areas is then combined to give a full yogic breath. Concentration on the movement of air, which completely fills the lungs, has also a pacifying effect on the mind and it helps to develop one-pointedness and relaxation. Using the savitri rhythm, it promotes harmony and relaxation of the body and the mind.

A TWELVE-WEEK PRANAYAMA PROGRAMME

This program is given as an indication for beginners. It is recommended that a progressive practice of breathing should be followed. This is done by regulation, timing and awareness of the breath.

The following instructions are given for guidance along with the table of practices.

1. Practise for one hour a day, if possible twice daily, on an empty stomach.
2. Follow the details of the practices given in each case.
3. Do not force the rhythm or strain the nervous system.
4. Practise kumbhaka from the fifth week.
5. Practise mudras from the sixth week.
6. Practise bandhas from the seventh week.
7. Practise shavasana at the end of each session, for at least ten minutes.
8. Keep the system cool and sip some water every fifteen minutes during the practice of pranayama.

Pranayama	WEEKS											
	1	2	3	4	5	6	7	8	9	10	11	12
Dhouti	*	*	*	*	*	*	*	*	*	*	*	*
Anunasika	*	*	*	*								
Sukha	*	*	*	*								
Vibhaga	*	*	*	*								
Mahat Yoga					*	*	*	*				
Surya					*	*	*	*				
Savitri					*	*	*	*				
Shvana					*	*	*	*				
Nadi Shodhana					*	*	*	*	*	*	*	*
Kapalabhati					*	*	*	*	*	*	*	*
Nadi Shuddhi						*	*	*	*	*	*	*
Ujjayi						*	*	*	*	*	*	*
Bhastrika							*	*	*	*	*	*
Sahita						*	*	*	*	*	*	*
Pranava							*	*	*	*	*	*
Naga									*	*	*	
Sitali									*	*	*	

CHAPTER 3

BANDHAS, MUDRAS AND KRIYAS

BANDHAS

The Sanskrit word bandha means to tie, to contract or to block and it denotes the process of controlling the prana in the subtle spinal centres. A bandha consists of a series of muscular contractions, which act on the nervous and the endocrine systems. In the breathing phase of kumbhaka or breath retention, bandhas are always performed with a view to channel the prana properly, to awaken the subtle centres and to control their energies. Bandhas are thus an indispensable corollary to the practice of pranayama.

The pranic energy is extremely dynamic and if it is not subjected to strict control, it tends to dissipate itself. Binding the prana in three main energy centres, the muladhara chakra, the manipura chakra and the vishuddhi chakra effects this control. These centres are important junctions of energy from which the subtle nadis radiate and transmit the pranic energy to all the vital organs of the body. When the prana can be concentrated, regulated and bound at these centres, the physiological effects of pranayama will be greatly enhanced and the inner perception of the vital energy will become possible.

When the prana is bound at the base of the spine, the process is known as mula bandha. When the prana is bound at the navel centre, it is known as uddiyana bandha and when the pranic energy is concentrated at the throat centre, the process is known as jalandhara bandha. When the three contractions are performed together, the process is known as bandha traya or the triple lock.

MULA BANDHA – ANAL LOCK

The process of contraction and release of the anal sphincters is described later in the technique of ashvini mudra. The Sanskrit word 'mula' means origin or root. This is considered to be the base of the spine or the lowest pole of the parasympathetic nervous system.

By the practice of this bandha, the downward movement of apana vayu is reversed and combines with that of prana vayu. This process energizes the sacral nerves and tones up all the organs innervated by them. The regular practice of this bandha reinforces the pelvic floor, produces youthful energy and confers strength and steadiness on the body.

This bandha can also be practised with asanas, such as bhujangasana, ushtrasana and dhanurasana.

Technique

Sit in padmasana or in vajrasana.

Inhale and during the breath retention phase, perform four successive contractions: of the outer anal sphincter, of the inner anal sphincter, of the anal elevator muscle and of the pelvic floor. Hold the breath and these contractions for a count of thirty seconds.

Exhale slowly and release the contractions in the opposite way: pelvic floor, anal elevator muscle, inner sphincter and outer sphincter.

The duration of the breath retention phase and of the contractions can be gradually increased with practice. A number of twenty contractions can be practised twice a day.

UDDIYANA BANDHA – ABDOMINAL LOCK

The word 'uddiyana' comes from the Sanskrit root 'ut' which gives the idea of flying. This term is used to indicate the movement of the diaphragm and the direction of prana in this bandha. In this process, the diaphragm is pulled up to its maximum position and the prana literally flies up. Through the practice of this bandha, the abdominal organs are lifted up by a powerful inner contraction.

The practice of this bandha is prepared by nauli kriya, which helps to evacuate the wind from the abdominal organs and strengthens the abdominal recti.

The regular practice of this bandha increases the digestive power, strengthens the abdominal muscles, slims down the waist and tones the internal organs of the upper and lower abdomen.

Technique

Ensure that the stomach is absolutely empty before starting this practice. Start the practice in a standing position. Lean the trunk slightly forward, place the palms of the hands on the thighs and keep the spine straight.

Exhale and, with empty lung retention, pull the abdomen in: lift the diaphragm as high as possible and as near as possible to the vertebral column. Keep this position for a count of twenty seconds.

Inhale slowly and gradually release the contraction. Repeat this process ten to twenty times.

When the movement has been mastered, practise uddiyana bandha in a sitting posture, like padmasana or vajrasana. After this, learn to combine mula bandha with uddiyana bandha.

JALANDHARA BANDHA – CHIN LOCK

The Sanskrit word 'jalandhara' is composed of 'jala' meaning net and 'dhara' meaning upward pull.

The Gheranda Samhita states that this bandha acts on a network of sixteen subtle centres and causes the subtle energy to move up from the base of the spine. Jalandhara bandha seals the air in the thorax, slows down the heartbeat, quietens the mind and produces an inner perception of the flow of prana.

This bandha reduces the tensions in the neck, creates hormonal balance in the thyroid and parathyroid glands while improving the quality of the voice and strengthening the throat area.

Technique

Sit in vajrasana or in padmasana.

Inhale deeply. Block the air in the lungs by a swallowing movement, known as aprakasha mudra. Place the chin in the middle of the sternum. This contracts the throat muscles and stretches the cervical area. Keep the full lung retention and jalandhara bandha for a count of thirty seconds.

Exhale slowly and release the bandha. Repeat this process ten times.

BANDHA TRAYA – TRIPLE LOCK

This bandha is a combination of the three practices previously described. The Sanskrit word 'traya' means three and 'bandha' means binding.

Bandha traya has an influence on the movement of prana in the spine. With a regular practice of this bandha, the subtle energy is brought gradually into the sushumna nadi, the central subtle channel of the spine. The important effects of this process have been described earlier in the chapter relating to the chakras and nadis.

Technique

After practising each of the three bandhas separately, practise them in pairs.

1 **Inhale**, hold the breath and perform mula bandha. Continue to hold the breath and perform jalandhara bandha. Hold this position for thirty seconds.
Exhale slowly and release the two bandhas. Repeat this process three times.

2 **Inhale**, hold the breath and perform mula bandha.
Exhale and continue to hold mula bandha while performing uddiyana bandha. Hold this position for thirty seconds.
Inhale slowly and release the two bandhas. Repeat this process three times.

3 **Inhale**, hold the breath and perform jalandhara bandha.
Exhale and release the bandha. With empty lung retention, perform uddiyana bandha and jalandhara bandha.
Inhale slowly and release the two bandhas. Repeat this process three times.

4 Perform the bandha traya.
Inhale deeply, and, on full lung retention, perform mula bandha and, then, jalandhara bandha. At the end of the retention phase, release jalandhara bandha but continue to hold mula bandha.
Exhale and on empty lung retention, perform uddiyana bandha and jalandhara bandha. Hold the three bandhas together for thirty to sixty seconds. Then, gradually release jalandhara, uddiyana and, finally, mula bandha.
Inhale slowly and deeply. Repeat the process of bandha traya five times and, then, relax with gentle breathing for two minutes in a supine position.

MUDRAS

The Sanskrit word 'mudra' means seal, lock. It has a concrete, literal meaning and a symbolic one.

On the physical and energy planes, a mudra represents a gesture either of the fingers, the hands, the neck and throat, the oral cavity and its organs, the anal cavity or the entire body, which helps to create a particular pranic circuit in the body during the practice of asanas or pranayamas. In general, mudras are performed in order to close body apertures and to contain the flow of energy in the proper channels.

In more advanced stages of Yoga, mudras are needed to control and guide the pranic energy which is being absorbed by the physical body in the course of the practice. They constitute both a safeguard for and an incentive to the flow of prana.

On the spiritual plane, mudras acquire a powerful symbolic meaning as they seal a particular stage of the Yoga practice and denote a manifestation of the kundalini energy moving through the body.

Fifteen important mudras are described in this section for their relevance to the practice of asanas and pranayamas.

Aprakasha mudra	Neck and throat gesture
Adhi mudra	Finger gesture
Ashvini mudra	Anal cavity gesture
Brahma mudra	Finger gesture
Chin mudra	Finger gesture
Chinmaya mudra	Finger gesture
Govinda mudra	Hand gesture
Hamsa mudra	Hand gesture
Kaki mudra	Oral cavity gesture
Maha mudra	Hand and body gesture
Mayura mudra	Neck and throat gesture
Namaskara mudra	Hand gesture
Viparitakarani mudra	Whole body gesture
Vishnu mudra	Hand gesture
Yoga mudra	Whole body gesture

APRAKASHA MUDRA – NECK AND THROAT GESTURE

This mudra is practised during the retention phase of the breathing process. During kumbhaka, the breath is held under pressure in the lungs and there is always a tendency to take another inhalation since the breathing centre in the medulla oblongata sends a signal for the intake of more oxygen.

Aprakasha mudra is practised in order to contain the pressure inside the lungs easily. This mudra is necessary for the practice of advanced pranayamas and for the practice of jalandhara bandha.

Technique

With retention of breath, perform a swallowing movement of the air after completion of the inhalation. This seals the breath at the throat and the retention is made easy. This mudra is practised before jalandhara bandha.

ADHI MUDRA – FINGER GESTURE

This gesture of the fingers is practised with pranava pranayama. It helps to send the prana to the upper lobes of the lungs and it is thus useful for clavicular breathing.

Technique

Place the thumb onto the palm of the hand and close the fingers around it. Place the fists, fingers down, near the groin or on the thighs.

ASHVINI MUDRA – ANAL CAVITY GESTURE

This mudra consists of a series of contractions and relaxations of the anal sphincter and of the anal elevator muscle. It allows the energy to be liberated from the muladhara chakra and it helps to harmonize the flow of prana and apana. This is a preparatory practice for the execution of the bandha traya technique. Its effects are mainly felt at the level of the pelvic part of the parasympathetic nervous system. It fortifies the pelvic floor and acts against the tendency of ptosis. Moreover, it decongests the anal venous system and reinforces the pelvic muscles. This mudra is very important in the practice of pranayama. Ashvini mudra produces vitality and strength and soothes the nervous system while preventing the organism from ageing.

Technique

Sit in padmasana, in siddhasana or vajrasana.

Inhale deeply and hold the breath. Press the chin onto the chest and, then, tighten the external anal sphincter, followed by the internal anal sphincter. While keeping the anal contraction, pull the abdomen slightly in and the diaphragm up. Then, release the two sphincters. Repeat this alternate movement of compression and release ten to fifteen times during one retention phase.

Exhale and relax. Repeat this cycle seven times. The best position in which to learn this mudra is to lie on the back with folded knees.

BRAHMA MUDRA – FINGER GESTURE

This gesture of the fingers is used during the practice of pranava pranayama. It helps to harmonize the flow of prana in the three sections of the lungs.

Technique

Place the thumb onto the palm and close the fingers around it. Bring the fists together, fingers pointing upwards, and place them on the abdomen, just above the navel.

CHIN MUDRA – FINGER GESTURE

This gesture of the fingers is used during the practice of pranava pranayama. It helps to concentrate the prana in the abdominal section of the lungs.

Technique

The tip of the thumb and of the index finger touch each other to form a circle. The remaining fingers are straight. Place the palms down near the groin or on the thighs.

CHINMAYA MUDRA – FINGER GESTURE

This gesture of the fingers is used during the practice of pranava pranayama. It helps to concentrate the prana in the thoracic section of the lungs.

Technique

The thumb and the index finger form a circle. The remaining fingers are clenched onto the palm. Place the hands near the groin or on the thighs.

GOVINDA MUDRA – HAND GESTURE

'Govinda' is one of the names given to the Krishna incarnation of the godhead Vishnu in the Hindu trinity. The purpose of this mudra is to promote a feeling of devotion and of reverence in the practitioners during the execution of certain asanas and pranayamas.

By joining the palms of the hands and raising the arms above the head, the channels of pranic energy under the armpits are cleared and there is an abundant flow of energy in the cervical area of the spine.

Technique

Stand with the legs slightly apart. Keep the hands together at the chest level with the palms touching each other as in namaskara mudra.

Inhale and raise the arms stretched above the head, keeping the hands in the same position. Retain the breath for a period of up to one minute.

Exhale and lower the arms and the hands. Relax.

Face East during the practice and repeat the same movement about ten times.

HAMSA MUDRA – HAND GESTURE

'Hamsa' means a swan in Sanskrit. This is thus the gesture of the swan. The energy circuit created in this attitude produces a good flow of prana in the middle and upper sections of the chest.

Technique

Stand with the legs slightly apart. Place the hands behind the back in the namaskara mudra and remain in this position for fifteen to thirty seconds.

KAKI MUDRA – ORAL CAVITY GESTURE

This gesture of the lips is practised generally with cooling pranayamas, like sitali, or with cleansing pranayamas, like dhouti pranayama. The Sanskrit word 'kaki' means a crow or a raven. In this mudra, the position of the lips evokes the image of a crow's beak. The classical Hatha Yoga texts consider this mudra to be a good healing technique for digestive disorders.

Technique

Sit in vajrasana. Place the lips in kaki mudra: contract the lips and allow them to pout. Slowly suck in the air for a period of fifteen to twenty seconds. Hold the breath for five seconds and exhale slowly through the nose. Repeat this cycle ten times and relax.

MAHA MUDRA – HAND AND BODY GESTURE

This mudra is described in the section on vajrasana.

MAYURA MUDRA – NECK AND THROAT GESTURE

This is a gesture of the neck simulating the movement of a peacock's neck. It releases the nervous and physical tensions that normally accumulate in the neck region and create pressure on the cervical vertebrae.

Technique

Sit in any pranayama posture or stand erect. Inhale deeply and with retention of breath, bring the neck to its rightly aligned position. This keeps the cervical vertebrae in position and releases the tension in the cervical nerves, which radiate to the arms.

NAMASKARA MUDRA – HAND GESTURE

This is a gesture that creates inner calm and peace.

Technique

Stand erect. Place the hands at the chest level and place the palms and the fingers of the hands one against the other in a sign of reverence for the inner Spirit.

VIPARITAKARANI MUDRA – INVERTED POSE

This mudra is described in the section on asanas.

VISHNU MUDRA – HAND GESTURE

This is the gesture of the hands needed for the practice of alternate breathing.

Technique

Hold the right hand in front of the nose. Place the middle finger against the bridge of the nose, at the important pressure point of the electrical energy detector on the roof of the nose. The index finger controls the right nostril and the ring finger controls the left nostril. The thumb and little finger are spread rigidly forming a V. This V should not be allowed to relax during the entire practice of pranayama as it helps to alternate the nerve currents. The thumb on the right controls the pingala nadi and the little finger on the left controls the ida nadi. The straightened thumb and little finger stimulate the nerves running up the arm to the armpits and thence to the cervical region. This helps in balancing the flow of prana.

YOGA MUDRA – LOTUS SEAL POSE

This mudra is described in the section on asanas.

KRIYAS

The Sanskrit word 'kriya' is derived from the root 'kr' which denotes the idea of activity. The kriyas described in this section are usually performed in connection with asanas and they represent a more intense but, at the same time, a more limited activity than the entire posture. These kriyas can be considered as the dynamic, fragmentary actions of a more general and comprehensive plan laid out in the enfoldment of the asana itself. Kriyas can be practised as preparatory movements for the asanas or they can be performed, at a more advanced stage of the practice, as a way of generating more prana within the energy pattern delineated by the asanas.

Thirteen important kriyas are described in this section for their relevance to the practice of asanas and the generation of prana.

Agnisara Kriya	Prana Generation
Ashta Sandhi Vimochana Kriya	Preparatory Movement
Baddha Hasta Kriya	Preparatory Movement
Bhujangini Kriya	Prana Generation
Dhanur Kriya	Prana Generation
Hala Kriya	Preparatory Movement
Nauli Kriya	Prana Generation
Pada Chalana Kriya	Preparatory Movement
Pada Hasta Kriya	Preparatory Movement
Pavanamukta Kriya	Preparatory Movement
Prishtha Tadana Kriya	Preparatory Movement
Sarpa Kriya	Prana Generation
Ushtra Kriya	Prana Generation

AGNISARA KRIYA – PRANA GENERATION

This is an activity of purification of the nervous system in the abdominal area by stimulating and regenerating the prana flow at the navel centre. In Gheranda Samhita, it is called the fire purification.

Technique

Sit in vajrasana or in padmasana. Inhale deeply and then exhale completely and relax the abdomen. Press the navel area towards the spine by pulling the abdomen in. Relax the abdomen and pull it in again. Repeat this cycle seven times.

This process of fire purification gives excellent results in the pranayama practice: it alleviates stomach disturbances and improves absorption and elimination processes. The manipura chakra gets fully activated and the vital organs in the trunk receive a rich supply of prana.

This kriya should be practised on an empty stomach. Since it generates plenty of body heat, it is advised to drink water or cooling juices. This should be practised early in the morning or late in the evening when the weather is cool.

ASHTA SANDHI VIMOCHANA KRIYA

This is the series of joint opening exercises, which are described in the chapter on asanas. These movements are extremely helpful when they are practised at the beginning of an asana session since they render the body flexible and more permeable to the flow of prana.

BADDHA HASTA KRIYA

This technique is used to improve and expand the chest, and to increase the breathing capacity. It is also used to develop the chest muscles, strengthen the arms and to reduce tensions in the head and neck.

Technique

Stand erect and raise the arms, bent at the elbows, to shoulder level. Clasp the hands, palms touching each other and fingers crossed, and keep the hands in this position at a distance of about twenty centimetres, from the chest. Inhale deeply, hold the breath and press the palms against each other for ten seconds. Release the breath and the pressure. Repeat this process five times.

BHUJANGINI KRIYA – PRANA GENERATION

This is a breathing technique, which produces a sound like the hissing of a serpent. It helps in removing tensions in the head and reinforces the nervous system.

Technique

Lie on the chest. Inhale deeply and then exhale through the

mouth with clenched teeth making a hissing noise. This kriya is practised in bhujangasana. On the ascending movement, the exhalation with the hissing sound is performed. On the descending movement, the inhalation is performed. This is the opposite of the classical posture. Repeat five times. Then, relax lying on the chest.

DHANUR KRIYA – PRANA GENERATION

This is a technique, which strengthens the legs, the arms and the spine. It provides good vigour and expands the chest.

Technique

Lie on the chest. Bend the legs at the knees, hold the ankles with the hands. Exhale and lift the legs and the chest up, resting the entire weight of the body on the stomach. Without breathing, move the body backwards and forwards, rolling on the abdomen. Perform about six movements. Repeat the process three or four times. Then, relax lying on the chest.

HALA KRIYA

This is a preparatory movement for the practice of halasana. This movement helps to massage the spine and it strengthens the back muscles. It is more intense than in pavanamukta kriya.

Technique

Lie on the back, inhale and lift both legs up simultaneously. Exhale, hold the ankles with the hands and bring the stretched legs nearer to the body whilst raising the buttocks. Inhale, raise the head and the upper back, resting the body on the buttocks. Exhale and perform a rolling movement with the back. Practise this movement ten to twenty times.

NAULI KRIYA – PRANA GENERATION

This is one of the most powerful practices of Hatha Yoga, which acts on the entire abdominal belt. It consists of a full rotation of the main abdominal muscles that produces a deep abdominal massage through a three-stage movement of compression and decompression. This, in turn, tones the navel centre and all the digestive organs. Moreover, the lungs benefit from the expulsion of the vitiated air, which takes place during the deep exhalation preceding the practice of nauli kriya.

This kriya is recommended as a daily practice for advanced practitioners. Nevertheless, persons suffering from high blood pressure and women in menstruation or during pregnancy should refrain from practising nauli kriya. This kriya helps the digestive and elimination functions and brings an abundant flow of prana to all the abdominal organs. It slims down the waist and gives lightness to the body. In the long run, it also facilitates the practice of pranayama.

In the Hatha Yoga Pradipika, it is stated that this kriya is the crown of the Hatha Yoga practice.

Technique

Stand with feet thirty centimetres apart. Tilt the body slightly forward and place the hands on the thighs, keeping the knees slightly bent.

Exhale fully, relax the abdominal belt and perform uddiyana bandha. Then, learn to isolate the abdominal recti muscles and the great abdominal oblique muscles. The central nauli movement is obtained by relaxing the abdominal recti muscles and contracting the great oblique muscles.

The full rotation movement is obtained by a succession of the previous activities and this is the real nauli kriya. Perform uddiyana bandha, contract the left oblique muscle followed by the left abdominal rectus muscle. Then, contract the right rectus muscle followed by the right oblique muscle. Perform uddiyana bandha again and relax. The quick succession of these muscle contractions gives the impression of a rotary movement that is characteristic of the full nauli kriya.

When this kriya is practised on the left side it is called vamana nauli and when it is practised on the right side, it is known as dakshina nauli.

PADA CHALANA KRIYA

This kriya involves the feet movements. It strengthens the ankles, tones the sciatic nerve and removes tensions in the neck and the cervical region of the spine.

Technique

Sit on the ground and stretch the legs. Breathe gently. Bend the feet backwards and forwards, at the ankles. Start with the left foot, and then the right foot and then bend both feet together. Perform five movements. Rotate the feet, separately and jointly. Lift one foot a few centimetres off the ground, then lift the other foot. When bringing the foot down, allow the heel to hit the ground. Relax.

PADA HASTA KRIYA

This is a preparatory movement for padahastasana. It helps to stretch the sciatic nerve gradually and it avoids an unnecessary pull of the leg muscles during the execution of the full asana. It also prevents strain in the back and helps to trim the waistline.

Technique

Stand erect and inhale deeply. Lift up the arms. Exhale through the mouth and bend forward, hands trying to reach the feet. On empty lungs, move the arms up and down vertically, gradually increasing the amplitude of the movement. Inhale and return to a standing position. Perform about five movements at a time and repeat the whole process five times.

PAVANAMUKTA KRIYA

This is a gentle rocking movement, which is performed in the pavanamukta position. It massages the back, reinforces all its muscles and strengthens the spinal nerves. This improves the digestion and eliminates toxins from the intestines. It is an excellent preparation for viparitakaranimudra.

Technique

Lie on the back. Inhale and bring the legs to the chest whilst holding the bent knees with the arms. Hold the breath and clasp the knees tightly against the chest. Exhale and roll the body backwards and forwards about five times. Lie and take a full breath before repeating the rolling movement. Repeat the process five times.

PRISHTHA TADANA KRIYA

This is a preparation for dhanurasana. It helps to reduce tensions in the thighs, buttocks and feet. It helps to overcome laziness. Moreover, it gives flexibility to the waist and tones the sacro-lumbar area of the spine.

Technique

Lie on the chest. Breathe normally. Bend the leg at the knee and move the heel towards the buttocks. Perform this movement slowly, with each leg alternately. Gradually increase the speed of the movement until the heels touch the buttocks. When the legs are flexible enough, the practitioners can hit the buttocks with both heels alternately. Repeat the movement about fifty times.

SARPA KRIYA – PRANA GENERATION

This movement is a variation of bhujangasana. It promotes spinal health and reinforces the sacro-lumbar joint.

Technique

Lie on the chest, lift the hands up and stretch them forward. Inhale and lift up the legs. Roll the body backward and forward on the abdomen with arms and legs stretched away from the ground. Perform the movement five times. Release the breath. Repeat the process three times.

USHTRA KRIYA – PRANA GENERATION

This movement strengthens the legs, the back and the lower abdomen. It improves the elimination function and stimulates the subtle centre at the navel.

Technique

Take the position known as ushtrasana. Inhale and remain in the position. Whilst in the position, perform abdominal breathing about ten times and then, relax. Repeat the process three times. Take the position again. Inhale deeply through the nose, release the breath powerfully through the mouth with the sound 'USH' and move the hips and the trunk slightly forwards. Return to the position of ushtrasana and breathe gently. Repeat the process five times. Then, relax and lie on the ground on the chest for about two minutes.

CHAPTER 4

FIVE SOLAR MEDITATIONS

Meditation cannot be taught, even less can it be explained as it is a state that manifests spontaneously when all the activities of the mind have subsided. It is an inner experience, universal in character but highly subjective in the way it is approached by the practitioner. The state of meditation is one of the higher goals of all the practices of Yoga. The practice of meditation however can be transmitted from master to disciple. It should then be qualified as objective meditation. It is a process of inner contemplation on a chosen symbol of the Ultimate Reality. The symbols are selected according to the particular path of Yoga that is followed and they should be in harmony with the practitioner's inner inclinations. They go from gross, outer symbols like the flame of a candle, the pictorial representation of a mandala, a flowing river to very subtle forms like an inner sound or an inner light. In the latter case, meditation is more like a higher kriya, a very refined form of intensive concentration. When practised with devotion and constancy, this concentration on the chosen object produces a slow but permanent transformation in the consciousness of the practitioner. With time and dedication, the individual consciousness starts to outgrow its limitations in a dynamic movement of expansion until it finally merges with the universal consciousness. This state is known as "samadhi", the ultimate state in Yoga.

In the solar meditation, union with the universal consciousness is attempted through a constant rotation of individual consciousness. This rotation simulates the apparent movement of the sun, which has given rise to time and space in our galaxy. It is determined by the four cardinal points, a zenith and a nadir as well as by the static, invisible centre of the entire movement. The mystical number seven, which is symbolic of the seven higher planes of consciousness, characterizes this circular mandala. Similarly, our inner sky, the "Chidakasha" is a medium of reflection for the spiritual sun, which can be perceived by the inner eye and which can be experienced in the silent core centre. In this centre, the meditator discovers the unity between self, the spiritual sun and the universe.

Solar meditation helps to eradicate the belief that there exists a separation between these three entities. By withdrawing the mind from the external world at a particularly favourable time of the day, the practitioner creates a space where the inner light can shine. The mind slowly returns to its source, the light that existed before time and space. There, pure forms take shape, which are a reflection of the divine creative power. By identifying oneself with any of these forms, one can experience a particular attribute of the Supreme Reality. The mind thus engrossed in this form, which is endowed with divine power, stops all other activities and is reduced to silence.

"Sandhya" or junction in Sanskrit is the moment chosen to withdraw the mind from the external world and to start the solar meditation. This period covers a span of 24 minutes before and 24 minutes after both sunrise and sunset. It is a moment full of cosmic and esoteric meaning and it represents the point of merging of opposites when night dissolves into day and day again into night. At this time, the cosmic vibrations are at their lowest point and the effect of this lowered rhythm creates a pause, a lull in the movement. For a very brief moment there is a cessation of the apparent dual movement of opposites. The entire creation finds itself in a state of perfect equilibrium and peace. In nature, this is the time when sun and moon meet and, in the human being, this is the pause between inspiration and expiration or the infinitesimal silence separating two succeeding thoughts. The purpose of the solar meditation is to catch that moment, to enter into it and, then, to prolong it as much as possible. By entering into this inner movement at that particular time of the day one gets a feeling of timelessness in which to experience the merging of what is static and what is dynamic. Indeed, light and darkness are two facets of a dynamic creation, in the same way as inspiration and expiration constitute the rhythm of biological life. But these opposites owe their existence to a source of light, which transcends them, the divine light which can be recaptured in the privileged moments of sandhya.

In the inner space enlightened by the spiritual sun the mind identifies with the solar inner journey. The four phases of this movement are coupled in pairs: sun rise and sun set, midday and midnight. At sunrise, it is a form of expansion: what is considered the "pravritti" in the Upanishads or the "uttarayana" in the Vedas, or the way of the bright ones. It is a movement through day and light marked by activity and progression. At sunset, it is a form of withdrawal: what is considered the "nivritti" form in Vedanta or the "dakshinayana" in the Vedas, or the way of the forefathers. It is the passage through night, steeped in darkness but enlivened by the appearance of light in the stars and the moon.

The zenith, the mid day point which is the extreme northern point, appears in the East-West direction. In the Indian calendar it corresponds to the outbreak of the monsoon rains when the sun's heat attains its maximum peak. In the chidakasha, the psychic sky, the zenith represents the sun in the meridian when it appears in full splendour to remove the darkness of ignorance. This is the way to spiritual fulfilment in the Vedic sadhana.

The nadir, the midnight point that is the extreme southern point, appears in the West-East direction. In the Indian calendar it corresponds to the transition between winter and spring when nature flowers again. On the psychic plane, the nadir is identified with the midnight sun when light appears in the deepest core of matter and displays its esoteric powers. This is the way to attainment in the Tantric sadhana.

To these four phases of the solar movement correspond four meditations to be practised at sunrise, midday, sun set and midnight respectively. Either the practitioner chooses one particular phase of the solar revolution and concentrates all the energy on that aspect of Solar Yoga or he/she embarks on an intensive course of sadhana and practises the entire cycle at the four different times of the day.

The movement towards the silent core centre represents the fifth dimension of the solar meditation. It manifests after a regular and constant practice of the fourfold movement of the spiritual sun in the inner space, the chidakasha. The circularity of this movement constitutes a mandala, a mystical circle, which revolves constantly upon itself until it reaches a state of perfect immobility. This movement towards the centre lifts the individual consciousness into a glowing realm of light, which has a purifying and dynamizing effect on the body and the mind. Expansion, peace, vitality and lightness characterize it.

These five meditations constitute a complete cycle of the inner sun's movement. Each cycle represents a day or a facet of the inner experience. With each enfoldment, a renewed energy is gathered with new inspiration and strength. This is not a mechanical process but a living experience that becomes fuller with each day of devoted practice. This dynamic meditation creates a feeling of fullness, a joy never felt before, an intuition of the timelessness of being and the vastness of its power. The periodicity and fluidity of the movement of the inner sun with its four phases give a feeling of the immense peace residing within that can be tapped at any moment in a state of profound communion with the eternal principle that supports the entire creation.

SUN RISE MEDITATION

Sit in padmasana or in any other meditation posture. Practise ten rounds of nadi shodhana and ten rounds of nadi shuddhi. With eyes closed, concentrate on the subtle heart centre in an attitude of calm expectation. At the beginning, thoughts, emotions and sensations will distract the inner attention. Bring them to the heart centre where they will dissolve. After some time, the heart centre starts vibrating with a life and a rhythm of its own. Deepen the concentration and visualize the rising rays of the sun in the heart centre. In waves of coloured light, they expand and gradually absorb the inner attention in their movement. Follow this movement of expansion with the entire being. From every ray emitted with the heart, feel a response coming from elsewhere in the form of a greater and brighter ray, which absorbs the heart ray into its powerful light. Progressively, all physical and psychic states are being absorbed in the light of these reciprocal rays until a state of full expansion is experienced.

If one retains the experience within, it will give peace and joy and a feeling of love spreading out to the entire universe and all living creatures.

SUN SET MEDITATION

Sit in padmaṣana or in any other meditation posture. Practise ten rounds of nadi shodhana and ten rounds of nadi shuddhi. Practise shanmukhi mudra in order to cut out sensory information and to allow the senses to withdraw from the outside world. Sunset is a moment of withdrawal and detachment. As the sun at dusk disappears on the horizon, so the mind withdraws from the senses and longs to rest in the Self. When the inner sound is perceived, release the mudra, close the eyes and visualize the calming rays of the setting sun in the subtle centre of the navel. Concentrate the inner awareness on that centre and see it as an island floating on a calm, vast ocean. See the seven rays of the sun returning to their source of energy and vanishing in that subtle centre. It is a transition into the inner world where the touch of an invisible presence is felt. That presence is the higher Self reflected on the calm waters at sunset. One concentrates on that Self until one dissolves into it and nothing remains of the image of the sunset except a vast expanse of Light. Remain in this blissful state as long as possible. And, when the senses gradually awake to the outer reality again and the mind is stirred into action, silently repeat seven times *Om* before opening the eyes.

MERIDIAN SUN MEDITATION

Sit in padmasana or in any other meditation posture. Practise ten rounds of nadi shodhana and ten rounds of nadi shuddhi. Repeat the Gayatri mantra seven times and imbue the mind with the feeling that the sun in the zenith is the ideal towards which one aspires, the truth that cancels the darkness of spiritual ignorance. Visualize a bright sun at the crown of the head and gather all the ascending energy at that point. There, feel the subtle particles of the sun's rays descending along the spine and drawing a path of pure light. It is a descent of energy that dissolves the impurities and breaks the limitations of the body-mind complex. As concentration deepens, feel the subtle centres along the spine vibrating like transparent spheres spinning upon themselves in endless space. Each one of them spins at its rhythm and emits a subtle sound. Their harmonious movement creates a sweet melody on which to focus the inner attention. Gradually, try to diffuse this music to all the cells of the body. After some time, the spheres of light remain suspended without a quiver, the inner sound comes to a complete standstill and true silence is experienced.

MIDNIGHT SUN MEDITATION

Sit in padmasana or in any other meditation posture. Practise ten rounds of nadi shodhana and ten rounds of nadi shuddhi. With closed eyes, repeat the solar mantras. Night is not synonymous of darkness or sleep for the searching soul. It is both a period of purification and initiation. The conscious passage through night gives more splendour to the light when it shines during the day. With full concentration, feel this movement into night like a current of energy gliding swiftly along the spine from the crown of the head to the base of the spine and rising again to reach the subtle heart centre. This centre then appears to the inner eye as a fixed screen of light on which the movements of energy draw pure geometrical forms. The downward movement of energy creates a triangle pointing downwards and the upward movement of energy produces a triangle pointing upwards. These two triangles meet in the heart centre. They enclose in their core a vibrant, powerful light on which to concentrate. This light is an emanation of the universal, centralizing power that sustains all created beings and enables them to gather and renew their scattered energies. With deeper awareness, centre the inner self in this light and try to experience the innate unity between the universal consciousness and the individual consciousness.

> *"To meditate in the active sense is to become what one meditates upon, obtaining the object under which the atman appears to the meditator"*
>
> — Chandogya Upanishad VIII, 2-10.

EPILOGUE

"Death never dies" (*)

"Remember that His Atman and your own Atman are One. The Atman that is never born and never dies Is for eternity. The body leaves us like a worn out garment. Try not to be attached to the body and do not weep because of it. Cry for God alone. Remember Him, repeat His holy name, contemplate on Him and read regularly the Holy Scriptures. Your sorrow will vanish when you dedicate your life to the Supreme." Sree Ananda Mayee Ma

On the sacred day of Uttarayana, in January 2002, a portion of the ashes of Sri Janakiraman reached India to be thrown, as per his will, into the river Cauvery at Siringapatnam. Giorgio, my husband, a faithful devotee of Sri Janakiraman and I travelled to India for the traditional rites to be performed by his son. We were taken in a small saucer-like embarkation made of coconut leaves and bamboo up to the point of the sangam marked by a statue of the divinity Narasimha in the middle of the river.

The peace and charm of the river banks with swaying coconut trees and thick, lush vegetation induced in me a state of contemplation about the spiritual beauty and richness of the fifteen years spent together with Sri Janakiraman. There was no sense of loss, no sense of separation and the human sadness had given way to an inner tranquillity that rested on the intimate experience of his constant loving and guiding presence.

During the return journey by car to Bangalore, an inner voice inspired me to turn around as the sun was setting on the horizon only to see the most extraordinary sight: instead of lighting up the sky in different shades of dusty pinks and reds, the sun was shooting

* Title given by Ram Alexander to his compilation of Swami Atmananda's diaries.

seven powerful rays into the sky. I was immediately reminded of the day in September when the first portion of Sri Janakiraman's ashes was thrown into the Mediterranean and a magnificent rainbow formed over the shore.

Our journey continued to the great temples of Tamil Nadu. In Kanchipuram, we were inspired to have a paduka puja performed for Sri Janakiraman at the Mahasamadhi of his Guru during his youth, the Senior Shankaracharya of Kanchipuram Mutt. We chose this sanctified place for the performance of Sri Janakiraman's tithi puja every year on the 18th of September.

On the way back to Chennai, we decided to stop by the ocean to give back to the waters the flowers of the paduka puja. At the chosen spot, there was a group of Christian nuns playing on the shores, quite an unusual sight in India! Immediately, my memory brought back to me the image of the day when Sri Janakiraman's body was cremated in Nice. We had given him a last good-bye with a heart of 108 yellow roses that we later brought to the sanctuary of Laghet where Sri Janakiraman often visited to offer homage to Mother Mary. When we entered the church, the nuns were singing and we placed the heart of flowers at the foot of the altar. The nuns in India echoed a strange resemblance to their sisters in France, both united as "One" in the Divine Mother.

There is no such thing as death for those who choose God as their refuge during their lifetime on earth and when they seemingly depart, their real presence remains and manifests itself in so many beautiful ways.

As my Guru, Sree Ananda Mayee Ma, once said to one of Her Western disciple " death must die". (*). The truth of this utterance reveals itself even more when the being who leaves the mortal coil has spent the life on earth in the love of God and the service of humanity. Then, the very essence of that being lives forever in the hearts of those who benefited from his presence, his teachings, his help or his friendship.

To confirm this point, I have dared to illustrate how deeply some of the persons, to quote a few, were touched by their association with Sri Janakiraman even if some of them might have spent only a few moments in his company.

" I have heard from Janakiraman's daughter what all you had done after Janakiraman left his body and I was just thrilled. You have

done exactly what was appropriate for great souls soaked in spirituality. I got the sense after my last trip to Nice that you and my brother are a single fused entity spiritually, living in two separate bodies. This concept will be difficult for non-spiritual people to understand simply for the reason no such thing ever exists in the material world. I see that you sense this dimension very deeply and you now have the full spiritual force of both Janakiraman and yourself in you and just carry on to whatever destination it leads to. You will savour the tremendous peace and harmony and the extraordinary level of spiritual energy that will vest in every one of your actions."

Srí Sankaran, younger brother of Janakiraman, himself a spiritual seeker and music composer:

" I will remember Sri Janakiraman as a very noble soul. His greatness was like the gentle breath of spring, invisible but irresistible. It touched all that was bare and bleak around him to splendour. It renewed everything around in pure Love. There was magnetism and an impalpable aura of lofty ideals and a mighty purpose about him, which left a deep impression upon me and all who came in contact with him, particularly young hearts and unsophisticated minds. Calm and reserved, benign and benevolent, he easily became the centre of respectful attention wherever he happened to be.

To have known Sri Janakiraman is a blessing indeed. When one meets such a noble soul, one does not even stop to ask if one has merited it. One just accepts it as a divine boon."

Nilesh Nathvani, friend and author of *Kailash Mansarovar.*

"Sri Janakiraman was one of my earliest mantra masters, way back in London during the sixties. His sincerity, humour, human warmth and joy of teaching, have long remained with me over the past thirty-five years. During my three-year pilgrimage as a wandering monk in India, and disenchanted with many 'gurus' there, I was hoping to spend more time studying with Yogacharya. But I was dismayed to discover that his ashram had closed and that he had moved to Italy and was teaching there. I always remembered him with love, and for me that is the sign of a true teacher. I found that his look lingered in the heart- the luminosity of his soul always shone from his eyes."

Mantracharya Muz Múrray – Ramana Baba- Inner Garden Yoga Centre, Caveirac, France.

"I was sitting in darshan waiting for Sai Baba at Whitefield and overheard an Italian devotee speaking about a Yoga Master who was treating patients with Yoga therapy. The next day I visited Sri Janakiraman at his home in Bangalore and observed his interaction with his patients. I was impressed by his logical and methodical yet simultaneously vibrant and intuitive approach. He explained that he was a cross between an aeronautical engineer and a mystical yogi. This second aspect was dynamically apparent when he was playing the veena and singing South Indian ragas.

My wife-to be and I spent forty days with him. We would have our private class each morning in which he would teach us his approach to each illness separately. Then in the afternoon and evening the patients would arrive and we would get a chance to observe him and take notes. It was a wonderful education that allowed me to help thousands of people here in Greece. Just about every evening we would chant bhajans for about half an hour with other devotees. Sri Janakiraman had a powerful voice and loved to chant.

I used to wonder at the way he would arrange his whole puja with meters of stringed flowers that he would have delivered daily and place on his icons of Baba, Christ and many other saints and gurus. He would feed beggars regularly. Also characteristic was his going off at 6 am on his Vespa to teach a few personal yoga classes which he had accepted around Bangalore. This was a time of learning and absorbing and Sri Janakiraman was an unlimited source of information and inspiration. We will be forever grateful to our teacher and friend."

Robert Elias Najemy, Holistic Harmony Trust, Athens, Greece.

"It was a shock to hear of the passing away of Yogacharya Janakiraman, as he has always looked so vital in photographs that there is a tendency to feel that he would be here forever. Though it is a great loss to the Yoga community worldwide, he has given much and I feel also that IYTA has been fortunate to have him for so long as a Full member of our Association."

Moina Bower, President of International Yoga Teachers Association, Sydney, Australia.

"All of us who knew Sri Janakiraman remember him with profound respect. We remember with affection the quality of his teachings and the light that irradiated from his person. For the Members of IYTA in Spain who had the good fortune to participate in his seminars, it has been an unforgettable experience."
Montse Barangé, the then President of International Yoga Teachers Association, Spain.

"Yogacharya Janakiraman besides being a divine friend had always helped my family and myself with his gifts of Yoga therapy. His masterpiece Solar Yoga inspired with his personality is with all of us and will continue to help us greatly."
P.R.S Mani, former Indian Ambassador, Bangalore, India.

"It is not easy to express in words the Being that Sri Janakiraman is. Since the 18th of September 2001, his Essence is felt stronger as time goes by and his Presence manifests in a wonderful way through events and things he loved, like the hidden language of flowers. His singularly fine vibration irradiates in my life and as I evolve, I become more aware of it on subtler planes of Consciousness. I am thankful to the Lord and to Guru Janakiraman that he appeared in my life sixteen years ago and has remained ever since. I welcome this gift every day with renewed joyful humility."
Reinhardt Scholze, psychotherapist and yoga teacher, Vienna, Austria.

"In 1982, I had my first life-transforming darshan of Bhagavan Sri Satya Sai Baba when Sri Janakriaman insisted that I should come with him to Whitefield. His loving words still echo in me today: 'Ponappa, we are in the path of Sakti and hence we will experience Baba's divinity in the form of vibrations. It is our duty to ensure through purity of body and mind that we experience it in subtle and subtler forms. You have now been propelled into a different frequency and are totally under the care and guidence of Baba'. I am forever beholden to Sri Janakiraman for his loving guidence in my practices of pranayama and meditation."
Sri Ponappa, friend and long-standing devotee.

"I am deeply grieved on hearing the news of the demise of Yogacharya Janakiraman."
T.K.V. Desikachar, Krishnamacharya Yoga Mandiram.

Caroline Rosso Cicogna in the presence of her Guru, Sreé Ananda Mayee Ma, Naimishar (U.P.), India, December 1980.

In the blessed presence of

1. Swami Chidananda, President of the Divine Life Society, Rishikesh, 1979.
2. Professor Gaurinath Sastri, New Delhi, 1980.
3. His Holiness the Dalai Lama, with husband Giorgio, New Delhi, 1980.

1. Sri Janakiraman and Carmelo Vranich, Yoga adept, artist, painter and friend who illustrated "Solar Yoga", at the AIYA in Trieste, 1987.
2. Sri Janakiraman and Caroline Rosso Cicogna at the AIYA, Trieste, 1992.
3. Sri Janakiraman and Caroline Rosso Cicogna-first encounter-Rome, 1985.

1. Sri Janakiraman with a bhajan group at the AIYA, in Trieste, 1987.
2. Yogacharya Janakiraman giving a Yoga seminar for the International Yoga Teachers Association, Spain, 1992.

Photo 9. Sun Temple of Konarak (Puri, Orissa, India). View from the South. Statue of 'Surya' in main niche. Kalinga style. Sandstone. Mid-13th century. By courtesy of A.I.I.S.

GLOSSARY OF SANSKRIT TERMS

Adham Pranayama	Abdominal breathing.
Adhi Mudra	Sealing gesture of the fingers that is practised with clavicular breathing.
Adhyam Pranayama	Clavicular breathing.
Agama	Classical Hindu texts dealing with the mystical worship of Shiva and Shakti.
Agni	The Vedic fire; the digestive power.
Agnisara Kriya	Cleansing process; action of stimulating the digestive fire.
Ajna	Command; the subtle nerve centre situated between the eyebrows; subcortical centre; the sixth chakra.
Anahata	Unstruck sound; the subtle nerve centre situated in the cardiac region; the source of vibration and movement in the body; the fourth chakra.
Anandamayakosha	The energy sheath enveloping the soul; the blissful sheath.
Annamayakosha	The sheath of physical energy identified with the physical body.
Anunasika Pranayama	Nasal cleaner.
Apana	One of the five major manifestations of vital energy that controls the elimination function.
Aprakasha Mudra	Sealing gesture of the throat practised with Jalandhara Bandha (Chin lock).
Ardhachandrasana	Half-moon Posture.
Ardhamatsyendrasana	Half-spinal twist Posture.
Ardhapadmasana	Half-lotus Posture.
Artha	Meaning, signification.

Asana	Posture; the third stage of Ashtanga Yoga.
Asanasiddhi	The excellence in postural practice.
Ashtanga Yoga	The branch of Yoga which is composed of eight stages, known also as Raja Yoga or the Yoga of Patanjali.
Ashta Sandhi Vimochana Kriya	The eight joint release method.
Ashvini Mudra	Sealing gesture of the anal sphincters.
Baddha Hasta Kriya	Binding gesture of the hands used in certain types of pranayama.
Bandha	Muscular lock applied during certain pranayama practices.
Bandha Traya	Triple lock applied during certain pranayama practices.
Bhadrásana	Bellows Breath: a classical type of pranayama.
Bhavana	Inner feeling.
Bhujangasana	The Cobra Pose.
Bhujangini Kriya	The hissing breath practised in the Cobra Pose.
Bijmantra	Core of the mystical syllable known as Mantra and which expresses its essence.
Brahma Mudra	Sealing gesture of the fingers used in the practice of the Cosmic Vibration Breath.
Brahma Nadi	Main channel of energy running through the centre of the spinal column.
Chakra	Centres of energy situated along the main axis of the energy sheath to which the important nerve plexi of the body correspond.
Chinmaya Mudra	Sealing gesture of the fingers that accompanies thoracic breathing.
Chin Mudra	Sealing gesture of the fingers that accompanies abdominal breathing.
Chitranadi	Grey H-shaped part of the spinal column
Cidakasha	The ether of consciousness.
Devadatta	One of the minor manifestations of vital energy: yawning.

Dhananjaya	One of the minor manifestations of vital energy remaining after physical death.
Darshan	Seeing; generally used with the sense of being in the presence of a saint and absorbing the blessing of such a presence.
Dhanurasana	The Bow Pose.
Dhanur Kriya	Rocking action in the Bow Pose.
Dhouti Pranayama	Cleansing Breath.
Gheranda Samhita	A classical work on Hatha Yoga.
Gomukhasana	The Cowhead Pose.
Granthi	Knots of subtle energy which prevent the free flow of prana.
Hala Kriya	Preparatory movement to the Plough Pose
Halasana	The Plough Pose.
Hamsa Mudra	Sealing gesture of the swan performed with hands clasped behind the back.
Hatha Yoga	A branch of Yoga based on the practice of postures and breathing techniques.
Hatha Yoga Pradipika	A classical work on Hatha Yoga.
Ida	The channel of receptive energy; subtle counterpart of the parasympathetic system.
Jalandhara Bandha	Chin Lock practised with certain types of pranayama.
Jayadeva	Bengali mystic poet of the 12th century, author of the Gita Govinda.
Jnana Yoga	A branch of Yoga based on knowledge.
Kaki Mudra	A sealing gesture of the lips in the form of a crow's beak.
Kapalabhati	The Brain Brightener; a type of pranayama
Karma Yoga	A branch of Yoga based on service and selfless action.
Kevala Kumbhaka	Spontaneous breathless state obtained after a rigorous practice of the science of pranayama.
Kosha	A sheath of energy.
Krikara	One of the minor manifestations of vital energy; sneeze or cough.

Kriya	Cleansing process.
Kumbhaka	Time interval separating inspiration and expiration, known as Antara Kumbhaka; or time interval separating expiration and inspiration, known as Bahya Kumbhaka; retention of breath.
Kundalini	The Serpent Power; the latent cosmic energy coiled at the base of the spine in the form of a sleeping serpent.
Kurma	One of the minor manifestations of vital energy that controls the movements of the eyelids.
Madhyama	Middle stage.
Madhyama Pranayama	Thoracic breathing.
Maha Mudra	A sealing gesture of the arms which promotes clavicular breathing.
Mahat Yoga Pranayama	Full yogic breathing.
Mandala	Mystic representation of the entire reality used as object of concentration.
Manipura	The subtle nerve centre situated in the navel region; the third chakra.
Manomayakosha	Energy sheath related to the functions of perception and awareness.
Mantra	Prayer, sacred formula, mystic syllable; a Vedic text or verse.
Mantra Yoga	A branch of Yoga based on the practice of sound vibrations.
Matsyasana	The Fish Pose.
Maya	The illusory cosmic power which veils consciousness and creates the sense of individuality.
Mayura Mudra	Neck gesture simulating the movement of a peacock.
Mudra	A sealing gesture creating a definite pattern of energy inside the body.
Mula Bandha	Lock of the anal sphincter used in certain types of pranayama.

Muladhara	A subtle nerve centre situated at the base of the spine; reservoir of the latent cosmic energy, known as Kundalini; the root chakra.
Nadi	A subtle channel through which the vital energy flows in the energy sheath, the Pranamayakosha.
Nadi Shodhana	Nerve Purifier; a type of pranayama.
Nadi Shuddhi	Nerve Purifier; a type of pranayama.
Naga	One of the minor manifestations of vital energy; belching.
Naga Pranayama	The Serpent Breath.
Namaskara Mudra	A sealing gesture of the hands used with certain types of pranayama and in prayer.
Nauli Kriya	A cleansing process acting on the elimination organs of the body.
Navasana	The Boat Pose.
Niyama	The second stage of Ashtanga Yoga: positive self-purification practices.
Om	The Cosmic Vibration at the origin of the universe.
Padachalana Kriya	Ankle movements.
Padahasta Kriya	Expiration activity in the Hand to Feet Pose.
Padahastasana	The Hand to Feet Pose.
Padmasana	The Lotus Pose.
Parashabda	The Supreme Logos.
Parvatasana	The Mountain Pose.
Paschimottanasana	The Head to Knee Pose.
Pashyanti	Unmanifested sound.
Patanjali	Author of the Yoga Sutras.
Pavanamukta Kriya	Rocking movement in the Foetus Pose.
Pavanamuktasana	The Foetus Pose.
Pingala	The channel of active energy; subtle counterpart of the sympathetic nervous system.
Prana	Energy in all its manifestations, especially bio-energy.

Pranamayakosha	The vital energy sheath.
Pranava	Name of the sacred syllable *Om*.
Pranayama	The fourth stage of Ashtanga Yoga: the science of breath control.
Pranava Pranayama	The Cosmic Vibration Breath.
Prishta Tadana Kriya	Leg movement in the Cobra Pose.
Puraka	Controlled inspiration.
Raja Yoga	The Royal Yoga; a branch of Yoga based on the science of mental control; also, Patanjali Yoga or Ashtanga Yoga.
Rechaka	Controlled expiration.
Sahasrara	Thousand-petal lotus, the symbolic expression of the highest psychic centre in the cerebral cavity; the seventh chakra.
Sahita Pranayama	The Compound Breath.
Samadhi	The eighth and highest stage of Ashtanga Yoga in which individual consciousness merges with cosmic consciousness.
Samana	One of the major manifestations of vital energy regulating the metabolic processes.
Samkhya	One of the traditional schools of Hindu philosophy, founded by Kapila.
Sandhya	Conjunction of day and night at sunrise and sunset, time especially appropriate for spiritual practices.
Sangita Ratnakara	One of the major Hindu musicological treatises of the 13th century.
Sarpa Kriya	Rocking movement in the Cobra Pose.
Sarvangasana	The Shoulderstand.
Savitri Pranayama	Rhythmic Breath.
Setubandhasana	The Bridge Pose.
Shabda	Sound, word; one aspect of manifested Consciousness.
Shakti	The energy manifestation of Consciousness.
Shalabhasana	The Locust Pose.
Shankaracharya	Hindu saint and philosopher; propounder of the school of Non Dualism.

Shanmukhi mudra	The gesture of closing the nine apertures.
Shavasana	The Corpse Pose.
Shiva	Pure Consciousness; also, the destructive aspect of the Hindiu trinity.
Shvana Pranayama	Dog Breath.
Siddhasana	The Accomplished Pose.
Shirshasana	The Headstand.
Sitali Pranayama	Cooling Breath.
Sukha Pranayama	Easy Breath.
Sukhasana	The Easy Posture.
Surya Pranayama	Solar Breath.
Surya Yoga	Solar Yoga.
Sushumna	The main energy channel situated inside the spinal column; subtle counterpart of the central nervous system.
Svadhishthana	The subtle energy centre situated in the pelvic region; the second chakra.
Tadasana	Standing stretching Posture.
Tantra	Eastern school of philosophy propounding the expansion of energy and consciousness
Trikonasana	The Triangle Pose.
Udana	One of the major manifestations of vital energy that controls the intake of air and food.
Uddiyana Bandha	Lock of the abdominal muscles practised in certain types of Pranayama.
Ujjayi	Victorious Breath.
Upanishad	The main scriptures of the Vedanta school of philosophy.
Ushtra Kriya	Breathing activity in the camel pose.
Ushtrasana	The Camel Pose.
Vaikhari	Manifested Sound.
Vajranadi	Subtle counterpart of the white filament inside the spinal cord.
Vajrasana	The Kneeling Pose.
Vayu	Vital air, nerve current or impulse.
Veda	The sacred knowledge incorporated in the whole body of Hindu Sacred Scriptures.

Vedanta	Traditional school of Hindu philosophy based on Non Dualism; the culmination of Vedic wisdom.
Vibhaga Pranayama	Sectional Breath.
Vijnanamayakosha	The sheath of intellectual and intuitive energies.
Vinyasa	A scientifically conceived sequence of Yoga postures or asanas.
Viparitakaranimudra	The Inverted Pose.
Virasana	The Hero Pose.
Vishnu Mudra	A sealing gesture of the fingers used with certain types of pranayama.
Vishuddhi	Subtle nerve centre situated in the pharyngeal region; the fifth chakra.
Vrikshasana	The Tree Pose.
Vyaghrasana	The Tiger Pose.
Vyana	One of the major manifestations of vital energy that controls the cardiovascular system.
Yama	The first stage of Ashtanga Yoga comprising a set of ethical principles of universal application.
Yogamudra	The Lotus Seal Pose
Yoga Sadhana	Methodical and intensive course of spiritual practices.
Yogasana	Meditative posture in which energy blocks are removed, mind is stilled and personality is harmonised.
Yogasutra	The classical work on Yoga by sage Patanjali.

SELECTED BIBLIOGRAPHY

Agrawala V., *Vedic Lectures*, Prithivi Prakashan, Varanasi 1981; *Sparks from the Vedic Fire*, Chowkhamba, 1962.

Aivanhof O.M., *Vers une Civilisation Solaire*, Ed. Prosveta, 1981.

Ananda Mayee Ma, *L'Enseignement de Ma Ananda Moyi*, Albin Michel, 1974.

Asimov I., *The Human Body*, New American Library, N. Y., *1964; The Human Brain*, Houghton Mifflin, Boston 1964.

Audibert P., *Les Energies du Soleil*, Ed. du Seuil, 1978.

Aurobindo, *The Complete Works*, Sri Aurobindo Ashram Trust, Pondicherry; *The Secret of the Veda*, Pondicherry, 1971.

Bailey A., *Initiation Humaine et Solaire*, Ed. Lucis, Gentve 1953.

Balu V., Balu S., *Divine Glory*, S.B. Publications, Bangalore, 1985.

Bernard Theos, *Hindu Philosophy*, Motilal 1981.

Carrel A., *Man, the Unknown*, Wilco Pub. House, Bombay 1959.

Charan Singh, *Divine Light*, Radha Soami Satsang, Beas, 1967.

Charon J., *L'Homme et l'Univers*, Albin Michel 1974; *L'Esprit, cet Inconnu*, Albin Michel, 1977.

Chaudhuri N., *Hinduism*, B.I. Publications, New Delhi, 1979.

Chidananda Swami, *Path to Blessedness*, Divine Life Society, 1975.

Coquet M., *Les Cakras*, Dervy Livres, 1982.

Coward H., *Sphota Theory of Language*, Motilal 1980.

Devi Chand, *The Yajurveda*, Munshiram Publ. 1980.

Diamond J., *The Life Energy in Music*, Valley Cottage, 1983.

Eliade M., *Le Yoga, Immortalité et Liberté*, Payot 1954; *Techniques du Yoga*, Payot 1975.

Feuerstein G., *The Philosophy of Classical Yoga*, Manchester University Press, 1980.

Frawley D., *The Creative Vision of the Early Upanishads*, 1982.

Gaurinath Sastri, *The Triune Path*, Varanasi, 1982; *History of Classical Sanskrit Literature*, Motilal 1974; *A History of Vedic Literature*, Calcutta, 1982.

Gitananda Swami, *Pranayama, the Science of Vital Control*, Satya Press, Pondicherry, 1972; *Correction of Breathing Difficulties by Yoga, Pranayama*, Satya Press, Pondicherry, 1972; *Yoga Samyama*, Satya Press, 1972.

Gopi Krishna, *Kundalini, the Evolutionary Energy in Man*, Shambhala, 1971; *The Secret of Yoga*, Turnstone Press, 1981.

Goswami S., *Laya Yoga*, Routledge & Kegan Paul, 1980.

Griffiths R., *The Hymns of the Rig Veda*, Motilal, 1973.

Gupta S., *Surya, the Sun God*, Somaiya Publ., Bombay 1977.

Guyton, *Textbook of Medical Physiology*, W.B. Saunders Cº, 1986.

Harshe R., *Satkarmasangrahah*, Kaivalyadhama, Lonavla, 1970.

Herbert J., *Spiritualité Hindoue*, Albin Michel 1947.

Iyengar B.K.S., *Light on Yoga*, Allen & Unwin, 1966; *Light on Pranayama*, Allen & Unwin, 1981.

Janakiraman S., *Practical Yoga Therapy*, Bangalore 1978.

Kelsey M., *The Other Side of Silence*, Paulist Press, N.Y. 1976.

Knipe D., *In the Image of Fire*, Motilal, 1975.

Kuvalayananda Swami, *Pranayama*, Kaivalyadhama, Lonavla, 1977.

Leadbeater C., *The Chakras*, Theosophical Publishing House, Adyar, 1973.

Mascaro J., *The Upanishads*, Penguin Books, London, 1970; *The Bhagavad Gita*, Penguin Books, London, 1970.

Masson A., *Le Soleil, l'Homme et la Santé*, Ed. Prosveta, 1980.

Muktananda Swami, *Swami, Play of Consciousness*, Harper & Row, 1978.

Muller M., *Sacred Books of the East*, Motilal 1981; *The Upanishads, The Vedanta Sutras, Vedic Hymns.*

Narasimha Swami, *Life of Shirdi Sai Baba*, Madras.

Osborne A., *Ramana Maharishi - Collected Works*, Rider, 1969.

Pandey L., *Sun Worship in Ancient India*, Motilal 1971.

Panikkar R., *The Vedic Experience*, Darton, Longman, 1979.

Prabhavananda Swami, *Yoga Sutras*, Vedanta Society of Southern California, 1953.

Rai R., *Mantra Yoga Samhita*, Chaukhambha, 1982.

Radhakrishnan., *Bhagavad Gita*, Allen & Unwin, 1948; *The Principal Upanishads*, Allen & Unwin, 1953.

Rama Swami., *Science of Breath: A Practical Guide,* Honesdale, Pa. 1979; *A Practical Guide to Holistic Health,* Honesdale, Pa. 1980.

Ruchpaul E., *La Demeure du Silence*, Gallimard 1973.
Sachdeva L., *Yoga and Depth Psychology*, Motilal 1978.
Sarngadeva, *Sangita Ratnakara*, Motilal 1984.
Sathya Sai Baba, *Sadhana, the Inward Path*, Prasanthinilayam, 1982; *Sathyam Shivam Sundaram*, Prasanthinilayam, 1980.
Sivananda Swami., *Practice of Yoga Sadhana*, Divine Life Society 1979; *Tantra Yoga, Nada Yoga and Kriya Yoga*, Divine Life Society, 1982; *Brahma Sutras*, Motilal 1977.
Srivastava V., *Sun-Worship in Ancient India*, Indological Publications, Allahabad, 1972.
Subbaraya Sharma Y., *Sri Kundalini Sakthi*, Bangalore, 1971.
Subramania Iyer N., *Sri Vidya Nityahnika*, Madras 1955; *Sri Vidya Saparya Paddhati*, Madras 1955.
Svatmarama, *Hatha Yoga Pradipika*, Theosophical Society, 1975.
Taimni I., *Man, God and the Universe*, Theosophical Publishing House, Madras, 1969; *The Science of Yoga*, Adyar 1961.
Tansley D., *Radionics and the Subtle Anatomy of Man*, Health Science Press, 1972.
Vajpeyi K., *The Science of Mantras*, New Delhi, 1979.
Van Lysebeth A., *Pranayama, la Dynamique du Souffle*, Flammarion 1971.
Vasu S.C., *The Gheranda Samhita*, Munshiram, 1980.
Vivekananda Swami., *Les Yogas Pratiques*, Albin Michel, 1970; *The Complete Works*, Advaita Ashram, Mayavati 1978.
Woodroffe J., *The Serpent Power*, Ganesh & C°, 1973; *The Garland of Letters*, Ganesh & C°, 1979; *Introduction to Tantra Sastra*, Ganesh C°, Madras 1969.
Yesudian S., *Yoga and Health*, Unwin Paperbacks, 1953.
Yogendra S., *Hatha Yoga Simplified*, Santa Cruz, 1982.

INDEX

1. English Terms

2. Sanskrit Terms*

* *The book contains many Sanskrit words, which are essential to defining yogic concepts. When a Sanskrit word appears for the first time, an equivalent meaning in English has been given. All Sanskrit words have been defined in a glossary. In this book, the transliteration of Sanskrit letters into Roman letters follows the standard system but no diacritical marks have been used.*

VEDIC HEALTH CARE SYSTEM

Clinical Practice of Sushrutokta Marm Chikitsa and Siravedhan Highlighting Acupuncture

Ram Lal Sah, Binod Kumar Joshi & Geeta Joshi

ISBN: 81-7822-041-5

THE YOGA COOKBOOK

Vegetarian Food for Body and Mind

Sivananda Yoga Vedanta Centres

ISBN: 81-7822-048-2

EROS, CONSCIOUSNESS AND KUNDALINI

Deepening Sensuality Through Tantric Celibacy and Spiritual Intimacy

Stuart Sovatsky

ISBN : 81-7822-179-9

STRETCH YOUR LIMBS FOR BALANCE

Yoga for Long and Healthy Living

Elise Browning Miller
Carol Blackman

ISBN: 81-7822-132-2

THE AYURVEDIC DIET

The Ancient Way to Health Rejuvenation and Weight Control

Dennis Thompson

ISBN: 81-7822-014-8

THE YOGA OF KNOWLEDGE

Based on Sri Aurobindo's Synthesis of Yoga

M.P. Pandit

ISBN: 81-7822-078-4

PRANIC LIVING AND HEALING

Luis S.R. Vas

ISBN: 81-7822-161-6

HEALING THE FUTURE

The Journey Within

Deepak Kashyap

ISBN: 81-7822-039-3

STEP-BY-STEP YOGA FOR STRESS RELIEF

Swami Shivapremananda

ISBN: 81-7822-046-6